Beyond Clinic Walls

Psychiatric Outpatient Centers of America (POCA) is an organization comprising Psychiatric Clinics and Community Mental Health Centers in the United States, Canada, and Mexico. Founded in 1963, some of its many purposes have been to: disseminate information of importance to its clinic membership, offer consultative services to new and established agencies, organize forums for discussing mutual professional and administrative problems, make available group insurance plans for member clinics as well as other group benefits, publish lasting literature in the field and a newsletter covering current information relative to legislation, etc. POCA holds an annual spring meeting which provides much of the material presented in these volumes. Though special services of POCA are available only to member clinics, the annual meeting is open to all interested professionals and non-professionals.

For further information contact:

MRS. MILDRED BERL
President—POCA
4327 Albemarle Street, NW
Washington, D. C. 20016

Beyond Clinic Walls

Edited by ALAN B. TULIPAN, M.D.

Faculty, The William Alanson White Institute
of Psychiatry, Psychology, and Psychoanalysis,
New York, N. Y.

and CAROLYN L. ATTNEAVE, Ph.D.

Research Associate, Department of Behavioral
Sciences, Harvard School of Public Health,
Boston, Mass.

and EDWARD KINGSTONE, M.D.

Sunnybrook Hospital, Toronto,
Ontario, Canada

POCA Perspectives No. 5

THE UNIVERSITY OF ALABAMA PRESS
University, Alabama

To
ERICH LINDEMANN, Ph.D., M.D.

Recipient, Fourth Annual Award,
Psychiatric Outpatient Centers of America*

Innovator, author, honored teacher, who has led out-patient psychiatry beyond clinic walls; reaching out to those in trouble so that they need never become patients; demonstrating that scientific problem-solving can be achieved with humanity, warmth, and genuineness.

*Previous recipients:

Gerald Caplan, M.D.
Rollo May, Ph.D.
Hon. William O. Douglas

Contributors

Chester Paul Adams—Twice Born Men, San Francisco, California.
Robert L. Bergman, M.D.—Chief, Mental Health Programs, Indian Health Services, U.S.P.H.S., Albuquerque, New Mexico.
Grace Burruel, MSW—Social Worker, La Frontera, Tucson, Arizona.
Betty Carter, MSW—Training Supervisor, Department of Psychiatry, Bellevue Hospital, New York, N.Y.
Nelba Chavez, MSW—Social Worker, La Frontera, Tucson, Arizona.
Sherrill A. Conna, M.D.—Director of Clinical Services, Youth Guidance Center, Worcester, Massachusetts.
W. Robert Curtis, M.A.—Program Director, Taunton Area Mental Health Program, Mass. Dept. of Mental Health, Middleboro, Massachusetts.
Paul Davis—Associate Editor, *Tuscaloosa News,* Tuscaloosa, Alabama.
George W. Dean, L.L.B.—Attorney, Destin, Florida.
Mathew Dumont, M.D.—Deputy Commissioner, Massachusetts Dept. of Mental Health, Boston, Massachusetts.
Thomas Fanning, M. Div.—Chief Chaplain, Bryce State Hospital, Tuscaloosa, Alabama.
Andrew Guthrie, Jr., M.D.—Asst. Professor of Pediatrics, Harvard Medical School; Chief, Children's Ambulatory Division, Mass. General Hospital, Boston, Massachusetts.

Arlene Katz, M.A.—Mental Health Coordinator, Mystic Valley Community Mental Health Center, Concord, Massachusetts.

Jack McCloskey, A.A.—Co-Director, Twice Born Men, San Francisco, California.

James E. Morris, Jr., M.D.—Superintendent for Clinical Services, Bryce State Hospital, Tuscaloosa, Alabama.

K. Patrick Okura—Executive Assistant to the Director, National Institute of Mental Health, Rockville, Maryland.

Peggy Papp, MSW—Director of Community Services, Nathan W. Ackerman Family Institute, Inc., New York, New York.

Elmer K. Parent, MSW—Social Worker, Community Care Program, V.A. Hospital, Bedford, Massachusetts.

Robert J. Ridick, MSW—Coordinator, Community Care Program, V.A. Hospital, Bedford, Massachusetts.

H. S. Sandhu, M.D.—Acting Chief, Ambulatory care Service, V.A. Hospital, Bedford, Massachusetts.

Albert E. Scheflen, M.D.—Professor of Psychiatry, Albert Einstein College of Medicine, Bronx, New York.

Guy O. Seymour, Ph.D.—Instructor in Psychology, Department of Psychiatry, Harvard Medical School; Director of Training, Psychology Internship and Group Therapy Programs, Boston City Hospital, Boston, Massachusetts.

Olga Silverstein, MSW—Staff Therapist, Nathan W. Ackerman Family Institute, Inc., New York, New York.

Sherry Stein, MSW—ENKI Research Institute, Encino, California.

Paul D. Steinhauer, M.D.—Assistant Professor, Department of Psychiatry, University of Toronto, Toronto, Ontario.

Povl W. Toussieng, M.D.—Professor of Psychiatry and Behavioral Sciences; Associate Professor of Pediatrics, University of Oklahoma College of Medicine, Oklahoma City, Oklahoma.

John R. Unwin, M.D., M.Sc.—Director, Youth Services, Allan Memorial Institute of Psychiatry, McGill University, Montreal, Quebec.

Contents

Preface

Action from principle, the perception and the performance of right, changes things and relations; it is essentially revolutionary, and does not consist wholly with anything which was. It not only divides states and churches, it divides families; ay, it divides the *individual*, separating the diabolical in him from the divine.

HENRY DAVID THOREAU

The community mental health field has undergone many transformations since its emergence from the self-imposed limitations necessitated by its embeddedness within the framework of *diagnosis* and *treatment*. Some of the changes have proved visionary, others magnificent failures. Innovations have often been initiated for the sake of innovation itself, and proved to be but near-sighted flashes of overinvested imaginations. Other programs were put into operation because they were effective for other places at other times and in other circumstances, but abominable failures in inappropriate settings.

The literature has been replete with "This is the way we did it at. . . ." papers which purported to be useful combinations, but which were neither validated nor validatable. Salutary immediate results rarely have been followed by studies designed to check on continuing efficacy. Nor can programs be validated by their repetition in other places, at other times, with other staff, for other communities. The variables are too pronounced, and there is no way of determining which of them might have been responsible

ix

for success or failure. In community programs, as well as in individual psychotherapy, indeed, the question of whether something works is a much easier question to answer than what caused the results. Who is to say if the key catalyst is a technique, an attitude, a personality, or even a fortuitous assemblage of congenial variables which happened to be there at the right time in the right place? The few inadequate instruments for proper measurement don't do the job, and, further, are rarely put to use when they might add objective knowledge. At least a symptom check-list, for example, might tell us whether a person is feeling better, though it certainly doesn't indicate whether he is living the personally transcendent life. So we know only that a procedure or a program appears to do some good. But we don't know, why, how, and for how long.

The fact is that immediate changes in mood, immediate amelioration of symptoms, immediate improvement in the feeling of well being—all can come about from a variety of means. A community can burst forth with positive energy through political change, the emergence of a strong and popular leader, a sense of unity arising from a common cause or a common disaster, or the optimism that accompanies the innovation of a program—any program, that promises the solution of a problem. Families and individuals "feel better" in these circumstances as well. Analogous is the seeming efficacy, for troubled people, by way of such vastly disparate stimuli as psychotherapy, primal therapy, scientology, LSD, hypnosis, membership in crusading political movements, encounter groups, religious sermons, nude marathons, "rap" sessions, Jesus movements, Liberation movements, and, yes, bowel movements.

The question of whether the results are palliative or curative is a pivotal one. Not that there's anything wrong with palliation, and if it can free people from obsessing about their pain long enough to devise more productive ways of living, that certainly is not to be frowned upon. But let us not forget that palliation is neither cure nor prevention. It is often a cover-up, a substitution of another thing that is time-consuming and mind-consuming, and thus a mask which happily covers the pain, rather than eliminates it. Such masks need constant replacement, as each, in turn, wears out—and this is exactly the way some people run their lives in order to escape from a recognition of their mediocrity, their pain, or their loneliness. Programs for the community can look marvelous because they make waves. But often, after a time, and in the clear light of day, the waves turn out to be evanescent ripples. The great dreams held out for the Community Mental Health Center movement have not been realized. "Action for Mental Health," that bible in 1961, is lying unopened on many a bookshelf.

It hardly seems appropriate for the editors of a book to exhort the reader to examine its contents carefully and critically. But as representatives of Psychiatric Outpatient Centers of America (POCA), they feel that such exhortation is in keeping with the aims of that organization, from whose meetings much of the material arises. POCA exists as an arena in which its member clinics can gain through an ongoing dialogue around community mental health as a fluid process; changing with the times and with social change, dependent upon and interdependent with the people and processes of the community itself. The frenetic activity within the arena is the stuff, the ideas, the seething cauldron, from which its subscribers (and the readers of this book) can pick and choose, take and discard notions and bits of activity that can then be molded and remolded in ways useful in each clinic's context.

The papers have been selected to give the reader a chance to capture an ambience, and sense a few beginnings. Between these covers, in microcosm, is a flavor of some of the happenings in the field at this particular time. There are research studies, narratives, editorial comments. By no means is this a compendium of strict scientific papers. The focus is clearly on the current trend toward breaking down the walls of the clinic in previously unforeseen ways—not through the construction of new walls, as in "storefronts" or "satellite clinics," but through a free-flowing collaborative interaction between clinic and community, where clinic does not necessarily mean "a" clinic, but a system of clinical attitudes pervading other aspects of community.

The intent is clear. The clinic is part of the community, not as a separate unit within it, but as a dynamic part of its economy, its politics, its sociology, and its people. The distinctions between medical, non-medical, and paramedical have become fuzzy. The authors and the subjects range among all lines of the community spectrum: doctor, lawyer, Indian Chief, writer, veteran, among others. The topics include flood, earthquake, war, poverty, family, etc.—and (if we can borrow them from the title of one paper) dinosaurs and octopuses as well.

From Dr. Toussieng's articulate plea for creative thinking, to Dr. Dumont's trenchant comments on the need for humanity, humility, and realism in our professional endeavors, there are embedded many pearls of differing colorations in this volume. Some of the material may strike familiar chords, some may appear innocent and naive, some will certainly be new and unusual, some relevant, some less so for the reader. In any case, a careful absorption of the contents will afford significant insight into what's happening——now.

A.B.T.
C.L.A.
E.K.

An Opening

Mental Health: In Memoriam

Paul W. Toussieng, M.D.

DEAR BROTHERS AND SISTERS,

Though I am grateful to have been asked to say a few words at this first stockholders meeting since Mother's death became publicly known, I find the assignment hard because my feelings are very complex. On the one hand, I find it sad and anxiety provoking to face up to the fact that our dear Mother, Ms. Mental Health, is no longer with us. What is going to become of all of us, her children, the "Mental Health Gang"? For we know that mother, even though she lived with him and went under the last name of "Health," never was actually married or otherwise related to Mister Medicine. Thus all of us children are really illegitimate—or "bastards" as people less friendly to us might call us. It is an open secret that we also do not all have the same father. Mother had a weakness for any man who had money and power and freely shared her favors with them. The man she kept introducing as Uncle Sam was clearly her favorite, and he has undoubtedly sired many, if not most of us. Yet, at the very same time that we no longer are able to hide mother's death, Uncle Sam has let it be known that he is through paying child support for us. (Between us, I'm not surprised. We really socked it to that nice guy for a long time. We fooled him cleverly enough with nice birthday cards like "Action for Mental Health," so that he did not catch on to what degree he was being had for almost twenty-five years!)

3

If mother were still around, she might have succeeded one more time to persuade Uncle Sam to continue supporting us. Knowing him as well as she did, she, for example, might have played on his terrible fear of illness. Our brother Rosenhan[10] has recently again documented how easily we can find major mental illness in anyone who is admitted to one of our corporate temples. (Because we are among ourselves, I am not using the name "hospitals," which we all know we use only to make it look to our friends and clients that we really are Mr. Medicine's children.)

Even so, I wonder whether even mother, in the long run, could have saved our huge family enterprise: "Salvation Through Mental Health, Inc." Having been born during Queen Victoria's reign, mother was a typical child of the Industrial Society and Era. For her there was no question that the mind could be sick just like the body could be sick. It never bothered her that while human bodies function essentially alike, though they may look very different, human minds come in such an endless, everchanging variety that we still are unable to find general laws that apply to all minds in the same way we have been able to with our bodies. It didn't matter to her that we still haven't been able to agree on a definition of exactly what "mind" is.

Instead, Mother was keenly aware of the heavy public responsibilities of psychiatry which, as our brother Szasz[13] so brilliantly has documented, required that she and her giant corporation assist governments by taking over, in the name of science, the witch hunts which the Inquisition used to conduct in the name of religion, and which, unfortunately, had fallen into disrepute. With her shrewd business sense mother perceived very early how well Dr. Kraepelin's fantasies would lend themselves to this delicate task. The scientific face which he gave to his speculations would provide an excellent and necessary alibi to appear as Mr. Medicine's legitimate wife while freely continuing her illicit love affairs with other influential men. Being able to go everywhere on Mr. Medicine's arm made it possible for her to meet many more such men. With her tremendous social skills she became an unmatched hostess who was tireless in pleasing her guests and always could come up with the mostest.

We all remember the glorious days when Mother expected to be asked to solve the problems between nations and of the world, and was letting it be known that she was available and ready for such assignments. Who can forget the times when Congress complained that Uncle Sam was not supporting us in style, and, over his protest, raised mother's child support and Aid to Families with Dependent Children? With all those beautiful memories reverberating in our minds, I almost feel guilty confessing that I, nevertheless, am glad that mother was allowed to die peacefully at this time rather than after her age would have sidelined her even more. The many years she had lived and loved had taken their toll. Even though she dressed up in mod clothes, her wrinkles, blue hair and bony knees mercilessly gave away her age. Worst of all, her Victorian grace, philosophy and way of life no longer at all fitted the times in which we now find ourselves. As unpleasant as this may be, it, therefore, behooves us to learn from what happened to mother, lest we ourselves, by continuing to identify ourselves with her and to live the way she taught us, become premature museum pieces and also are left behind by the new times.

Mother was born into a stable colonial society, where change was gradual and predictable. What the governments and the elite wanted in those times was to have an ample supply of stable workmen and employees, so that their countries could continue to steadily increase their Gross National Products. In this way, the white Christian Nations which ruled the world would eventually be able to match their economic power with their colonial and military powers. However, just as things were really beginning to roll, unrest arose between the working classes and the elites. Production suffered from strikes and other works of the devil.

Finally, the governments had no other recourse but to start a series of international wars, which diverted the workers' attention and allowed the governments to assume far-reaching powers over all their citizens. During these wars, the governments more and more came to realize the value of the services offered by mother and her brood, particularly by those of her sons working in our Military Branch. By World War II that branch had accumulated a lot of experience. Soldiers trying to cop out from fighting were talked into returning to their battles in larger numbers than ever before, so that the enemy could kill them as planned. (After all—what good is a war without a lot of "blood and guts"?) After World War II, when there was a lull in the fighting and national economies temporarily had to be switched back to peacetime production, it was logical for governments to expect that mother's enterprises would be able to keep workers productive and on their jobs. Mother responded by immediately creating a new Industrial Branch. An intensive public relations campaign further bombarded the market.

In her 1958 report to the Joint Commission on Mental Illness and Health, our sister, Marie Jahoda,[4] crowed:

> . . . under the guidance of voluntary and governmental agencies, the public has taken hold of the term (Mental Health) in spite of (or, perhaps, because of) its ambiguity. Funds are being raised and expended to promote mental health; educational campaigns are being conducted to teach people how to attain this goal for themselves, for their children, for their community.

Clearly, the millions were beginning to flow into mother's coffers, and made it absolutely necessary to rearrange and restructure the family enterprise. The present multibillion dollar conglomerate, "Salvation Through Mental Health, Inc.," was born.

In 1962, one of our conglomerate's most persuasive salesmen and revivalists, brother William Menninger,[9] titled his address before the College of Physicians of Philadelphia "Mental Health, Everybody's Business." He proudly noted that it now had been established that 17½ million Americans needed salvation through mental health. He promised that Mother would do away with crime and delinquency, with "the famous three A's of industry— alcoholism, accidents, absenteeism," with the painful facets of family life, with the problems of students in the educational systems, with problems in courts of law, with the tensions of life for all of us, with mental illness, and that she would reduce the high cost of caring for the mentally ill, if society would just give her the necessary wherewithal. Listening to what brother Will said it was clear that the Devil's days were numbered if only Mother received enough donations.

Well, Mother got the money and our conglomerate enterprises grew and prospered. She could count on making thousands of new converts daily. Their donations built many a palmshaded shelter for us, her humble and busy offspring. Only her fertility matched Mother's tireless energy—we have become a family of many thousands, not even counting our own families and our nearest kin. Why is it, then, that we today not only mourn the passing of our beloved Mother, but face the future with unbecoming anxiety and trembling?

Though she was too old to do so herself any more, Mother would have approved of, and even encouraged, our taking a hard look at what has happened to our revival and salvation market, so that we again can find a rich lode mine. Clearly, the Devil has been at work, and there can be no doubt about his identity: Albert Einstein. His theory of relativity, which made all phenomena four dimensional by including time, destroyed not only Newton's centuries old stranglehold on science, but fundamentally changed the way in which we had to view ourselves, our fellow human beings, and man in general. Our own salvation movement has, until recently, stubbornly resisted taking a look at this. Thus it was our nephews in sociology and anthropology who owe so much of their know-how to us, who first studied the full implications of the new view of man for our business enterprise. In the process they unfortunately were able to figure out, by sheer deductive reasoning, that Mother was dead and had been dead for some time. All our efforts to shield her body from public view and all the other tricks we had used to conceal her death suddenly stood exposed—as did we. That could not be and was not healthy for us as revivalists, particularly after it turned out that Mr. Medicine neither would, nor could, protect us.

Exactly what has this, the new view of man, done to us? The answers to this question depends on whom you ask. One of our more senior brothers, Edgar Levenson,[6] Director of Clinical Services at the William Alanson White Institute of Psychoanalysis, Psychiatry and Psychology, studied what happens if we include the time factor into our credos. He found that even the most holy words and the most holy concepts will continue to change meaning as time passes, regardless of how we try to counteract or ignore this. He came to realize that Freud's Dora, if examined by one of our brothers or sisters today, would be called a schizophrenic, not a typical hysteric. Hence our wonderment where all those nice hysterics from yesteryear have gone: today they are schizophrenics.

Levenson shows us that neither the mechanical (work machine) paradigm of Freud's era, nor the updated mechanical model, the communication model of Sullivan, Erikson, and others, any longer can deal with the postindustrial, electronic era of today. In this era of rapid, constant, unpredictable changes, this era where everyone is constantly flooded with information from all sides, attention to content is simply no longer possible, nor even desirable. We need to look at the overall context, the overall "gestalt." This he calls the "perspective paradigm."

Levenson still finds it necessary to cling to some "ism," some theory (Lévi-Strauss', Piaget's, Foucault's, etc., "structuralism") but his clinical examples make it quite clear that he, when he is with his clients, is fully aware of, and takes the full consequences of the fact that, in the new context, "therapist" and "patient" continuously mutually reinvent each other. Thus he now ignores the content of the contacts with clients and looks at the overall context—the system into which he finds himself being ensnared by his clients and the setting in which he meets them. It should be very obvious that not in any way can this context be fitted into a health-illness model. The goals which we pursue with our clients in context will be elusive indeed.

Some members of our family, like brother Jose Lombillo[7] and his associates in Naples, Florida, have already dropped the old rituals of evaluation and diagnosis. Together with their clients they determine not only what they will be working on, but also decide what goals they will seek together and what criteria they will mutually use to measure to what degree they have accomplished those goals. In this they are making use of brother Kiresuk's[5] "Goal Attainment Scaling," which fits the new era well, but eliminates the last illusions of Mr. Medicine's paternity. For in these procedures there is no room, or even possibility, for concepts such as "mental health," "mental illness," etc. Sister Carolyn Attneave[1] and brother Ross Speck,[12] while developing what they call "network intervention," have learned to leave the analysis of a problem, as well as the figuring out of a solution, entirely to the family tribe they ask to gather. They, themselves, offer no opinions, nor do they make any prescriptions.

Our cousins in sociology, such as Goffman,[2] as well as our own aforementioned brother Rosenhan,[10] have shown us to what degree the setting in which we work determines how we will see our fellow human beings, let alone how we then subsequently will end up "treating" them. Hence the whole world now knows that our concepts of "mental illness" and "mental health" are pure figments of our imagination and merely have been invented by us to help us appear to be the legitimate children of Mr. Medicine. I'm grateful that mother died before this truth leaked out to a larger public.

The only comfort in this situation may come from Margaret Mead,[8] who sees the whole adult generation of today as being in an outdated, and therefore phony, position. She calls all of us adults today "immigrants from another era" and promises us that we will never fully grasp what it is like to grow up in an Einsteinian world with television. No wonder that a thirteen-year-old boy, whom I was supposed to "treat" through psychotherapy, instead awed me by building an extremely complicated Hi Fi amplifier in his sessions with me. He was as blasé about what he was doing as I was about diagnosing his resistance to treatment and managed quite effectively to make me feel as outdated as parents who can't help their kids with the New Math.

We, the children of Mental Health, are in danger of becoming permanently uncomprehending spectators if we, in reverence to our dear departed mother, continue to consecrate ourselves to her styles of thinking and working. Thus, while mourning her passing, we may instead want to join the times we are now in, rather than to continue to worship mother's heroes: Newton, Queen Victoria and Kraepelin. This will require that each one of us change in certain fundamental ways. For learning new and clever techniques will not get us into new times, only a new way of being-in-the-world. In the Einsteinian world all of us are engaged in interchange with others—objectivity, partial involvement and detachment are not feasible in that world.

Following man's fate through the Darwinian, Einsteinian and Freudian "revolutions," Sydney Harris[3] shows how each of these "revolutions" further dethroned man. Man could no longer view himself as the child of God, the center of the universe, or as acting only on the basis of conscious premises. Harris leaves out the ecological revolution, which now drives home to man how dependent he is on this planet's biosphere—the very area he had planned to exploit and master. In this situation, Harris sees man in need of becoming a "fuller person," just like the acorn tries to become the "most" oak tree it can be. "Becoming what we are meant to be" to Harris is the core meaning of the "authenticity" which he believes man today must have. To work towards that goal, then, is a task both for the helper and for the client. However, seeing the clients and ourselves in this light no longer leaves room for concepts like "mental health" or "mental illness," which by their very nature are cross-sectional concepts, concepts which attempt to exclude time. What we will need instead are longitudinal, relative concepts which can fit into a four-dimensional space and can comfortably harbor concepts such as "process," "systems," etc.

Gazing into the lovely face of a child sleeping between his two peasant parents, Saint Exupéry[11] decided he looked like Mozart. Almost instantaneously he was gripped by horror as he thought of what would happen to this little Mozart once he was put into the "common stamping machine." Saint Exupéry sighed: "When by mutation a new rose is born in a garden, all the gardeners rejoice. They isolate the rose, tend it, foster it. But there is no gardener for men."

What I should like to propose here today is that we honor Mother's memory by deciding to become gardeners for all men, including ourselves. This means realizing our own potentially noxious or even lethal behaviors as well as the other ways in which we stunt or inhibit our own and other people's growth. Once we have really allowed ourselves to see what we are doing to ourselves and others, we can better tend the garden of humans. There will then no longer be space for preconceived ideas as to what the goals of growth should be or where it should go. We will know and understand that we stunt or inhibit ourselves as we force others into patterns which do not fit them. Acknowledging our dependence on nature in this manner will keep us from interfering with it as little as possible, while nurturing and respecting it. Thus we may support and cheer that growth and change which constitutes the hyphen between birth and death.

Our dear Mother, Ms. Mental Health, has reached the end of her hyphen and is no more. Thanks to the way she has brought us up, we have become massproduced, stamped out Mozarts rather than Beethovens, Bachs, Chopins, etc., etc. However, the spark of life is still in us, and thanks to our resilience we may still bounce back to our original shape and resume some growth. As we turned our back on Mother's grave, left the cemetery and walked back out into the world of the still alive, we entered the world of relativity, of four-dimensional space, of interdependence of all things. Mother was no part of that world, nor could she ever be. Her name will blaze on the marble monument which will mark her grave. However, trying to cling to Mr. Medicine's family no longer means anything in the world in which this stockholders' meeting take place. I, therefore, respectfully move that we change the name of our conglomerate from "Salvation Through Mental Health, Inc.," to "Mozart to Mozart, Acorn to Oak, Assistance Corporation, Inc." I believe Mother would have been the first to second this motion, though probably for the wrong reasons. May her buckchasing soul continue to find hundred dollar bills wherever she is now!

REFERENCES

1. Attneave, Carolyn. Personal Communication, 1972.
2. Goffman, Erving. *Asylums: Essays on the Social Situation of Mental Patients and Other Inmates.* Garden City, N.Y., Doubleday Anchor, 1961.
3. Harris, Sydney J. *The Authentic Person: Dealing With A Dilemma.* Niles, Ill., Argus Communications, 1972.
4. Jahoda, Marie. *Current Concepts of Positive Mental Health.* Joint Commission on Mental Illness and Health, Monograph Series, No. 1, New York, Basic Books, Inc., 1958, 5.
5. Kiresuk, Thomas J., and Sherman, Robert E. "Goal Attainment Scaling: A General Method for Evaluating Comprehensive Community Mental Health Programs." *Community Mental Health Journal,* Vol. *4* (6), 1968, 443-453.
6. Levenson, Edgar E. *The Fallacy of Understanding: An Inquiry into the Changing Structure of Psychoanalysis.* New York, Basic Books, Inc., 1972.
7. Lombillo, Jose R., Kiresuk, Thomas J., Sherman, Robert E. "Evaluation of the Effectiveness of a Community Mental Health Program." Mimeographed.
8. Mead, Margaret. *Culture and Commitment: A Study of the Generation Gap.* Garden City, N.Y. Natural History Press/Doubleday & Company, Inc., 1970.
9. Menninger, William C. "Mental Health, Everybody's Business." *Transactions & Studies of the College of Physicians of Philadelphia,* Vol. *30,* July 1962, 11-18.
10. Rosenhan, D.L. "On Being Sane in Insane Places." *Science,* Vol. *179,* 19 January, 1973, 250-258.
11. Saint Exupéry, Antoine, De. *Wind, Sand and Stars.* New York, Harbrace Paperbound Library, Harcourt, Brace & World, Inc., 1967, 242.
12. Speck, Ross V. and Attneave, Carolyn L. *Family Networks,* New York, Pantheon Press, 1973.
13. Szasz, Thomas S. *The Manufacture of Madness.* New York, A Delta Book, Dell Publishing Co., Inc., 1970.

PART I

Mobilization of Community Resources Subsequent to Profound Disaster

Mobilizing in Response to a Major Disaster

K. Patrick Okura

On June 23, 1972, the Susquehanna River, fed by the torrential rains of Tropical Storm Agnes, overflowed its banks and broke the dikes holding back its waters from Luzerne and Wyoming Counties in northeastern Pennsylvania. What has been called "the greatest natural disaster in American history" ensued.

At the time of the flood, Luzerne County had a population estimated at 342,000 people, most of whom had deep roots there and many of whom were Roman Catholics and members of specific European ethnic communities. A quarter of the population were older than 55 years. Seventy-eight percent of the people lived in towns or cities, of which Wilkes-Barre, the county seat, was the largest, and the county's economy was an urban one; during the previous decade manufacturing had displaced mining as the primary employer of labor.

Wyoming County immediately to the north, in contrast, was rural and agricultural. Its population was estimated at 19,000 people, only 11 percent of whom lived in urban areas (mostly in Tunkhannock, the county seat), and its 500-odd farms dominated the local economy.

The flood finally crested on the evening of June 26 and the Susquehanna thereafter rapidly receded to its normal boundaries, though some parts of Luzerne and Wyoming Counties remained inundated for several weeks afterward. The damage it wrought in the two counties was immense. Though fortunately there were only a handful of deaths, almost 400 homes were totally destroyed, 15,500 sustained major damage, and 5,500 others received minor damage. Because of the residential damage, between 70,000 and 75,000 people were forced to move to other quarters. One hundred fifty manufacturing firms suffered greater or lesser harm, most of their more than 11,000 employees rendered temporarily jobless. Three thousand commercial enterprises were similarly affected. Bridges were down, roads were impassable, telephones were out, and other vital common properties were rendered useless. For a time, water transportation was more efficient than land transportation in the affected areas.

In the mental health area, the Office of the Administrator of the Luzerne-Wyoming County Mental Health/Mental Retardation (MH/MR) Joinder, which operates public mental health services in the two counties under the supervision of the county boards of commissioners acting jointly, and MH/MR's Mental Health Center No. 1, both co-located in downtown Wilkes-Barre, were flooded out, and damage was later estimated at more than $200,-000,000. In addition, about half the MH/MR staff personnel were flooded out of their homes.

James H. Lawler, the MH/MR Administrator, initiated 24-hour emergency psychiatric service at the unaffected Wilkes-Barre and Nanticoke State General Hospitals on the morning of June 24 and at the same time arranged emergency communications with several of the federal and state relief units already on the scene. The following day, after assessing projected mental health needs and because part of his staff was unavailable owing to transportation and personal problems, he won authorization from the Luzerne and Wyoming County Commissioners to hire 12 college graduates as temporary workers; half of them began work on June 26 and the remainder on June 27 or 28. After brief training and orientation they were assigned as members of nine four-person teams of experienced mental health teams, three of which were headed by psychiatrists. The teams' initial effort was to make contact with emergency shelter and medical-unit chiefs to make known the availability and range of MH/MR's psychiatric services, their location, and ways to communicate with them. The teams also dealt with problems of mental illness as they encountered them in the shelters and medical units. During the week that the teams focused on the centers, each managed to visit between seven and nine centers during its 12-hour working day. The following is Mr. Lawler's report about that period, as detailed in MH/MR's July 23, 1972 proposal to the National Institute of Mental Health for a longer-range mental health service, training, and evaluation program:

Teams headed by psychiatrists covered the larger shelters (150 to 2,000), which did not have medical components. The non-psychiatrist teams covered smaller shelters (housing 10 to 150). A large number of problems and psychiatric emergencies were encountered and handled. By July 2 the psychiatric in-patient units at both Nanticoke and Wilkes-Barre General were filled. Numerous OBS, disorientation, depression, anxiety reactions, situational disorders, arteriosclerotic conditions were manifesting themselves in the shelters. Temporary psychotic episodes due to lack of food and sleep were also encountered in this first week. A number of mentally retarded and disoriented children were manifesting acting-out or withdrawal symptoms. Reactions due not only to lack of privacy in shelters, but also to lack of diabetic, cardiac and psychotherapeutic medications were frequent. Agitation, irritability, and hostility symptoms were expressed by others. Intervention verbal counselling was a primary mode of support . . . due to a need for ventilation and acceptance of the reality of the crisis. On June 28 the city day-curfew was lifted and many shelter residents visited their homes for the first time, and with this the physical manifestations of psychiatric and emotional difficulties increased.

Because he realized that the dozen college-graduate temporaries were too few and insufficiently trained to meet MH/MR's needs, the Administrator on June 26 asked the Pennsylvania Department of Public Welfare to supply additional, trained staff. The Department arranged for six psychiatrists and 24 social workers, registered nurses, and caseworkers to volunteer their services, and they reported for work in the affected area on July 3, staying for one week. The 12 college-graduate temporaries were released on or before August 31 as funds for their salaries ran out.

Initial NIMH Involvement

Although various investigators in the National Institute of Mental Health had interested themselves in the emotional sequelae of previous disasters and the Institute was well versed in research on crisis intervention, it had not intervened in the aftermath of any disaster before the Rapid City and Susquehanna flood because it had not been organizationally structured to do so. An internal reorganization coincident with these two disasters now allowed it to do so for the first time: several activities dealing in one way or another with crisis intervention, including the Center for Studies of Suicide Prevention, were to be merged on July 1, 1972, into the Mental Health Emergencies Section, which could deal with a situation such as that in the Wilkes-Barre area.

As the flood began to recede, we received several calls from State and local officials requesting assistance. We responded immediately to the call for help by dispatching a mental health team of four headed by Dr. Harvey Resnik, Chief of the newly established Mental Health Emergency Section, to Wilkes-Barre to examine and deal with the mental health needs of flood survivors. After two days of touring the stricken city and its environs, conferring with local mental health workers and rescue officials, and camping out in an armory, the team concluded that there would be long-term psychiatric sequelae of the flood, that NIMH would have a useful and important role in dealing with them, and that the organization of an NIMH-sponsored program should be undertaken at once. Dr. Resnik then helicoptered to Philadelphia to confer with colleagues in Regional Office III and arrange for the execution of several immediate measures, and then returned to NIMH in Rockville, Maryland, where he reported to Dr. Bertram S. Brown, NIMH's Director.

During the early weeks of July, officers at NIMH fleshed out the present mental health program in Luzerne and Wyoming Counties through correspondence, quickly arranged meetings among interested parties, and—above all—telephone calls. The final shape of the program was clear by the last week in July.

The Program Contracts

The NIMH program was to consist of three parts: services (which would account for most of the funds spent), training, and evaluation. Because the program's quickly hired frontline workers would have no schooling in crisis intervention, they would have to be trained, and because it was hoped that the nature and extent of the mental health problems the program would encounter as well as its effectiveness in dealing with them would serve as guidelines for action after future disasters, the program would have to be evaluated.

On July 23, at the invitation and with the assistance of NIMH, the Luzerne and Wyoming County Commissioners, on behalf of their Mental Health/Mental Retardation Joinder, submitted a proposal to NIMH requesting funds for a year-long program of mental health services to residents of the flood-affected area. Project Outreach, as the program was to be called, was to be headed by a project director who would report to the MH/MR Administrator and, besides the project director, would have a staff of six supervisors (one community organizations representative, two social workers, one casework supervisor, and two casework trainees), 50 Human Service Aides (later called Human Service Counselors), and three clerks—a total of 60 persons. The salaries of all but 38 Human Service Aides, equipment and supplies, rent, telephone and postage fees, travel expenses, and other costs of the service portion of the program were to be paid through a $249,908 NIMH-MH/MR contract, and the salaries of the remaining 38 Human Services Aides were to be paid through an NIMH staffing grant of $231,242.

The training and evaluation functions were contracted for through the Eastern Pennsylvania Psychiatric Institute in Philadelphia which was to receive $5,000 for its overhead services. In turn, it subcontracted with Community Crisis Corner, Inc., of Gainesville, Florida, for $61,590 in training services and with the Community Mental Health Research and Development Corporation, of Buffalo, for $57,500 in evaluation services.

The Program Begins

Project Outreach was activated on August 10. Initially, its staff consisted of only two members, Edward F. Heffron, the project director, and Martin Marshall, the community organizations representative. During their first week and a half on the job—in makeshift quarters in downtown Wilkes-Barre that they were to occupy until the end of October—Messrs. Heffron and Marshall interviewed applicants for the first 20 Human Service Aide positions, which paid annual salaries of $5,007, $5,268, or $5,803.

A number of approaches were used in recruiting the aides, the first of which was publicity in the local media associated with the awarding of NIMH funds to the project. Others were referral sources including public and private social agencies, churches, unions, governmental units, the Pennsylvania State Employment Bureau, private employment agencies, and federal units, and the community grapevine. Newspaper advertisements and street posters were later to be used in recruitment. Personnel selection was guided by considerations outlined in the project proposal: the Human Service Aides should "be indigenous to flood-affected areas, and/or indigenous to Luzerne-Wyoming Counties, and/or be directly, personally affected by the disaster, and/or have experience since June 22 in the delivery of crisis intervention mental health services."

The 20 trainees chosen comprised 13 men and seven women ranging in age from 20 to 56 years and in education from high school completion to master's degree. The majority were recent college graduates without previous professional experience. Representatives of ethnic groups prominent in the area as well as Vietnam veterans were among the 20, who were almost evenly divided between married and single persons.

The first training course was held at Retreat State Hospital at Hunlock Creek. The instructors were all associated with Community Crisis Corner, Inc., an organization closely connected to the University of Florida at Gainesville.

During the first two and a half days the trainees were told the purpose and philosophy of Project Outreach, instructed in the nature of crisis and disaster and the theory and practice of crisis intervention, and asked to read explanatory materials supplied by the staff. Another day and a half was devoted to specific Human Service Aide duties and administrative policies and practices. The trainees spent the mornings of the fourth and fifth days in the field with supervisors to gain personal experience with the problems they would later face, and the afternoons of those days discussing their findings and reactions to them with the training staff. Much time in the training sessions was devoted to sensitivity-oriented team building, which was judged highly effective in creating a feeling of unity and mutual purpose among the trainees.

On August 28 the newly minted Human Service Aides took to the field full-time, concentrating their efforts during the first week or 10 days in one relatively small area of the Wyoming Valley. The reason for this was basically twofold: the supervisory staff wanted to gain needed knowledge about the community's receptivity to outreach work, the effectiveness of the canvassing or door-to-door approach, the kinds of needs that existed, the nature and speed of the recovery process, and the advisability of assigning aides to two-person teams; and, second, the area in which the aides were first deployed had been undersupplied with social services. Most service programs at that time were concentrating their efforts on evacuees in temporary trailer sites, leaving a gap in services in areas where evacuees were returning to their homes. The area in which the aides first worked was characterized by returning residents, an unusual proportion of the elderly, and a strong sense of neighborhood identity.

During this early period the Human Service Aides canvassed freely in their assigned area, sometimes meeting people on the street and sometimes knocking on doors to talk to residents. Later each day they would review their day's encounters with other aides and supervisors, thus sharing experiences and gaining advice on difficult matters. Approximately 200 contacts were made during the period, few recorded in writing.

On the basis of the aides' reports during the initial week of operations, Mr. Heffron and his fellow supervisors reached two organizational decisions that are still in effect. First, the aides would work in pairs to allay certain anxieties that had developed during the first week, enhance their feelings of security, and encourage their continued willingness to involve themselves in potentially difficult situations. Second, it was decided that teams composed of paired aides would work in five geographically defined areas for administrative convenience and to let the aides develop a useful sense of identification with a locality and responsibility for the people in it. Team assignments were made with an eye to developing internal balance; hence, consideration was given not only to whether workers lived in their assigned areas but also to personality, sex, age, and education. A supervisor was put in charge of each team.

Early Facts and Fears

To prosecute their work effectively, it was urgent for Project Outreach's leaders and their consultants to identify and project the short- and long-term mental health effects of the disaster and, at the same time, to deal firmly with misinformed rumors about those effects.

Early on, according to the MH/MR proposal to NIMH of July 23, 1972, mental health workers "observed a number of persons manifesting some degree of psychological and emotional disturbances. A fairly common manifestation was depression, disorientation, and inappropriate behavior (laughter and giggling upon receipt of news of loss)." The intake figures compiled by Mental Health Center No. 1 in Wilkes-Barre for the 18-week periods from June 24 to August 28 in 1970, 1971, and 1972 reflect these observations quantitatively. The intake for the period was 260 cases in 1970, 283 cases (an increase of 8.8 percent over the previous year) in 1971, and 343 cases (an increase of 21.2 percent over the previous year) in 1972. Of the 15 problem categories noted in the records, noticeable differences were observed in two areas. In 1971, 33 cases were classified as "thought and affective disorder," whereas 102 cases were so classified in 1972, an increase of 209 percent. On the other hand, 25 cases were classified as "disturbance of social relationship" in 1971 compared to nine such cases in 1972, a decrease of 64 percent.

It is clear from an Associated Press dispatch published in the local press on September 26 that there was some disagreement among the area's psychiatrists about the extent and future of mental illness resulting from the disaster. One Mental Health Center staff psychiatrist, was quoted as saying that his clinic was treating greater numbers of persons for depressive syndromes (he guessed the increase to be 45 percent) and that the affiliated Children's Service Center in Wilkes-Barre was busier than ever. "That's because the children have been scattered from their neighborhoods because of the housing problem and are upset by attending school in unfamiliar surroundings," he said. A psychiatrist associate agreed: "The adults are thrust right back into the cleanup, but the children only hear the discussion of the tragedy and they can't get involved." In contrast, the chief psychiatrist at the local Veterans Administration hospital derided those observations: "Children are having a wonderful time. They're running around home trailers, riding bicycles all over the area, buzzing around, helping out," called Project Outreach "money down the drain." "People need financial help, that's all they need," and scoffed at a possible increase in suicides: "I know the people here. They are not the suicide type."

Indeed, the possibility of a rash of suicides was widely bruited, and both Project Outreach and NIMH went to some pains to disprove rumors to that effect in the community, the local press, and the national media. In late August or early September Messrs. Lawler and Heffron visited the Luzerne County Coroner, to learn how many people had taken their lives since the flood, and later had the pathologist give a signed declaration of his negative findings to two visiting NIMH officers, finally releasing them to the press: "We have had three suicides since June 23, when the Susquehanna inundated a large portion of the valley, and that's no increase. In my opinion, none of the three is attributable to the disaster. We've had 19 suicides to date this year, and that's about normal. I don't think these people are going to take their lives. They're tough. They are used to hard work, and they will work, not quit." That apparently squelched the suicide rumor.

During the months since Project Outreach began, its leaders have tried to work closely with the press and community leaders to explain their work and the nature of the mental health problems the area faces in the wake of the flood. Several news conferences have been held; the local press was invited to attend the dedication of the project's new offices in a modular building on the grounds of Wilkes-Barre's Treadway Inn on October 16 and it was covered thoroughly in the papers, even though the offices were not occupied for two more weeks. Community leaders and the heads of other relief agencies have been visited, a general flyer about the project was prepared for release to the public, and posters have been tacked up throughout the area explaining how any member of the public can get the project's help. Mr. Heffron and his colleagues believe that these steps have allowed the project to maintain a high profile in the community.

The literature about the emotional sequelae of disasters clearly indicates that during and immediately after a catastrophe, the medical problems that are encountered are somatic rather than psychiatric, but that from the first week afterward and for some months thereafter a variety of greater and lesser emotional problems is evident in the stricken area. Such was the experience in Luzerne and Wyoming Counties. During the flood and in the few days after the waters receded, the area's people were busy saving themselves, their possessions, or both, and coping with urgent problems of readjustment; while shock was clearly apparent, there seem to have been few other symptoms of mental disequilibrium in that period. Depression stemming from property loss and—perhaps more important—acute anxiety about housing and the coming of cold weather began manifesting themselves in early July and became more noticeable as the weeks progressed. Some of the early problems that Project Outreach workers encountered subsided as housing and job conditions began returning to normal, and other, perhaps longer-term problems that will be discussed below began appearing. NIMH and Project Outreach officers nevertheless realized that the emotional sequelae of the disaster would have to be dealt with for some time, and so continued their work.

Further Operations

The second training course, attended by 21 Human Service Aide candidates, was held from September 11 to 15. The same staff of instructors that had given the first course was in charge. The selection procedure was similar to that used in recruiting the first group of aides except for a greater amount of newspaper advertising, and about 50 persons were interviewed. The 21 chosen for training comprised 11 men and 10 women aged 19 to 62, with an average age of 30. Whlie several were recent college graduates, there was a greater diversity of backgrounds in the second group: it included a reformed alcoholic, a nutritionist, a beautician, a teacher, a former security guard, and several laborers. All 21 trainees completed the course, which was judged as successful as the first.

The second phase of training—in-service programs—also began during the second Human Service Aide course when, on September 14 during the absence of the trainees on a field exercise, the first group of 20 aides was brought back to discuss their first two and a half weeks' encounters and reactions with the training staff in depth. On the afternoon of that day the first and second groups of aides met and mingled in an attempt to promote unity among them.

Immediately after the second training course the new aides were assigned to the existing teams in the five geographic areas established earlier, and the teams continued their work of door-to-door canvassing and visits to people who had been referred to them in one way or another. Each worker wore a name tag identifying him as a Project Outreach aide of "MH/MR," but he avoided telling clients that he was a mental health worker because of the adverse reactions they would sometimes display when confronted with known mental health representatives. The aides continued to return to a designated place in midafternoon for group conferences in which they could share their experiences and gain the advice of their supervisors about difficult cases. During the second aide group's first full week on the job the teams made 603 individual contacts, responded to 86 separate referrals from other agencies, and talked to more than 50 community leaders at all levels.

Two significant administrative developments occurred during the weeks after the second group of aides began their work—the project's supervisory apparatus took definite shape and careful records began to be kept. Neither had occurred before because of the fluidity of the early weeks, the urgency of the work at hand, and the intimacy of the project's workers that sprang from their small number. A progress report Mr. Heffron submitted to NIMH in late November spells out these developments:

Possibly because of lack of time and previous experience, supervisory staff were hired on the basis of their education, background, and estimated ability to handle supervision of paraprofessionals. None of the supervisory staff has previous administrative or supervisory experience. The original philosophy was to allow supervisors to function rather independently with the social workers to provide the clinical backup and direction as required. During the initial weeks there was no particular desire or observable need to develop a hierarchy of supervisory staff below the Project Director. If the program was to remain flexible, mobile, and innovative, it was felt that the total responsibility should remain initially with the Project Director, with all supervisory staff functioning as "equals." This approach essentially allows the "cream" to rise and makes the chief administrator's decision on lines of authority much easier. This process was used in appointing the two casework trainees.

As the program developed and some 40 of the staff completed training and entered the community, the supervisors had to assume the responsibility for a team of aides. At this point, the "inequality" of the supervisor started to become apparent. This inequality refers to the fact that a natural kind of hierarchy began to develop based on experience, training, and other factors. At the same time, there began to exist a need for a slightly more structured approach to maintain the operation of the program.

For several weeks following the second training program, each team met with its supervisor daily for general orientation, guidance, and assignments. Also, one member of each team telephoned the Project Outreach office twice daily for any additional instruction. Workers were encouraged to contact the office whenever they required guidance or information. An effort was made to have at least one supervisor in the office at all times. One member of each team is still required to telephone the office daily, and each team now meets with its supervisor at least three times weekly.

As the weeks passed, the need for a somewhat refined record system became more apparent. A specific intake form and procedure were developed whereby referrals from the community or other agencies pass through the intake supervisor to the team supervisor to the workers, who follow up on the request. At the same time, any previous contacts with the individual or family are noted to provide continuity and avoid duplications. The few notes taken during client contacts are made on notepads. The Intake and Proposed Plan Sheet is prepared shortly after each contact, but only if any service is provided or contemplated. Workers retain the intake sheets until they consider the cases closed and have justified such recommendation to the satisfaction of their supervisors. Until late October it was not possible for the supervisory staff to be fully informed concerning worker case loads. In late October, Project Outreach workers were required to submit all intake sheets to the supervisory staff. On this occasion, all cases were recorded administratively to establish centralized control and files. Open cases were then returned to the workers.

Henceforth, a three-copy client information sheet will be prepared on each contact, whether worker-initiated or referred from other programs. Each client information record will be followed up with an intake sheet report. One copy of the client information sheet is to be retained in the office, a second by the team supervisor, and the third by the worker . . . .

Yet another development in the program was the initiation of evening and weekend coverage on December 26. The supervisory staff had been preparing for it for some time, and part of the preparation was the second in-service training session, held on October 5. Dr. McGee spent that morning with the supervisors working out a tentative plan for the extended coverage and that afternoon briefed the entire staff on the techniques of crisis intervention by telephone, which have been used widely and successfully elsewhere in preventing suicides. As part of the training session he played tape recordings of actual such telephone conversations in which the identities of the callers were concealed. The project office is now manned from 5 p.m. to midnight on weekdays and from noon on Saturdays and Sundays until 1 a.m. the following day by three workers, one to respond to telephone calls and two to act as a crisis intervention team on a rotating basis. Every aide participates in the rotation.

Staff changes also occurred during the closing months of 1972.

Several Human Service Aides resigned, two were promoted to casework traineeships, a woman with a master's degree in social work was hired as a supervisor, three women and two men joined the staff as aides, an agreement was signed on November 8 with the Mercy Hospital School of Nursing in Wilkes-Barre to allow 18 junior nursing students to spend at least one day a week with Project Outreach teams as participant observers, and a handful of master's degree candidates in social work at Marywood College in Wilkes-Barre were hired as half-time aides. Although the social work students function as Human Service Aides, they cannot become involved in dealing with clients when continued service is indicated because of their   part-time status and so turn such clients over to full-time aides.

As of January 5, when Project Outreach submitted its most recent progress report, the staff comprised the Project Director, two social workers, one casework supervisor, one community organizations representative, two casework trainees, 44 full-time aides, six half-time aides, and two clerk-typists—a total of 59 persons.

The most pressing personnel problem has been the continued resignations of Human Service Aides to take higher-paying jobs elsewhere in the area. One of the aides from the original group of 20 resigned before the second group joined the staff; a few candidates who were offered positions in the latter group either declined after a day or two of further job-hunting or failed to report for training, and at least three members of the second group resigned within a few weeks of the date they began work. "A check on the status of these individuals made it quite clear that in the month between the hiring of the two groups the economic picture of the area had changed considerably," Mr. Heffron wrote in his second progress report as early as October 13. "The influx of new programs and additional support for existing agencies put Project Outreach in a competitive hiring position. Almost invariably, these people indicated that they had decided to take other jobs at higher salaries." He and his fellow supervisors felt the answer to this problem was obviously higher salaries, and so proposed abolishing the original three-step scale for aides ($5,007 to $5,803) and substituting a two-step scale of $6,000 for 30 aides and $6,500 for 20. Since the proposed increases would go beyond the Presidential wage guidelines, they were submitted to the Philadelphia Regional Office of the Pay Board on December 18 for approval.

Despite salary frustrations, the aides are "providing services in an increasingly efficient manner," Mr. Heffron recently reported. "As a result of their field experience, and to a degree because of the type of supervision offered them, they are highly confident of their own abilities to provide service in difficult situations. Some of these situations include working with acting-out psychotics, severely depressed persons, several potential suicides, and some aged facing death because of terminal illness. The aides now consider themselves seasoned and competent, yet they remain spontaneous and eager."

Relations with Other Organizations

Of necessity, Project Outreach had to maintain close contact with other emergency organizations in the area. Relations among these organizations were not always smooth, as Mr. Heffron observed in an early progress report: "As recovery operations progressed, coordination of all activities became a monumental task, exacerbated by lack of experience in coping with emergencies and further intensified by manifestations of state and federal rivalries. According to local sources, this seriously hampered the recovery process. Nevertheless, federal and state officials active in flood recovery efforts attempted to work together despite political complications."

Project Outreach's relations with two organizations—the Department of Housing and Urban Development and the local United Services Agency—are particularly noteworthy.

By late October, HUD had provided housing to about 14,000 families in Luzerne County in several programs, the most significant of which for Project Outreach were 24 HUD-operated sites housing 2,000 families and 11 commercial sites subsidized by HUD housing 300 families on the one hand, and the provision of trailers—usually located on damaged personal property—to 1,700 more families on the other.

At the housing sites that HUD either operated itself or supervised, site managers and resident advisers in a ratio of one per hundred families were in charge and responsible for arranging whatever social services the evacuees required. Initial progress reports from Project Outreach indicated that it had managed to establish a degree of rapport with the site managers and resident advisers in gaining access to troubled site residents, but recent progress reports tell another story. The most recent report states:

> Continued attempts by Project Outreach to gain access to the HUD group sites were fruitless. Official HUD policy bars any canvassing on the sites and, as a result, Project Outreach can enter only on the request of the resident adviser. This policy is of increasing concern to Project Outreach inasmuch as reports indicate a great deal of hostility, frustration, anxiety, and depression among the park residents. Project Outreach is now trying to gain access through the auspices of the United Services Agency and the Pennsylvania Department of Public Welfare.

Another source of friction between the project and HUD was the latter's decision in mid-fall to recall the trailers or "camper units" that it had lent many families, usually to live in on their own property while their damaged houses were being repaired. HUD noted that the units were not suitable for winter living and announced that they would have to be vacated by November 28. "As the date of withdrawal approaches, the anxiety of the residents increases, especially since many will not be able to return to their own homes and therefore must move to a HUD group site or make other arrangements," a Project Outreach report in mid-November noted. By the end of the year, however, HUD had changed its mind. "As a result of considerable public pressure, HUD developed a new policy whereby a decision on camper trailers would be made in each individual case, thereby taking specific problems and situations into account," Mr. Heffron reported. "This alleviated much anxiety."

Another interorganizational problem that affected Project Outreach's work was the uncertainty and occasional vagueness of its relations with the Pennsylvania Department of Public Welfare and a state-funded agency established on October 1 called the United Services Agency. In mid-September the state deputy secretary of public welfare for the region embracing Wilkers-Barre was relieved of his duties because of inefficiency. The lack of responsiveness from the Department of Public Welfare before and after his reassignment caused Project Outreach some concern. At about the same time state officials developed a plan to set up the United Services Agency to coordinate several social service programs, including mental health, in Luzerne and Wyoming Counties. Funding of the mental health program, among others, was to be shifted from the counties to the state, and the executive directors of the participating local agencies were to become part of the USA central staff and serve as technical consultants to the directors of several multifunction centers that USA would establish.

The uncertainties surrounding this plan left the bicounty Mental Health/Mental Retardation Joinder and its subordinate Project Outreach in doubt about their future status throughout the fall and early winter. But, apparently to assure his future, the MH/MR Administrator opted to accept an offer to become director of the USA's proposed Hazelton-Nanticoke center as of January 1. Project Outreach's organizational relationship with USA apparently has still not been fully resolved.

Evaluation and the Future

As noted above, the Community Mental Health Research and Development Corporation of Buffalo entered a subcontract with the Eastern Pennsylvania Psychiatric Institute of Philadelphia to evaluate Project Outreach. After reviewing the project's first 70 closed cases filed in late October, the firm submitted its first, essentially descriptive report to the Eastern Pennsylvania Psychiatry Institute and NIMH on November 15. It is scheduled to submit its final report on the project sometime during the summer of 1973.

By the beginning of this year the Project Outreach staff had contacted 9,504 persons. Both the project and the evaluation staffs have noted changes in the nature of the problems being encountered. "To a great extent, the majority of problems discovered by the aides during the first three months dealt with concrete needs, most often related to housing," Mr. Heffron reports. "These people were angry, frustrated, anxious, and quite often depressed. As the weeks passed and the early problems resolved themselves, a whole new set of problems seemed to surface. Project Outreach aides have reported finding an increased amount of drinking as well as increased tensions within families or among individuals housed together because of the flood. They also report increased feelings of isolation among many people in both the communities and group sites."

Two breakdowns of interest covering an unspecified but apparently recent period are given in the latest progress report:

1. Problems dealt with by Project Outreach

Problem Type	Pct.
Mental-health related	37
HUD, Small Business Administration, and other recovery agency-related problems	20
Housing	19
Physical health	9
Aging and related problems	8
Domestic and child welfare	5
Mental retardation	1
Serious alcoholism	1

2. Ages of Project Outreach clients

Age	Pct.
Under 20	2
20-29	7
30-39	10

40-49	17
50-59	17
60-69	28
70-79	14
80-89	4
Over 90	1

Project Outreach's funding is scheduled to end in early August 1973. The experience it gains during the coming half-year should be of vital importance in planning for and carrying out emergency mental health programs following future disasters.

An Earthquake Shakes up a Mental Health System

Sherry Stein

The Earthquake

On February 9, 1971, an earthquake in the San Fernando Valley, California caused the death of 64 persons, destroyed numerous homes and office buildings, 3 hospitals, a juvenile detention facility, and a dam. It uprooted trees, tore apart a new concrete freeway, and wrought damage totaling one billion dollars. Hardest hit was a 25-square mile area where a new $30 million 888-bed hospital was damaged to such an extent that it had to be abandoned. In the hospital complex was the Olive View Mental Health Center: one building housed 100 psychiatric patients in open wards on the 5th floor; the other building had 2 floors, and housed 50 patients in locked wards. The earthquake caused the five-story structure to drop 8 feet, 4 wings splitting off from the core building like a schizophrenic reaction. The 2-story building was converted into a 1-story structure when the 2nd floor "slid down like an elevator" (as described by a patient) thereby becoming the 1st floor.

One amazing reality is that from the 888-bed hospital, only three lives were lost in the upheaval. Another amazing reality is that 131 patients with psychiatric problems walked to safety in an orderly and controlled fashion after being tossed out of bed and cast into darkness, challenged by the destruction of exits, and withstanding the terrifying rumble of the earth's motion and the screeching of shifting walls.

At the time of the earthquake, a staff psychiatrist on duty reported that his first reaction was to contact the fire department on the grounds. When he found the equipment inoperative because the firehouse doors were blocked, he went to the Mental Health building and found that the occupants were already gathering in a nearby parking lot. He noticed that the patients were amazingly calm, and wondered if they were in shock. An order came from someone indicating that patients should be taken to one of the old one-story buildings that seemed intact. He thought that it would be safer to be out in the open, but followed instructions. By then, inpatient treatment staff arrived and took over. One of the psychiatrists reported that she drove up to the hospital shortly after the earthquake and sat there looking at the destruction in a stunned way for "fully five minutes" . . . annoyed with herself that she delayed going into action for as long as five minutes! One of the patients described the experience later in this way: "I was already up, grabbed my robe, but left my good slippers. My 70-year-old roommate was a 'moaner' and kept moaning through-out. I saved her life, but she just kept moaning and did not appre-ciate what I did for her. She doesn't even know that I saved her life. There was a lot of broken glass and a lot of rumbling, and it was very dark. The nurse and some of the men patients led the way down the stairs from the 5th floor and it was just like the movie 'Lost Horizon' where we seemed to be walking in clouds of plaster dust on broken glass. We were hugging people we didn't even know. The nurse got some records while she was calling out instructions. She asked me to help get the other patients under control. I wasn't frightened. It was my time to help someone where so many were panicky."

A psychiatric resident and a fireman went into the mental health building and brought out some medication and some of the card files which contained patient identification data. One staff member commented that he would not have taken such a risk because the tilted building presented a grotesque appearance which was intimidating. Psychiatric staff gathered patients together on the lawn and organized a system to determine where they would be sent. When it was announced that they were to go to the state hospital, a few patients became agitated, protesting against going there, but soon responded to reassurances by staff. A few patients were given tranquilizing medication.

The Study

Our earthquake study developed when ENKI staff shared personal reactions to the earthquake experience with one another: those who were single apartment dwellers shared experiences with their neighbors; those with families became immediately engaged in the safety of their children, spouses, and even pets; those whose children were grown and out of the home seemed immobilized, contrary to their usual patterns of responding immediately to danger. I was one of those who felt immobilized, but believed that I would have been quick to act if my children had been at home. Without this responsibility, I assumed a passive role and waited for my husband's directions. This was not at all in character for me! Within an hour after the earthquake, we were at my husband's Home for the Aged, where we viewed the reactions of another population in a group-living situation. Here we found 230 residents, average age 84, calmly eating breakfast by candlelight. It seemed that their "togetherness" contributed to their relative serenity.

Because of these reactions, ENKI staff speculated as to how groups of psychiatric patients, a population presumably already in stress, would react in terms of immediate or delayed trauma. We wondered what might be learned about the behavior of people who are grouped together in a setting that is destroyed in 30 seconds by an earthquake. It was our conviction that documentation of reactions of people in an institutional system at the time of the catastrophe, along with a follow-up study, would provide valuable clues for planning preparedness programs.

Attempts to obtain funding for the initial study and for follow-up interviews were unsuccessful. It is ironic that federal funds were immediately available for inquiry into the environmental aspects of the earthquake, but not for inquiry into people's adaptation to disaster.

Having worked with Erich Lindemann, I recalled his concept

about "hazardous events." After the Coconut Grove fire in Boston, he found that people who had lost loved ones in the fire, and had sought therapy in handling their grief soon after this event, were able to withstand later crisis with greater inner strength. Those who had no exposure to therapeutic intervention at the time of crisis were less able to adapt to subsequent crisis events.

ENKI was interested in exploring crisis concepts further in relation to events at Olive View. We had been in the process of studying the Olive View program prior to the earthquake, as part of a research project on California's new mental health legislation. When Olive View was destroyed, ENKI decided to find the program wherever it had relocated. First, it was necessary to find where the patients had been taken. Since there was little telephone communication, the primary news source was from transistor radios; however, even these reports brought confused and contradictory information about Olive View patients. ENKI staff went to the Los Angeles County Psychiatric Hospital where the patients reportedly were to be sent. Although the hospital was preparing for them, they did not arrive.

We learned later that some patients left or were sent home directly from Olive View; 40 patients with drug problems were sent to a university hospital; and 76 psychiatric patients were sent to Camarillo State Hospital located 50 miles away. Transportation was provided by people from the community responding to the Center's request.

Of the 76 patients transferred to the state hospital, 6 left immediately, and others were soon discharged, so that 3-6 days after the earthquake, we were still able to interview 41 patients in the state hospital. There were a few patients who were not available because they were on home visits. Families were interviewed in all but 6 cases, and 2 patients asked us not to contact their families.

As a safeguard in planning our approach for interviewing patients, we decided to lead gently into the discussion of the earthquake in order to ascertain patient reaction. After a few test interviews, it became clear that these discussions gave rise to no adverse patient reaction. In fact, patients were eager to talk of their feelings about the earthquake experience. Some patients discussed the earthquake with staff or families, but a number had not talked about it at all. We learned that there were no general hospital guidelines as to whether or not discussion of the earthquake experience should be encouraged, and there was great variation in practice. On one ward, medical and nursing staff deliberately avoided all mention of the earthquake and considered our interviews with patients a potential jeopardy to their equilibrium. However, it was our feeling that planned discussion would tend to decrease ongoing tension.

Patients whom we interviewed could be divided into three general groups: (1) those who were on voluntary status and in contact with reality, (2) those who were hospitalized on an involuntary basis for 72-hour observation, and (3) those who were certified as dangerous or gravely disabled resulting in hospitalization for 17 days. Some patients said they decided to remain at the state hospital for treatment "because there was no other place to go." Although a few subsequently changed their minds, they found that they could not leave because discharges were not processed during the 4-day holiday which began on February 13, six days after the earthquake. Although some patients and families did not like this, they accepted it as one of the rules.

In spite of Olive View's request for a separate ward at the state hospital so that its patients and staff might remain together, this plan did not develop. Patients were placed in a number of different wards and were incorporated into the state hospital's program. Patients and staff spoke of the loss they felt in being separated from relationships that had been an integral part of the therapeutic Olive View community.

One of the most frightening features of the earthquake experience, according to all patients, was the darkness; and this suggests the urgent need to plan for emergency lighting in disasters. Other disturbing aspects were the rumbling noise of the moving building, the plaster dust, and the cold weather. Most of the women grabbed robes, but not slippers, and were assisted by the men who, for the most part, put on pants and shoes. Many were troubled later that their personal possessions were lost in the rubble. Many patients said they were not frightened during the earthquake, but were upset afterwards when they saw the destruction around them. Tension and uneasiness increased as they sat, cold and hungry, waiting to learn what would happen next. One patient reported:

> I was so doped up the night before, I was unaware there was an earthquake. I thought I'd had a wild dream, and that I was thrown out of bed because of the dream, so I simply returned to bed. Even when I heard people screaming, I was still unaware that it was an earthquake. It was like being derailed from a roller-coaster. Someone yelled that we should meet at the nursing station, so I put on my boots and pants, though I was still foggy. I followed others to the station where the nurse told us to hold hands and go downstairs. By the time I got downstairs, I realized there had been an earthquake. But since the building was still standing, I asked if I could go back for my glasses. I had no fear then. It took a couple of days to realize what had happened. I might have been in shock then. I still feel nervous and restless. (5 days later)

Most of the patients were concerned about their families but did not try to contact them, waiting instead for them to call. This suggests that these patients were not inclined to act on their own initiative. They tended to follow instructions well, indicated by their good response to evacuation directions by staff. In planning for preparedness education programs, consideration should be given to measures which will tend to help the passive isolated individual as well as the person who readily tries to find help.

Almost all family members voiced concern about their inability to locate the whereabouts of the patients for as many as four days, although they called the police, local newspapers, the County hospital, the County Department of Health, the Red Cross, ministers, and other resources. The language barrier was a key problem for some families of Mexican descent. A few families drove out to Olive View, found the patients, and took them home; while others who drove out were unable to get through the police lines. At least two relatives living in the East flew immediately to Los Angeles to try to locate the patients. One of these heard that all of Los Angeles was devastated. Some families, tuned to transistor radios, were frightened to hear about the deaths at the nearby Veterans

Administration Hospital which was sometimes incorrectly identified as Olive View Mental Health Center.

Patients commented that the earthquake was particularly startling to them since it occurred while they were asleep (6:02 a.m.). It seemed to be an exaggeration of a confused state: "I thought I was dreaming"—"I just pulled the covers over my head." Many felt immobilized but responded when they heard staff calling out instructions for them to gather at the nursing station. One patient said:

> I was in the two-story building—the building where the second floor fell gradually down onto the 1st floor. I was terrified, couldn't see anything except furniture falling. I called out, "What is it?" and someone said it was an earthquake. My bed had rolled to the door, jamming it. We got out to the hall somehow through the dark and dust and falling plaster. I reached into my bathrobe pocket for cigarettes and had none, so I dashed back into the room to try to locate them, but did not stay long. On the bus driving to the state hospital, the main topic of conversation was the fact that there were no cigarettes .

Another reported that she was having delusional thoughts but was able, nevertheless, to try to reassure and calm other patients. Several prided themselves on their heroic behavior. One woman told her husband that she could not remember the earthquake, but by the time we saw her, two days later, she remembered being "scolded for preaching about the Ten Commandments and justice." One of the medical staff recalled that she was one of the few patients who was agitated and was given medication before being placed in the bus transporting patients to the state hospital.

For a number of depressed patients, the earthquake seemed to act as a brief shock treatment that enabled them to respond to directions, get out of the building, and help others. One patient had been hospitalized a few hours before the earthquake, and was so hyperactive and uncontrollable that he was placed in restraints—a practice used only in extreme situations. At the time of the earthquake, a nurse disengaged his restraints, and told him that an 18-year-old catatonic girl could not get out of the building without help, and it was up to him to direct her. He escorted her safely out, remained coherent for a few hours, then regressed. When he improved a few days later, he clearly recalled these events. It seemed that this experience was something in the nature of a shock treatment for him. Some patients who regressed subsequently improved rapidly.

Olive View patients whose medical records noted them to be delusional, agitated, or extremely hostile prior to the earthquake were under heavy medication. By the time of our interview within the next few days, almost all were able to talk calmly and rationally with us. In fact, except for one patient in a catatonic episode and one who said she was "Jane Doe," all patients were in contact with reality and were able to identify themselves. By the time of our interview on the fourth day after the earthquake, "Jane Doe" was able to give us the name and address of her brother, and this information was given to the hospital.

Almost all patients contrasted the differences between the beautiful, modern Olive View facility, where 3 or 4 persons shared a room, and the less attractive state hospital with 30 in a room. They were troubled to be in a setting with a great number of patients with chronic illness and regressed behavior symptoms, in contrast with those at Olive View Mental Health Center where "you could hardly tell who was patient, staff, or visitor."

Despite the interruption of their treatment program and the transfer, at a point of crisis, to a less attractive facility located further from families, we found that the patients whom we interviewed made a remarkably good adjustment at the state hospital. We felt that this was related to the fact that the single outstanding characteristic most meaningful to all patients was that Olive View's staff had "cared" about them. They said that staff members were "beautiful," "great," "effective," and had "not panicked." Staff evacuated patients safely with calm but firm instructions and were concerned about their needs. For example, some of the staff pulled up their cars for patients to sit in after being evacuated, because it was cold outside. Patients commented: "The staff had been on duty all night and stayed on with us until 2:00 or 3:00 in the afternoon. They were fantastic. They really cared." "Most of the patients stayed calm—maybe they were in shock—and the nurses were 'beautiful' in the way they got them all out." This points up some of the qualities found to be meaningful to people involved in sudden environmental disaster. The glow of the universal feeling that "they cared" was still very strong 3-6 days after the earthquake, at the time of our interviews. The fact that staff cared for them appeared to help patients readjust to a new setting and transfer the good feelings about staff to the personnel of the state hospital.

During the two weeks following the earthquake, there were more than 200 aftershocks registering up to 4.4 on the Richter scale, compared with the earthquake reading of 6.6. The fact that Olive View patients were removed from the area, and did not experience the repetition of the shocks, probably contributed to their overall adjustment. ENKI staff felt these Olive View patients were less fearful during the aftermath of the earthquake than those of us who remained in the area where the aftershocks continued.

In general the patients seemed to react during the disaster with a great deal of stability, seeking leadership from staff to effect their rescue, attempting to help each other. They seemed to adapt unusually well to a unique experience. It might well be that the enormity of the earth's disturbance lessened the quality of their own disturbed feelings.

Olive View Mental Health Center

Some of Olive View's services were slow to reorganize after the earthquake. Of the 150 inpatient beds, only 3 beds were relocated in other setting in the community, while all new admissions from the San Fernando Valley were referred to the state hospital. Emergency and outpatient services were set up temporarily in other County programs, and were later relocated at Olive View site in old buildings that had been only minimally damaged. Some personnel were shifted to other County programs, and some chose to resign rather than accept other assignments.

It is necessary to understand the pre-existing Olive View personality to understand the impact of the earthquake on staff. Olive View Mental Health Center was like a family of professionals who had moved into a lovely new home and were planning together to bring about a gratifying way of life for psychiatrically disturbed persons and for each other. There was a tremendous let-down for staff when their beautiful home was destroyed and their program could not continue intact.

The day treatment program survived the earthquake intact. About two hours after the earthquake, a half-dozen patients from that program arrived at Olive View and arrangements were made for the group to meet on the following day. They used one of the old buildings, although there was no heat, electricity, or water. Portable toilets were set up outside the building, and staff brought hot water in thermos jugs for instant coffee.

Although it was colder inside the building than it was outside, warmth radiated from patients and staff in their pride that even an earthquake had been unable to destroy their program.

Comments on Findings

1. Olive View patients were distressed by the failure of the electric lights system as well as the auxiliary emergency electrical system. Regulations should require battery-operated systems for lighting and for communication emergencies. We have grown so accustomed to the magic of world-wide communication that we have neglected to develop adequate local emergency systems for communication, resulting in great trauma for families who attempt to locate victims of disaster. It is essential that disaster communication systems be multi-lingual.

2. There is a need to develop plans for coordination among mental health systems for emergency care procedures during disasters.

3. Follow-up crisis consultation to the staff of institutional systems after sudden catastrophic incidents would facilitate individual, group, and system equilibrium. We found that mental health systems, as well as individuals, undergo functional *depression*.

4. It seems important that patients involved in disaster events should be provided with the opportunity to participate in organized discussion in order to minimize anxieties. When no warning precedes

a disaster, people do not have time to prepare themselves and the shock is dramatic and immediate. Erich Lindemann's studies have shown that avenues for directed catharsis are needed to prevent delayed emotional reaction.

5. Olive View's patients were convinced by the staff's valiant efforts to lead them to safety that the staff really cared about them. In the past, some of these patients found it difficult to see themselves as persons who could be loved, but the dramatic demonstration that "staff cared" touched them and enabled them to become engaged in new relationships. It may be that some psychiatrically troubled people require unusually strong demonstration of positive feeling in order for them to respond to the therapeutic process.

6. ENKI began this study with the premise that persons in treatment for acute psychiatric conditions might react to disaster events with less hysteria than the general population because of their generally passive nature, or because of the influence of medication. We found that Olive View patients did, in fact, respond very well. It seemed that they reacted to the challenge of rescue, to strong leadership, and to group identity with a common problem. It was true that these psychiatric patients fared well under earthquake conditions, but perhaps, for reasons other than those we had anticipated.

7. It was our impression that an individual in a group situation tended to be propelled into action more quickly with less immediate shock than an individual who was alone. We believe that organization of people into groups and assignment of tasks and responsibilities during catastrophic events tends to minimize stress reactions. Therefore, it seems valid to suggest development of pre-planned systems to organize groups with delineated and assigned tasks to be implemented at a time of disaster. The theme of assigned responsibility might be compared with Erich Lindemann's concept of task orientation, although it is used here in a different context. He used the task orientation concept in terms of assessing a child's ability to function. This theme could be the basis for development of a systematic approach of pre-planned task assignments for any organized group such as a neighborhood, apartment complex, factory, office, or any institution.

In summary we feel that disaster preparedness should include planning for individuals and community organizations to deal with immediate or delayed emotional stress to minimize trauma after emergency situations.

Update—February 21, 1973

A major earthquake again rocked the Los Angeles County area. The epicenter was located in neighboring Ventura County and was only 1/10 to 1/20 as great in intensity. Estimates of damage to homes and businesses were about one million dollars, and three people were injured.

Radio and television reports of reactions of people in Los Angeles County varied from those who were more frightened with each new quake, to those who were adjusted to continuing earthquakes as a routine way of life. There were no clues as to why each person developed a different set of attitudes.

For me, the second earthquake of my life resulted in none of the fear and immobility that the first one produced. As my husband and I stood in the doorway, within the first 10 seconds of the 20 seconds that it lasted, I said immediately, "Oh, this one is not as bad as the last one."

I am certain that this optimistic fearlessness could be directly attributed to the therapeutic benefit which I experienced in writing this paper. Therefore, I would like to thank POCA for helping me experience earthquakes with a brave new attitude.

Twice Born Men

Chester Paul Adams and Jack McCloskey

I spent twenty-seven months in federal prisons. When I went in I had a family, a home, and a clear picture of what I wanted to do with my life. During the months I was locked up I learned a great deal about what prisons do to people who work for them as well as to people who are locked up in them. I learned those things in what I thought was an objective way—watching my fellow inmates and the employees, learning that the guards were in as much of a prison as I was. None of that knowledge meant much to me. It was just something that stuck in the back of my mind. I knew the ways I adapted to oppression, struggled against coercion, and kept my mind free. And I watched my brothers in those same struggles winning and losing. What I learned was what prison reformers have always given lip service to—that prisons program prisoners in negative ways that insure that prisons stay in business. When I got my parole and began to get ready to go home, an old man sat me down and said, "Son, you've been away from the world for a while, and it's all changed. Nothing you knew is and everything you thought wouldn't happen has." But I didn't believe him. I just packed my gear, headed out the front door, and headed home. I tried to. When they let me out, home was where they told me to go but I couldn't find it. I looked and looked but I must have put it down in one of those long hallways and forgot where I'd left it. Wherever it was, it was someplace else. So I got a job as a cook in a town on a beach and for six months I tried to find out what had happened to my direction, manhood, ability to love or even feel. For six months I sat there until one day my friend David came by and told me that there was a job to be done in San Francisco and nobody knew how but me and would I quit sitting on the beach and come do it. When I moved to San Francisco, I started with a bunch of people on a political initiative to stop the war in Southeast Asia. I found out that out of the forty thousand California residents who worked on that campaign, the ones who worked the hardest and seemed to be most like me were a group of Vietnam Veterans. And so we became friends.

A couple of the Vietnam Veterans I got to know had put together a rap group and were getting together every Wednesday night to work on this thing called "Post Vietnam Syndrome." They were working on defining what it was and why the Veterans Administration and professional therapists had either refused to see it or employed methods that were ineffective if not additionally damaging . . . and what things they were doing to heal themselves. I had had some paraprofessional training in group facilitation methods here, in New York, and some experience working with groups of chicanos and junkies in the southwest before I went to prison and had set up groups while I was locked up. Besides, I still had this numbness, and pain and dreams. When the vets told me about PVS it was like hearing someone talk about me. The symptoms were the same. So I guess that's what we want to tell you about now.

Post Vietnam Syndrome

It appears that a significant proportion of Vietnam veterans, especially those who were extensively involved in active combat, have serious problems readjusting to civilian life. These problems may not become apparent for six months to two years after return to civilian life and are manifested by job instability, difficulties in relating to other people, depression, social alienation, anger and resentment, emotional irritability, poor control over aggression, alcoholism, and drug addiction. These symptoms are a sign that considerable time may be needed in order to master the mental conflicts associated with overseas war experience and come to terms with the complications of our present turbulent civilian society.

There are four main factors that underlie this problem: (a) Estrangement from home values and behavior due to military life overseas, (b) Closing of ranks at home during the veteran's absence, (c) Brutalizing of the soldier by combat experience, especially in guerrilla warfare, and (d) Ambivalent welcome to the veteran by a home society in unstable equilibrium, with precarious control over its own violence.

(a) *Estrangement Overseas.* The soldier in Vietnam, like the volunteer in the Peace Corps, must learn a new way of life that in many respects is alien to his home culture. He becomes accustomed to ways of relating to others and managing the details and rhythm of his life that are different. He learns new manners and develops a liking for new foods and different people and surroundings.

When he comes home he feels a stranger, and it takes him quite a time to relearn (or unlearn and replace) his old habits and values. This is particularly difficult if the problem was unexpected, and if while he was overseas he had built up a sentimental picture of the peaceful gratifications of home to make up in fantasy for the privations and dangers of his military experiences. Not only is it a shock to discover that home life also involves much difficulty, but he sees many of its aspects with the eyes of a stranger and perceives complications in areas that he previously took for granted. He may share with other young people the cynical rebelliousness that is currently so common, an attitude that may have been particularly stimulated by his military experience.

(b) *Closing of Ranks at Home.* The social circle in the family, among friends, and in the work situation has usually taken up the slack in the man's absence. Life has gone on, and his old roles may have been allotted to other people. His room at home may have been kept empty, and his place in the affections of his close family may not have been filled, but his old friends and girl friends may have developed other relationships, his place at work may have been taken by another, and his favorite seat in the local bar may have become someone else's favorite seat. The veteran may have to work hard to break back into the circle again, and since he may have meanwhile changed his own interests, he may be uncertain in his motivation and therefore less effective in doing so. He may also be weakened by his frustrated longing for the warm ties with his old military buddies that he contrasts with the cool relationships he finds awaiting him back home, where so many of the men of his age have not shared his experience. Apart from anything else, he is two or three years older and has missed the opportunity for the smooth development linked with the passage of time that he would have enjoyed if he had stayed home.

These two sets of problems are expectable in the case of any overseas experience, but for a Vietnam veteran they are aggravated by the following:

(c) *Combat Brutalization.* Our combat forces in Vietnam were trained to kill, and in order to do so effectively they learn to dehumanize their enemies. Since much of the fighting is at close quarters under guerrilla conditions and the Vietcong and North Vietnamese combatants mingle in civilian clothes with the local population, the boundaries of this dehumanization are difficult for the men to define—much more so than in traditional warfare, where the enemy is in uniform and fights in circumscribed units and situations so that the inhibition of normal humane feelings can be compartmentalized to fit such conditions. In Vietnam there appeared to be a tendency for our men to generalize their hostile responses on to local civilians and even South Vietnamese and other Asian fellow combatants. The vagueness of these boundaries of suppression of normally forbidden savage impulse makes it especially difficult eventually to regain civilized control.

Many Vietnam veterans not unexpectedly continue to have great difficulty after they come home in asserting consistent mastery over their violent impulses, and in overcoming deep feelings of disgust and guilt associated with their former combat behavior. Particularly difficult is the process of allowing themselves once again to experience empathy and compassion for the difficulties and sufferings of other human beings, after these feelings had been systematically suppressed in order that the men could maintain mental balance during combat. Once these humane reactions have been frozen it is difficult and painful to thaw them out.

(d) *Ambivalent Reception By The Public.* Most of us are currently uneasy about the issue of violence and its control. Our civilian society is driven by social and racial tensions, and polarized by conflicts about law and order on the campuses and in the streets. Public opinion is deeply divided in regard to the merits of the Vietnam war and this has aroused particularly violent reactions and counter-reactions among the peers of the returning veterans.

The result of all these factors has been a less than optimal reception for Vietnam veterans among the general public, and a widespread fear that they may unleash their violence on the home front because of a resentment about their lot or because they take sides in a community conflict, and thus upset our current precarious equilibrium. We have the impression that this fear sometimes leads to a defensive denial that the veterans have significant problems in readjusting to living back home, and this contributes to a lack of public initiative in providing services to help them deal with the transition, which in turn exacerbates their situation and increases their resentful hostility.

The Veterans Administration gave the disenfranchised veteran of the Vietnam era a label "Post Vietnam Syndrome," but few Vietnam era veterans are successfully treated in VA programs and fewer will approach an agency of a government they feel manipulated by. Existing VA programs seem for the most part to be based either on a highly manipulated environment or chemical control—bases which seem defeating given the experiences of the Vietnam era veteran.

During the last several years (since late 1970) a handful of progressive professional psychotherapists and researchers in Psychiatric advocacy have studied the problems of the Vietnam veteran, some few after many months participating effectively in group experiences. Those who have (Robert Jay Lifton, Chaim Shatan, BettyJo League, George Soloman, Charles Levy) have clearly indicated in their writings that professionals are effective in such groups only if they are ready to put themselves on the line personally, a kind of subjectivity which seems to go against much training for professionals. However, only through sharing situations of emotional risk familiar to combat veterans can professionals gain trust and rid themselves of authoritarian roles resented by the veteran because of military life.

Robert Lifton tells us that there are three principles that have proved effective in veteran group experience. One is the simple principle of affinity which develops from a coming together of people who share an overwhelming historical or personal experience that no one else can fully share. A second principle has to do with "being there," a sense of presence, of full engagement and integrity, and of openness to mutual impact. The third principle is that of self-generation. The groups themselves create much of their own direction and form.

Our work for the past seventeen months has been to establish, sponsor, and promote therapeutic readjustment centers for returning military veterans and to provide such persons with assistance that will aid them in regaining self confidence and the confidence of their fellow man, and to assist them in confronting and grasping reality. That is what we set out to do and is part of what we do now, but the process of getting from one place to another involved a great deal of learning and growing and not a few mistakes.

In late 1971 about thirty Vietnam veterans began to meet to discuss their common abilities and disabilities upon return to this country from Southeast Asia. Some had paraprofessional training and many others did not, but all had been attempting to deal with their rage, depression and alienation for some time and were ready to try to work it out together. Because a number of the men had undergone ineffective therapy in existing institutions since their return, and because they all shared a distrust of objective professionalism in any field, the meetings were first restricted to veterans only, with no professional consultants or group leaders.

However, the group grew. As time passed it became evident that persons who had experienced the coercion, regimentation, violence, and dehumanization present in prison settings had parallel problems and the group began to deal with veterans of two fronts. As our strengths and weaknesses found definition, our families began to have input and needed support and we began to relate to them within our group experience. As the group developed, it defined itself. Thirty became an untenable number of people for one group, so more groups formed. Each group has, through skills shared by the paraprofessionals, structured itself.

Perhaps the best demonstration as to whether individual members have benefited from the meetings is the statement by one of the members after approximately three months of sessions, "We started out yelling at each other, not really listening and dealing with what was being said. Now at least we're talking and trying to understand what was said." This aptly stated discovery is typical of the changes that enable people to cross the bridges back into other social contexts as individual human beings.

For some individuals these group discussions on a once a week basis proved to be enough. They were able to make good use of other opportunities for training, employment, social, and family life. Within a few months members were able to find their own sense of direction and companionship not only within the groups, but also outside of them.

However, it became evident to the participants that some group members had difficulties too great for a once a week meeting to cope with. Much discussion and energy went into attempts to find alternative ways to have a significant impact on various problems of this nature. Daily sessions of the groups and individual sessions were explored as possibilities.

Primarily due to the time factor and individual scheduling conflicts, daily group sessions proved impossible to manage effectively. It was also the consensus of each group that, regardless of their sense of responsibility for one another, some "head trips" could only be tackled by the individual himself. Until this could be done, perhaps even supplementary group sessions with individual therapeutic contacts would prove inadequate. However, the demands of urban living seldom allowed the time and relaxed freedom for the basic self-exploration. The distractions and interruptions were not only distracting but disturbed any healing processes.

It seemed obvious that what could prove of assistance to the individual in solving his inner conflicts would be to provide an environment which would be free of the demands of city life. Such an environment would allow the individual to devote his energy (psychic and physical) to resolving his inner conflicts without having to expend time and energy with the tensions which pervade urban life.

With the cooperation of the group called People's Union, many members of this project were allowed to work on a farm and hopefully gain insight as to their conflicts and relationships. The endeavor seemed successful because, as the external stresses were alleviated, the group members found contact with their own beings and creativity expressed through their work on the land.

Out of this exploration developed the plan for combining the urban group sessions with planned periods of several weeks on the farm. The combined benefits of outdoor labor and continuing supportive but reality-oriented interpersonal contact seemed to provide a time and space which could not be attained within the context of daily city life. The rural group experience supplements but does not replace the urban group. Both are needed in proper sequence, usually: urban group/rural group/urban group.

Our program is broken into modules of four weeks with provision for recycling at each stage. Each stage leads to specific growth and the last, hopefully, into the maturity and self-confidence which allows an individual to evaluate daily situations, consider alternatives, and make choices suitable to himself. Movement from stage to stage will take into account the readiness of the person, the consensus of the group affected by the move, and the opinion of the paraprofessional and professional (if any were consulted).

The first stage is urban, involving entry and familiarization with the philosophy of the group, development of sufficient trust for effective participation and the beginnings of growth and reawakening. Decisions regarding the form of this group will come from its members.

The second stage involves residence in the rural group for four weeks, participation in work and therapeutic programs under the direction of the group and one paraprofessional therapist in residence. Sufficient labor will be required to maintain routine operations of the farm in exchange for board, room, and services. The degree of involvement in farm operations will depend on the individual. Although one of the goals of this stage of the program is that of learning to cooperate and work with others on the farm, it is not the intent to place heavy emphasis on farm labor.

The third stage is built around return to the urban setting. It includes a four week program focused around re-entry and survival within urban settings. It will deal with planning in relation to the individual's need to deal with employment, academic or vocational training, use of community resources, an establishment of residential (family?) base. The third stage is not designed to be "therapeutic," but referrals are available.

The fourth stage seems to us to be crucial to our personal development as well as to the growth of the groups. It depends upon "alumni" acting as senior members of groups to assist new members, giving both emotional support and practical advice. Obviously this is not a mandatory part of the program but depends on the energy and direction of each individual as he finishes the third stage. However, this makes possible a continuity of contact for individuals and also enables the program to benefit from each experience. The resulting social network provides ties with the community for all participants.

At the fourth stage, we feel those who desire to develop any therapeutic skills which assisted them during their process of growth should have that opportunity. It is our hope that a professional therapist, in addition to being available for referral and group work, will be available both for consultation with the professionals and for guidance of individuals in the fourth stage toward appropriate research materials and workshops. We recognize the value of contracting for a consultant with the best available credentials and a specific interest in innovative programs for groups previously unreached.

We also recognize that different parts of this program seem similar to a number of modern therapeutic developments. However, there are essential differences both in philosophy and technical approach. For instance, while the urban and rural groups develop a therapeutic milieu, it is not Milieu Therapy, which implies a highly controlled, manipulated environment. The latter, though effective for many persons, is not so for both veterans and ex-convicts whose problems stem from their experiences in other highly controlled, manipulated environments and whose distrust of authoritarian reward systems would defeat the processes which make professionally established Milieu systems effective.

Similarly, the need for confrontation and encounter with the self and others as well as deep understanding of personal emotional conflicts and dilemmas suggest aspects of the newer marathon, group, gestalt, and encounter therapies. While we realize the need for correct understanding of these techniques, we do not lose sight of the needs of our particular program. The important elements in this project are the men who have been through a common experience. While learning to understand and trust one another, they can adapt what they need to their specific predicament.

Post Institutional Syndrome

As we continue to work, and our program develops, we have discovered that the scars left by Vietnam and the prison experience are not unique, as we once thought. Families of veterans and ex-prisoners first approached us for help with similar scars and then veterans of other than combat experience, including women who had been in the military. Our groups now include persons from mental institutions. Also, we recently met a therapist who had recently lost her vision and was undergoing symptoms of what previously, we would have felt applicable only in veterans and ex-prisoners. What is beginning to emerge is a commonality in American experience of institutional oppression. In one way or another most persons in America have experienced the alienation, the insular reaction to institutions. Many feel the supressed rage at their impotence to affect change in the techno-systems supremacy and a hostile resistance to the channeling of energies into dehumanized functions. Most people's institutional experiences are non-coercive in style. In other words, the institutions that dysfunctionally and negatively affect people leave no more choice than prison or the military, but they deny and disguise any element of coercion. This can be seen in many schools, government organizations, churches, and nuclear families. Oppression is subtle; and yet people are forced to do things they do not want to do and about which they feel guilty and build walls of insulation.

What is institutionalization? We think it is a surrender of the dynamic power of identification, a misdirected concern, with safety and order as ends in themselves. Its results are the drying up of general and personal interest and an unhealthy exaggeration of detail at the expense of the whole.

There seem to be three stages of institutional decline which correspond inversely to the normal stages of a healthy social development. First there is a loss of the will to adventure, to accept adult challenges which involve a worthwhile risk. The group or person no longer thinks of the goal, but only of the status quo. There isn't a purposeful growing towards adult goals.

The second stage sees an increase of the intensity of life within the group or person, to the detriment of life outside. There is a narrowing of confidence to immediate cliques and related persons, a gang mindedness which includes distrust of those outside the group. This is an adolescent stage, prestige- and power-conscious, passionately subjective and only secure within itself.

The last stage is one in which even this limited security is lacking. The totally institutionalized person or group has become as dependant and as resentful of dependence, ambivalently, as a child whose helplessness isolates it from the wholeness of life and paralyzes its social functioning.

Thus is the adult component of people restricted and mutilated while the irresponsible greedy child and the emotion-driven adolescent take over his role, his right to expand and be responsible.

We are often asked and have spent much time considering why, if most Americans encounter and are affected by institutionalization, veterans and ex-prisoners seem to have such greater difficulty adjusting to life in America. Several answers seem certain: Degree of coercion, intensity of experience followed rapidly by admittance into a world which seems contradictory, and peer group acceptance. There seems little doubt that isolated, highly controlled, intense, coercive, violent experiences cause people to reshape their values and realities, and that those new values and realities seem out of context when they are thrust into the mainstream of

America after several years of absence. What plays on our minds often is the insistence by those people that their intense experiences were caricatures of what they find in much more subtle form at home.

The victims of institutionalization who are referred to us or find their way to our facilities require getting in touch with those real adult perceptions about themselves and each other, and then learning how to put those feelings and the subsequent perceptions about survival in America to work, to produce a life that has meaning and substance.

We call ourselves "Twice Born Men." The choice of name has a curious source. Daniel Berrigan, while a fugitive, wrote a letter which was circulated throughout prisons in this country. He wrote of the psychological wrongs committed by prisons and the military. Cynically, he wrote of such institutions as perhaps unwittingly being a vast network of living laboratories which segregate certain rare, spontaneous spirits, its staff more or less skilled in the deepening of men's abilities to survive. He wrote about fear and the ability to deal with it. He called men who came out of dehumanizing situations in command of their lives "Twice Born Men." We find that dealing with fear, not conquering but unmasking and learning to deal openly with fear, puts us well on the way to being alive and real about our lives. Dealing with the parts of our lives that have become deadened and dysfunctional allows us to begin the search for those homes none of us really felt we came back to.

PART II

Special Community Services and Service Systems

The Community Care Program: An Answer to the Challenge of Community "Back Wards"

H. S. Sandhu, M.D.
Robert J. Ridick, M.S.W.
Elmer K. Parent, M.S.W.

One of the greatest, certainly most difficult, and perhaps ultimately most important of challenges in the mental health field today is to develop methods and means for effectively treating the "chronic patient," (usually "chronic schizophrenic") so that he may return to and remain in the community. Successful programs of stabilization and rehabilitation have generally focused upon interest in and involvement with the patient as a person (the idea of caring for people rather than simply maintaining them). This essential ingredient, often seen in programs in the late 18th and 19th centuries, was lost with the rise of huge impersonal and insensitive mental hospitals in the early part of this century, and led to "permanent residents," "custodial care," and "back wards."

With the development of the organic therapies (and particularly the neuroleptic drugs) increasing numbers of previously hospitalized patients have returned to the community, and much has been written and spoken about "treating in the community" and "alternatives to institutional care." Community mental health programs, however, have also shown many inadequacies in dealing with this group of patients. Not only has there been the same lack of interest in the "patient as a person" even here, but also the pervasive lack of treatment and rehabilitative facilities and resources for this group of patients has contributed to a general inability on the patient's part to adjust to the outside, and a resultant increase in the rate of rehospitalization. Sanders points out that patients in a hospital setting often establish roles which they cannot translate to the community. Studies of statistics showing a high rate of repetitive hospitalization required by chronic schizophrenic patients revealed that (1) there is no correlation between what goes on in the hospital and the patient's adjustment in the community and (2) chronic schizophrenic patients' adjustment in the community is dependent upon a stable supporting social group for the patient. He also points out that of great importance is the location of the living accommodations and a low skilled job. Mowry argues that a large part of the inertia shown by chronically disturbed patients is the result of the active acceptance of a sheltered, dependent life provided for these passive individuals by publically supported hospitals, and that "reinforcement of this inertia results from the very nature of institutional psychiatric therapy, since dependency is handled as if it were always evidence of the continuing and active original illness."

David Daniels terms the chronic, relapsing, institutionalized mental patient the "marginal man" and points out the following characteristics of this group: lack of residential stability or adequate living accommodations; a long history of institutionalization in some form; frequent loss of or alienation from family, spouse, or other human resources; and poor employment history. He cites a number of internal resource deficiencies that compound these external problems: poor impulse control, with short-term rather than long-term goals being characteristic; poor self-image and self-esteem; ego disorganization; pervasive mistrust; and defensiveness, combined with apathy, despair, estrangement and lack of commitment. Daniels argues that it is "through social organization that man must obtain gratifications, develop identity, and find validation and confirmation of his social environment, especially his family and community groupings . . . for any man to change and grow, he must have the situations that provide some stress and challenge, yet also opportunity and support."

The Bedford VA Hospital is a neuropsychiatric facility of some

900 inpatient beds, with active inpatient and outpatient psychiatric programs. We registered approximately 55,000 outpatient visits last year and have nearly 1,400 active outpatients on our rolls at present. As a result of the clinical goal of providing the best possible treatment to meet veterans' needs, the development and maintenance of community programs for outplaced veterans has been of prime importance for a number of years. Since 1949, a comprehensive community care program has been an integral component of the hospital's after-care services. The program was begun with the emphasis on a reduction in the length of hospitalization, and the prevention of rehospitalization by providing additional resources to help the veteran readjust to and live in the community, be he a long-term elderly chronic patient who, although no longer in need of hospital care, found himself with no family interested in him, with parents too old or dear, with a wife who had learned to live without him or with no other close relatives; or the younger patient for whom living in a home other than his own offered the therapeutic means by which he could relearn how to live comfortably and usefully in the community.

Recently there have been many expressed concerns that not only do the communities into which patients are discharged have negligible and inadequate resources and programs for treatment and rehabilitation, but also that foster homes and community placements have simply become the "back wards" of the community. Murphy reports that the same conditions of regimentation in activity and social isolation found in mental health institutions are also present and found in foster homes that patients are released into. In this study on 50 foster homes in Canada, researchers report lack of interaction with the community on the part of the patients in the home, lack of interaction with the family, loss of initiative, and a real need for professional assistance in the foster home programs and guidance for the foster home sponsors. It is just such a condition and just such a challenge that the community care program at Bedford has dealt with from the beginning and even more so today.

The community care program at the hospital has gone through an extensive developmental process in reaching its present stage and ability, not the least of which has been the educating of the hospital staff to the therapeutic value and potential of community living and of re-educating patients to a life outside of institutional walls. Along with this has been the discovery, promotion and organization of community resources utilizable in this context, with stress laid on families, social agencies and newspaper publicity to emphasize the "therapeutic" rather than the "custodial" approach. As the nationwide rise in outplacement of "chronic" patients and the move towards an active, intensive community-based treatment program progressed, our program has had to increase its supplementary services and resources with corresponding broadening and increase of personnel. Family care home sponsors have been picked for their warmth, understanding, interest, patience and desire to help, as well as for the harmony of their family life, their willingness to work with patients, and attitudes conducive to making the patient an integrated member of the family. They are closely followed and supervised by multidisciplinary therapeutic teams made up of psychiatrists, social workers, nurses, recreational therapists, occupational therapists, dietitians, all working to promote a comprehensive rehabilitative aftercare effort with the veteran. In 1965 Bedford became the leader in the VA in its total number of placements of psychiatric patients in homes other than their own, and since then has been able to maintain this distinction. At present, the program follows over 675 patients in over 100 community residences.

Our program is based on the belief that patients, staff and sponsors can work together in new ways to achieve maximum rehabilitation of patients in the community. Its assumption is that the patients, their families, the hospital, the staff members, the community care facilities and the sponsors are interrelated in a total system. Changes in or interventions at any one point do cause changes at all points. This assumption and the multi-disciplinary approach allows us to view specific situations and deal with them in a broader multi-dimensional fashion, thereby avoiding the piece-meal and fragmented responses so often found. This shift in perspective from just the individual to individual-within-a-total-system leads to a redefinition of professional roles and prerogatives and the development of trust and respect among the participants in the system.

We view the patient and his individual program of after-care in the context of a social phenomenon. Mental illness and health are not just the result of individual and family dynamics but a composite of social forces, including institutional organizational factors and resource availability. The interaction of these with a patient's personal situation may place the solution to his needing care not at the level of his inadequacies but on institutional factors. If then the individual turns out to be one among many with the same needs, the solution will necessarily lie in intervention at the social institutional level. This perspective has required us to re-examine customary assumptions about where to direct our interventions in helping individuals. The broader view afforded by a systems approach has opened up existing and challenging vistas for action, social change and personal development.

Many of the pitfalls of "foster care" described by the Canadian study mentioned above have not developed as a result of this basic approach. An alternative to back wards in the community has been developed through an improved staff-patient ratio with multi-discipline involvement of those professions which were utilized within the institution. This staff is then charged with the task of working toward completing the job that was left undone within the institution as well as eradicating the delusion that the job was complete. Not only have various mental health disciplines been incorporated and integrated within Community Care as full participants in foster care, but also other services such as housekeeping and engineering are called upon as well. All professions are increasingly trying to close the gap between the theory of community involvement and the reality of too little involvement. As the disciplines push toward this involvement and as our health system opens to accept this involvement, Community Care programs have a ready population in need of a staff. Community Care must be ready with an appropriate invitation to its treatment partners. At least partially, that is how the multidisciplinary program at Bedford emerged. The following vignettes illustrate the characteristics of the population and the program.

John is a 49 year old man with a history of "seizure disorder with psychosis" dating from 1946 and hospitalization from that time. His seizures have been controlled with medication. His behavior for years has been characterized by staring, preoccupation and general uncommunicativeness and an inability to participate actively in hospital programming. He required considerable supervision of his hygiene. All questions were answered with monosyllabic responses. John was outplaced to a group personal care, boarding home three years ago. Multidisciplinary, community follow-up has been provided to him. He now fully manages his own hygiene. He participates in group functions organized for our community residents. He has made positive relationships within the community. He recently dined at the home of a local family and later introduced his sister to that family. He is by no means "cured" of his chronic condition but he is relating to his surroundings to a degree that astonishes his family and gives them hope that he will improve even further.

Jack is a 57 year old, WWII veteran with a history of successful community adjustment prior to the war. He developed tinnitus under extreme combat conditions. Auditory hallucinations of a persecutory nature later developed as well as delusions and hostile, threatening behavior which alienated his family. He initially was a severe management problem with elopements, verbal outbursts, and general intolerance for organized treatment programs or work assignments. He gradually became more manageable and was involved in many of the hospital treatment programs. His auditory hallucinations and delusions persisted. He often was observed gritting his teeth because of the amount of press he experienced. He was outplaced to Community Care three years ago with the goal of promoting further progress by involving him in programming within the community. Increasingly, Jack has had diminished press from his symptoms to the point where he is undergoing his longest time span without hallucinating. His mood has thus changed remarkably and his affect is now more related to life around him than to his intrapsychic distress.

The above are taken from a community of 7,000 people in Western Massachusetts where over 40 chronically ill veterans reside, including the two men whose vignettes were presented. There are five "personal care residences" in the town. Two are licensed boarding homes with 15 patients in each. All of the homes have intact families except one boarding home which has a paid residential caretaker as well as other staff. The homes are visited minimally once each week by two staff members and monthly and bi-monthly by other staff. Team meetings are held to review the status of patients and the direction of efforts by the various disciplines. The social worker acts as coordinator of the team with each professional maintaining his autonomy and contributing in his area of expertise.

In the attempt to carry on the efforts that were begun within the hospital, a number of activities geared at increasing levels of patient interaction were instituted. The first was a bowling league organized by the recreational therapist. Initially few patients were willing to participate. The bowling alley proprietors were skeptical and the sponsors responded that patients were not interested. The staff perceived an overall fear of failure on the part of all concerned. Multistaff participation was then instituted to maximize encouragement and support to the patients. Patients not ready for participation were encouraged to be observers. Some resorted to hallucinations and delusions as defenses against their fears. The bowling program served as a concrete issue to focus on in group meetings with the homes and increased verbalization was evident on such an issue versus attempt to discuss intrapsychic or purely interpersonal issues. After two years, active participation has increased from 5 to 25 participants. Most sponsors participate and the bowling alley proprietors have become committed to the program and to the men. Two bowling banquets were held. The local American Legion donated their hall and patients have reciprocated by becoming Legion members. The alley proprietors contributed 15 large trophies as well as small trophies for each participant. This league now functions with or without staff attendance and has given participants a taste of success. All participants have increased their bowling averages and several have bowled single strings of over 200.

Many other programs and activities have been initiated and are in various stages of development. Nursing involvement quickly uncovered numerous problems that warranted their expertise, particularly around hygiene and supervision of medications. Patients were evaluated for self-medication capabilities. With nursing support, over fifty percent of the patients in one of the large homes mentioned have been successfully given self-medication regimens. Sponsors and patients alike are now comfortable with these changes.

Occupational therapy projects were also started within the homes. Projects relevant to self-care were emphasized, though projects were tailored to fit the patient and included painting, sculpturing, woodworking, and others. Sponsors were assisted in utilizing residents to participate in home beautification projects including housepainting, gardening, groundskeeping, remodeling, etc. All projects are geared to provide successful ego building experiences. Some of the projects have secondary gains for the sponsors thus aiding the sponsor to value the initial efforts at engaging patients in tasks. Often sponsors initially feel that it would be easier to complete the task oneself, but as performance in the patient improves the sponsors' initial attitude disappears. Increased empathy and concern also ensues.

In one large home several patients are now doing much of the housekeeping and cooking. One patient is fully employed within the home.

A sheltered workshop was also initiated within several of our settings. One interesting finding was that some patients who performed inadequately in the hospital workshop performed quite effectively in the home workshop. Steps have been initiated for 8 of the 40 veterans to begin employment. Also, a volunteers program is being initiated.

Interaction between homes in the community has been encouraged and stimulated. Joint picnics, deep sea fishing trips, and fresh water fishing trips are held. The VFW has initiated several functions and has also enlisted members. Joint Christmas parties, as well as within each home, are held annually. Informal dining out with staff on visitation days takes place and card games are sometimes initiated. Carry over value is sought and enjoys increasing success.

What have been the consequences of such programming? To the sponsors it has meant increased commitment to principles of rehabilitation and an increase in emotional investment in their residents. Sponsors reflect an increasing attitude that they are therapeutic partners with the staff and they show considerable enthusiasm in the patients' progress. Anecdotes are enthusiastically related about evidences of progress on practically all the patients. The feeling of having been a contributor to that progress is joyfully shared.

Too much evidence of idleness and lack of assimilation continues to exist. But the evidences of positive change abound and staff, sponsors, patients, and community residents are enthusiastic about the changes. Some progress was noted in the vignettes. Many other examples are evident in that same community group. One chronic patient recently was able to return to his family on a permanent basis. Another returned to apartment living. Some men have taken independent vacations; others are contagiously (sic) planning to do the same. Evidences of progress, however, small or great, can be related about each patient. All are quick to state their preference for living out of the hospital.

Other communities have been similarly dealt with by our teams. Two YMCA programs yielded the secondary benefit of improved hygiene through regular showers after mildly competitive sports. This shower regimen had considerable carry over value. Salvation Army, Social Clubs and other community resources such as fraternal organizations, clergy, physicians and the VNA, have also been utilized. One large group setting now has a "moving out" group for those patients ready for more independent living settings.

For the Community Care Staff, the consequences of sharing in effecting planned change for the chronic care patient has been that of high morale and enthusiasm. The introduction of new disciplines to Community Care is initially quite threatening to existing staff. Fear of being scapegoated for the withdrawn, asocial condition of the patients is prevalent. Also, overlap of expertise in mental health functions precipitates some fears of encroachment. Planned fostering of a truly collaborative team approach focusing on the patients' needs enhances each discipline's effectiveness and promotes personal satisfaction. Overlap in skills thus becomes an asset promoting growth in patients, staff and sponsors through a consistency in approach. There is no shortage of problems in meeting patient needs. Working together to effect planned change is both effective and rewarding.

In summary, the need for an ongoing, comprehensive after-care program within specific alternative living situations for many is well recognized and is being provided by the Community Care team at Bedford VA Hospital. The aim is maintenance of remission as well as providing continuing growth and rehabilitation leading to some degree of social restoration. In service of this goal a spectrum of placements now exists varying from small one patient foster homes to large multiple placement dwellings, all under close, professional supervision and guidance by multidisciplinary outreach teams. As patients being discharged from chronic hospitalization often lack many basic skills in dealing with life in the community, and in turn communities lack the ability to deal with the returning patients, new methods, new knowledge and better preparation of professionals and sponsors with integrated, comprehensive treatment plans have been required and will continue to be required to meet these needs, within the context of the patient's total social system.

REFERENCES

Daniels, David N., and Kuldan, John M. "Marginal Man, The Tether of Tradition, and International Social Therapy." *Community Mental Health Journal,* Vol. *3,* No. 1, Spring, 1967.

"Foster Homes Seen as New 'Back Wards'." *Psychiatric News,* Nov. 1, 1972.

Hogarty, G. "The Plight of Schizophrenics in Modern Treatment Programs." *Hospital and Community Psychiatry,* Vol. *22,* No. 7, July, 1971.

Mowry, Robert S. G. W. Fairweather (Ed.), chapter in *Social Psychology in Treating Mental Illness: An Experimental Approach,* New York: Wiley, 1964.

Pendleton, Bernard. "Rip Van Winkle Goes Home." *Bedford Research,* Vol. *11,* No. 1, Winter, 1965.

Redding, Robert. "Some Dynamics in the Family Care Placement of Adult Psychotic Patients." *Social Work,* Vol. 7, No. 2, April, 1963.

Sanders, David H. "Treating Mental Illness in the Community: An Alternative to Institutional Care." Paper presented at the Conference on the New Hospital Psychiatry, Madison, Wisconsin, June, 1969.

Community Human Service Networks:

W. Robert Curtis

Should the mental health worker move beyond the clinic walls? What should he do outside those walls? These are important questions. However, a more basic question might be asked: "Should the mental health clinic have walls?" By walls I mean the outside perimeter with several controlled gateways that separate the mental health clinic from other human service systems and from the social environment.

In my opinion there are a number of reasons why these walls must change significantly, if not actually come down. Perhaps most important is the fact that the mental health system has been given (or we have taken) too much responsibility. There is no way that we can deliver effective services to the large number of children, adolescents, and adults whose symptoms suggest they have serious problems. Although we tend to measure the size of this population by the number of people requesting our services, there is considerable evidence that over 20% of the population is in need of human service.[1] It is clear that we need more resources. However, it is even clearer that these resources will not come in the form of new money or new personnel, at least not for the remainder of this

[1] Dorothea C. Leighton *et al., The Character of Danger,* Basic Books, New York, 1963.

decade. Changing the walls so that we can become part of a larger resource system is probably essential for our survival. Simply resolving duplication of service with other agencies, sharing our skills with other caregivers, and consulting around difficult cases are all noble activities; but they both perpetuate the walls and perpetuate the almost exclusive use of service models that focus inside of the individual. The walls, gateways, and inner sanctums serve to reinforce this psychological model by keeping the social environment out. From within the clinic it is difficult to identify the problems that are kept active through an interaction in relationships between individuals and between individuals and the social environment, and even more difficult to intervene in the social process.

If we are to expand services successfully without an increase in budget, we need to distinguish between those problems which can most effectively and efficiently be resolved by focusing inside of the individual with our traditional models, from those that can best be resolved by focusing on the interaction in the social environment. Frequently problems of runaways, marriage, alcoholism, juvenile delinquency, school, or drug abuse are kept active through experiences in the interpersonal relationships between the person with the "problem" and his kin, friends, neighbors, employer, and community caregivers. Unfortunately, from within the clinic walls we have little access to this social environment and few models for intervening in the social process.

Ironically, the mental health worker may be in the best position not only to make these distinctions but also to design new human service systems within the community to resolve these social problems. Mental health workers are the largest group of human service personnel with the exception of educators. They have the mandate, the largest wealth of skills and knowledge about human behavior, and are potential leaders.

Each community or neighborhood[2] has a system of human services which is available for solving problems or maximizing

[2] Defined here as a naturally occurring geographic location with a population generally less than 10,000 and a clearly defined social process to which people report they belong.

growth. These services, however, in no way resemble a system. They might more aptly be described as a non-system, for their outstanding characteristics are duplication, isolation, competition, and lack of coordination. The services exist, however, and despite their fragmented form provide a wider base of resources than most of us recognize. They fall roughly into three dimensions of resources: state human services,[3] community caregivers, and community citizens. (See figure 1.) State human services in Massachusetts officially include the six specialties of welfare, mental health and retardation, public health, rehabilitation, corrections, and youth services. Not falling under the official umbrella of human services but certainly in the human service business are employment, education, and community affairs. There are approximately 30 state human service personnel available to deliver services in each community of 10,000. However, few of these personnel ever enter the community. Instead, they deliver their specialty services in area or regional facilities.

In this same community of 10,000 there are between 300 and 400 persons paid by the community (in the case of a neighborhood, by the city) or privately, to deliver human services. These community caregivers include teachers, school counselors, special education personnel, school administrators, clergy, social agency personnel, privately supported mental health workers, police, recreation agency personnel, court personnel, the staff of nursing and rest homes, hospital personnel, physicians, public health nurses, etc. Like state human service personnel, most community caregivers are primarily interested in their specialty and are seldom encouraged to relate their specialty service to a community human service network or to the social environment outside the individual. The frequent experiences of failure and isolation, which results from a narrow definition of problems, has led to a significantly large group of frustrated community caregivers.

The third dimension of resources are citizens. Although they are frequently used as volunteers in various agencies their effort

---

[3] Included in state for the purpose of simplification are federally paid personnel; some directly, others indirectly through the state.

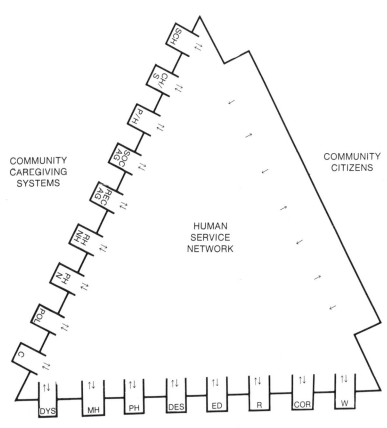

COMMUNITY
CAREGIVING
SYSTEMS

COMMUNITY
CITIZENS

HUMAN
SERVICE
NETWORK

STATE HUMAN SERVICES

SCH	Schools		DYS	Youth Service
CH/S	Churches/Synagogues		MH	Mental Health
P/H	Physicians/Hospitals		PH	Public Health
SOCAG	Social Agencies		DES	Employment Security
RECAG	Recreation Agencies		ED	Education
RH/NH	Rest Homes/Nursing Homes		MR	Rehabilitation
PHN	Public Health Nurse		COR	Corrections
POL	Police		WEL	Welfare
C	Court			

is most often the kind of work below the role of the mental health professional. Consequently, with so few meaningful roles to experience, most of the potential volunteers are still uninvolved. There are two critical functions which citizens can bring to human services that money cannot purchase. The first is an environmental network for identifying problems that are not receiving services, unearthing new resources, sanctions for delivering direct and preventive services, and planning community programs. The second is manhours and the corresponding relationships for certain important roles within a human service system, such as big brothers or sisters, foster parents, day care workers, or members of a problem solving team.

As mentioned earlier, these resources form a non-system of human services. In their present state they reach only a fraction of the individuals that could be served if the resources were reorganized. I would like to suggest five directions in which the mental health worker should move to begin the process of redesigning clinic walls to become an integral part of a human service network.

Decentralization

Decision making, budget preparation, and deployment of personnel for most state and city human service systems systematically exclude input from the social environment of the community or neighborhood. This environment is intimately tied to almost all human problems, yet is rarely considered when services are being designed. The mental health worker should play a leadership role in creating mechanisms which encourage citizens to participate meaningfully in designing human services.

This necessitates moving the decision making process down to the level where services are needed. Decentralization to the community and neighborhood level is imperative if we hope to involve consumer boards that accurately represent the community, to unearth the potential resources for human service hidden in each community, to involve citizens and caregivers in meaningful roles within the system, to reach a larger percentage of people experiencing problems, and to develop local prevention programs.

Furthermore, the mental health worker should help distinguish between the separable services which can be delivered to an individual (financial aid, individual counseling, some aspects of vocational training, a hospital bed, chemotherapy, etc.) which may very well be delivered more effectively and efficiently on a centralized level from the inseparable services which focus on the relationships in a person's social network and consequently should be delivered within the community social system. Clearly personnel delivering inseparable services must leave the area and regional facility and become integrated in the community environment. It should be noted that, although long term solutions to decentralization will require new legislation, in many cases much of it can be implemented right now administratively. In fact, legislation can only make decentralization possible. For it to work there must be commitment and motivation to build relationship on a community level.

Coordination

The mental health worker, in the role of a human service coordinator can focus on two dimensions: individual needs and specialty system isolation. Each individual has a number of needs which are met through the tasks and processes in the interpersonal relationships of his social network. If these needs are not met, problems develop which become manifest through the individual's behavior. Human services have been designed by the community and state to resolve these problems; however, each service frequently attends to only one unmet need which it defines as its specialty. The whole individual, all of his needs and relationships, are seldom focused on, particularly as a process over time. Consequently the problem is not adequately defined and most of the potential resources for resolving it are excluded. The role of a coordinator in this dimension is to bring together the whole social network to achieve an accurate definition of the problem (focusing on the interaction of needs and relationships) and to ensure the integration of services with the whole individual. The power of such a process cannot be underestimated, particularly in a society where there are so few times that an individual experiences all of his roles, needs, and relationships being accepted.

Specialty system isolation calls for a parallel role for the human service coordinator but is on a larger level of social organization. Rather than coordinating the process of a social network for problem solving, the human service resources are coordinated within a community. Each community is rich with specialty systems. However, each operates in isolation from the other despite having the same goal of meeting human needs. In this dimension the human service coordinator becomes a generalist or integrator. His role is to build relationships across specialty systems. At times it will simply be for the purpose of coordinating one case. At other times he will be designing a more formal system for long range planning or for filling in gaps in service. The most complicated task, and perhaps the most important, is building a human service network in each community. In this network state agencies, community caregiving systems, and citizens can share their resources and cooperate on those services their specialty system can not effectively deliver in isolation.

In the Taunton Area, rather than developing out patient services, consultation and education, prevention, and day care through a centralized mental health clinic, our energy has been invested in building a human service network in each community and neighborhood. Because mental health is only one agency along the state human service dimension, great care has been taken to build this system as a human service network in which we participate as an equal member rather than a mental health empire. This task has not been easy. Mental health has a reputation that is difficult to live with because of its previous and existing empires and its association with illness. It is also difficult to distinguish between the democratic self-determination of a community and the value we place on a network of human services. To insure community self-determination the mental health worker has formally become a human service coordinator who is accountable to a human service board which represents the community.

Coordinating the development of this network, consequently, has taken a different form in each community. However, in the five communities and neighborhoods where we have focused most intensively there appears to be a pattern of movement towards a formal human service center. In this center the vast resources identified in figure 1 can be brought together in a human service partnership. The community center becomes responsible for delivering inseparable services, identifying the frequency of problems in the community, and having a thorough knowledge of existing resources. Furthermore, it provides a vehicle for changing the wasteful practices of duplication, competition, isolation, and lack of coordination. It also serves as an advocacy system for any individual who is being excluded from services as well as supporting social change on the community level in the areas of housing, jobs, and missing services.

Community Organziation

Roland Warren makes a distinction between two processes active within a community. One he calls the vertical axis and the other the horizontal axis.[4] The vertical axis is the specialty and interest system within each community whose process is characterized by authority in their upward accountability to an area, regional, state or national organization. The horizontal axis is the social relationships between people and groups and is more characterized by choice and equality.

A lasting human service partnership between these two axes cannot be built unless a board is designed to represent the horizontal axis within the community. This requires organizing a volunteer group of citizens representing an accurate cross section of the community on the dimensions of consumer groups, class, occupations, values, race, and ethnic origin who can speak for the community. This group can not only give sanctions to and support a human service center, but also can identify the 2,000 potential volunteers for delivering inseparable services. Mental health workers do not make particularly good community organizers. There are, however, two other alternatives. One is to motivate communi-

---

[4] "Toward a Reformation of Community Therapy," *Human Organization,* XV, No. 2.

ties to organize themselves by developing a formula for matching state resources with community resources for the purpose of building a human service network and make this board (its representation and power) a condition of the contract. A second is to use mental health blocks to hire community change agents.

Training and Sanctions

If community caregivers and citizens are to have a meaningful role in the delivery and design of human services they must be seen as equals. Each partner brings important resources to this partnership which must be shared to broaden each specialty system. The mental health worker has a wealth of skills, information, and knowledge about human behavior but it often remains within the closed system of mental health. Likewise, community caregivers have specific skills, information and knowledge relating to their specialty system and citizens know a great deal about the needs, sources, and processes of their community.

Mechanisms for sharing among the three partners need to be designed. Training programs offered by mental health workers can facilitate this sharing if they recognize the important contributions of all the trainees as they move toward broader responsibility as a partner in resolving human problems. Citizens and caregivers recognize a need for training in the areas of human needs, community process, group process, interpersonal relations, problem development, etc., which the mental health worker can provide. In a community of 10,000 people there are over 150 citizens and caregivers who would attend these training sessions with very little organizing. Unfortunately, mental health workers often forget that they can also benefit from the skills of the other two partners, and through the subtle communication of a superior role they generate little interest in training or sanctions.

New Models

Many new models need to be designed for delivering service in the interactional process of the social environment. Rather than focusing exclusively on the psychological process within individuals these models need also to focus on variables such as money, power, and values. The mental health worker plays an important role in the development of these models because of his special knowledge of the individual. It is important that each of these new models be founded in an understanding of the individual as well as the social environment.

In conclusion, I would like to report briefly about an interactional intervention model we have designed which may serve as an example of the kinds of models that may be developed. It is called team problem solving in a social network. There are two systems in this model: the social network and the team. The social network is anchored to a situation or problem where individuals and relationships linked to an individual whose behavior is of some concern are brought together as a social group. The participants include the primary actors of kin, neighbors, friends, and secondary actors of community caregivers, state human service personnel, employer, etc.

The network comes together as a group to consider how each of their relationships are contributing to keep the problem active and then to assume some responsibility for changing these relationships. The problem solving team is the intervenor or facilitator. The team is a trained system of three or four community persons from the three dimensions of resources. They meet weekly with the social network until the immediate problem is resolved and continue to support the network as the members attempt to utilize the problem solving skills learned with the team on their own. In the past three years 449 social networks have met with problem solving teams in the Taunton Area for an average of six sessions for each problem.

The members of the problem solving team are continuously experiencing opportunities for sharing; for gaining new knowledge, skills and information; and for using these tools as they work together on the team and relate to others in their specialty or their own social network. The team experiences the satisfaction of using their combined skills to resolve more effectively those problems that could not be alleviated by one specialty system.

In addition to the direct services to social networks the team concept provides a meaningful role for citizens and caregivers in the overall human service system. Their increased knowledge about human behavior, human needs, and the absence or presence of human service resources in the community allows citizens and community caregivers to participate as an informal equal in the decision making processes of the human service system.

REFERENCES

Leighton, Dorothea C. et. al., *The Character of Danger*, Basic Books, New York, 1963.

Warren, Roland, "Toward a Reformulation of Community Therapy," *Human Organization, XV*, No. 2.

Role Problems in Community Psychology Internship Training in Community Agencies

Guy O. Seymour, Ph.D.

Robert Curtis presented a closing example of the model that he had been thinking about and using. I would like to give an opening example of a model that I had thought a lot about until I started to try it out in real life. In the one particular agency in this example, the model worked out as it was supposed to. That is the rare occasion, not the usual one. Anyhow, let me tell you about it because I think it is an interesting model.

The philosophy behind the program is that different minority groups (however you define minority groups) have different cultural and life experiences. It's a long struggle as a member of a minority group grows up through the educational system—through high school, through college, through graduate education. You know, I started on my Ph.D. five years before I got it and in those five years a lot of things happened. As you go through the educational system, the tendency is to become distant from your minority group identification. You become more identified with the majority group because the majority group runs educational systems.

It was my belief then that there was no viable way to deal with that, and with this came a particular and personal pain at losing that identification myself (even my speech patterns are becoming acceptable at this point).

It hurts to lose my identification, and my feeling was that what we as minority group professionals need is some mechanism for re-alignment or reaffirmation of identity. What I needed for myself was to be working with some people who had not yet lost much of their identification, and perhaps by doing that both they and I would get something from one another. There were people who needed training to deliver psychological services and to consult to community agencies. Why not have them work with their own minority group population? Not that it should be exclusively Blacks working with Blacks or Puerto Ricans with Puerto Ricans, but to have the interns work mainly with their own folks in order to maintain their personal identification, deliver meaningful service and learn their trade in the process.

The model for training that we now use is not one that is very heavily tied to clinical treatment, nor very heavily tied to the hospital situation, although I am convinced that clinical skills are essential tools of the professional psychologist's armamentarium. Right now let me talk about what happens to the intern in the community agency as the program was designed. The perfect example. The rare thing. Then we'll talk about the problems.

I had been working with a Head Start Center since the summer of my second year in graduate school. It was part-time, a half day a week, the kind of thing that Bob Curtis was talking about in terms of utilizing all available resources to their fullest possible capability. In this first year I maintained contact with the Center and in the beginning brought along an intern with me. At first, S.B., the intern, met extensively with myself as the senior member of the consulting team. During these meetings she was briefed on the nature of the Center, its personnel, problems and social dynamics. Following these meetings, she was introduced to the Center and its personnel (after they had had some weeks to anticipate and discuss her coming). During her initial period of familiarization with the center, the intern spent her time between classroom observation, talking with teachers and playing with the children, and in meeting with and going on outreach work with the social service staff.

Gradually she increased her participation and took on more responsibility. I decreased my time, and I decreased my activity at the Center. She began to do several things: one was consulting with the teachers on the children that they had in their classes, whom she was familiar with because she had been spending time playing with them in the classroom; another was talking with the teachers and the Social Service staff about the relationship between the parents and the siblings and the child in the center. She also developed Child Centered conferences with total or partial staff information exchange and planning more appropriate psychoeducational activities to have in the classroom. She did this in concert with the staff, not so much as an expert but as somebody who has been in the classroom and had some experience with what was going on and who knew something about human development. She conducted staff workshops on child development and on practical approaches to family dynamics in dealing with disruptive behavior in the family. In turn, the teachers and the Social Service staff could use that material and that knowledge in helping the older siblings who needed to learn to deal with the younger children and themselves and their parents. We sought and hoped for a mutual process up and down the line. Then together S.B. and I held mental health oriented discussions for staff, and then had separate ones for parents. Subsequently, at mid-year the center held a conference and we were integral parts of the planning and delivery. It included staff, parents, some other professionals in the field, people from outside the agency, people from the central OEO and OCD funding offices, the local CAP offices, etc.

Now during this time the intern had become more and more responsible for most of the things that I used to do when I was fully involved with the center. She's done some things that I had never done and never had the time to do or never thought about doing, and I've learned from that in terms of my own growth too. I find that it's a learning process for me and for her, as well as for the people she's working with. I don't need to think of myself working with her in the same kind of way with the center anymore. It's very different now and she has grown into an effective, fairly autonomous professional who uses me as supervisor and consultant with very little dependency.

The process of entry and the underlying assumptions on which work with the agencies is carried out is founded in a close working relationship between the interns, their supervisors, the community agencies and program staff. The model used for introducing trainees to working with community agencies is the same as that developed in the Boston City Hospital group work training program. Each trainee is assigned to either a staff member, advanced trainee or supervisory staff member who is working with community agencies. Initially, the role of the trainee is that of an observer-participant in the consultation or system-oriented activities of the senior member, although they are perceived by the agency as a team. Gradually, with continued evaluation and feedback from each team to the project director, increasing responsibility in certain areas is shifted from the senior to the junior member of the team. Finally, when a trainee reaches a sufficient level of proficiency he becomes the senior member in a new pairing with a less advanced trainee, and the new team will function under the continued supervision of a staff member and in consultation with the project director. This model has the following advantages:

a. It maximizes the supervisory experience since the senior member of the team has first hand knowledge of the agency, its functions and its problems, and it provides the junior member with the opportunity to become familiar with the agency while under close and active tutelage.

b. It provides advanced trainees with the experience of supervising others.

c. It provides continuity in consultative efforts and introduces the consultant to the agency in a gradual manner thus facilitating the work itself while, at the same time, introjecting fresh personnel with fresh viewpoints into the system in the least threatening fashion possible.

d. It facilitates the transition from trainee to professional status with appropriate role development models while ensuring a broadening of the program staff's outlook.

e. It alleviates the concern, particularly of community agencies, that new professionals beginning independent work either do not know enough or do not have enough influence. Since the senior consultant is present for a good portion of the time to provide the initial bridge to agencies, agency personnel have an opportunity

to observe a trainee at work before the latter does so independently.

f. It builds in a mechanism to free up the senior staff member's
time for work in other areas or agencies, enabling the expansion
of expert psychological practice by minority group professionals
and the development of further resources for training.

g. It allows for the spreading out of each trainee's time in the
assignment so that the heavy burden of community service and
involvement is shared and actual functioning is enhanced.

That was the model and it worked. The intern learned. Teachers
and staff at the agency learned. The parents learned. Child care
was enhanced in that setting. But it did not work in a majority of
the other agencies where we had interns attempting the same thing.

I'd like to share with you some of the problems we encountered
in trying to implement this "succession-apprenticeship" model of
training in community agencies and ask for your suggestions and
criticism so that in the future the program will work better, or at
least differently.

It's frustrating to have a nice model that you've seen work well
in a few situations and not at all in many others. Essentially, I see
the problems of implementing the model as mainly related to the
issues of role identification and expectations of perceived roles.
An intern has several roles: as a learner; as a practitioner of something that is not well understood by people who work in community
agencies; as a helper; and as a teacher both of his or her teachers
and of the clientele served. But there are also expectations held by
others as to who and what the intern is. Some of these are appropriate to the intern's role. Most are not. Many times agency personnel expect the intern to be (or at least quickly become) what
they perceived the senior team member to be, both as an individual
and as a professional (whatever that is), and those perceptions
are fraught with inaccuracies and the "magic" of esteem built up
over many years and forged in crises that are very unlikely to recur.

Interns also have expectations of the people they work with and
for. Here, too, there are difficulties. And finally supervisors and
program staff have expectations of agencies, interns and one
another, some of which are also unrealistic and inappropriate. In

my own self-righteousness, I choose to call these role confusions and unrealistic expectations "resistance." In fact, though, they do serve to impede and resist the effective performance of the work to be done and to divert energy and time to non-legitimate concerns.

There are three sources of this "resistance." Resistance comes from the agencies (of course we all blame the victim first). It comes from the agencies in the sense that the leadership feels threatened by people with credentials. They feel threatened by people who are somewhat different from themselves. As an example of that, in one of the Centers, an intern who was very much 'avant garde' in his dress and self presentation went in and had a couple of meetings with the director, and with the chief psychologist. When he was introduced to the staff, which was composed mainly of middle-aged black females, they were up in arms. They accused him of being a homosexual: "What kind of presentation is this for young, black male children to see a black male psychologist who's effeminate?" The guy just happens to dress differently and to carry a handbag.

Such differences are very difficult for agencies to tolerate in the community. Especially when the differences between the intern and his/her senior team member are clearly noticeable. Their 'traditions' and therefore their existence is threatened; their legitimacy is perceived to be threatened.

As has been pointed out earlier the model that we use really depends on the intern coming into agencies that their supervisors have been working in. They eventually take over most of that function, thus freeing up the supervisors to do other kinds of things. At times the supervisors had provided fairly traditional kinds of psychological services and the agencies wanted to use the interns similarly. Getting agencies and interns and supervisors to see the utility of both the more traditional ways of functioning and innovative activities and modalities of practices has been another area of the difficulties created by changing roles.

At other times the new interns want too much. They expect to be Jesus Christ with a large S on the front that says Savior. They expect the agency will be grateful for getting this professional psychologist in there. An intern may think he's going to do such a tremendous job that all their problems will disappear.

There is a fourth aspect of role confusion that has recently come to light which could pose some serious political problems. In two particular agencies the intern is beginning to be used as a source of power. When they talk with other agencies that do similar kinds of things they set themselves up as the leader of that movement. The rationale is that since they have a black professional psychologist who consults with them that of course makes them better than the other agencies. Therefore they should have more influence: they should have more power. The intern thus becomes perceived as a political asset and is elevated to a special exalted status in the eyes of the agency he works for and with respect to its associates. More subtle kinds of resistance come from the interns. Now we're not blaming the victims; we're just blaming the people who are part of the victimization. They say, "You know, this kind of work demands too much time. We can't afford to be going to meetings in the evenings from 7:00 to 10:00. What will happen to our other kinds of pursuits, academic, social, whatever?" They feel sometimes that the demands are too many.

At the same time they would like to take over both the program and the agencies. I've seen this happen with one particular intern, who feels that he really runs the agency "from behind the throne" because he consults with the director, and with the director of Social Service and the educational coordinator, and to the director of the job counseling. Although he's never actually said it, his manner indicates that he feels he runs that agency. Given the ease with which agencies will acquiesce to the suggestions of a consultant this attitude could be very dangerous in enhancing the dependence of an agency on an intern—something quite contrary to our desired goals. In a sense, this presents an impediment to truly effective intervention because that attitude precludes serious learning and genuine respectfulness. At these times the interns feel they know everything, which is connected to the third main kind of resistance for the interns: the attitude that they don't have to learn anything. You know, "the supervisors are nice to have around because it provides a method of entry into the system, but there's not much we have to learn—at least from them. Besides, they're old-fashioned." The attitude presented is that program staff and supervisors have little ability to communicate with community residents because they've been trained in the 'wrong way' or have gotten too far away from the street situation. I believe that this kind of resistance results from the conflict between the role of student and the demand to be a competent practicing professional with sufficient knowledge and autonomous skill to respond adequately to a variety of trying situations.

The last source of resistance is the program staff resistance. Here I'm spreading around the blame. We have two other professional staff, the associate directors, besides the secretary, who really runs the show, and the program staff is not without fault. Not that I myself resist. Heaven forbid that I should have role problems. At this time I choose to see it as staff resistance.

Seriously, though, most of the problems in this area have to do with the fact that I had originally conceived of the program and of the model and have not modified it very much. It's mostly in my head and it's very hard to get it out to other people; hard to get it out to agency personnel or to staff, to supervisors or to the interns. It's hard to communicate it because just doing that engenders a sense of loss. It's a 'giving up of my thing.' So I resist it. What I feel is emerging right now is that I'm becoming more of a benevolent dictator rather than just a dictator, and I feel that of course benevolent dictators are needed.

Someone has to run the show and be the place where "the buck stops." Because I haven't been able to fully divulge all the details of the functioning of the program with its many different facets, others do not always know what is expected of them or what they can expect of me. This does create misunderstandings and interferes with the smooth operation of both the service delivery and the training components of the program. However, it does bring us all closer together in the resolution of some of the issues that crop up and enables others to truly have input to the concretizing of some of our goals. This, however, serves as reinforcement in a subtle way for delaying the full laying out of the concepts behind our work, and herein lies some of the conflict or staff resistance. It is my hope that there will be a complete unfolding of what's in my mind before the end of this, our first year, and fortunately my staff are skilled at getting information.

In closing, let me say that the intent of this training program is to provide both enough structure to ascertain that interns achieve a functionally competent level of skill in those activities associated with the profession of psychology and enough flexibility to respond to the individual needs and future career plans of minority group and non-minority group students. Our goals are to present them with the opportunity to deliver services to those populations with which they are most closely identified and in the places and settings that are most accessible and attuned to the needs of those populations. In the context of this service delivery we want them to be able to ethically experiment with modifications of present psychological techniques and to develop innovative mechanisms in providing service and assessing their effectiveness. In all this, the major learning experience must come both from their clientele and from minority group professionals whose own skills are aligned with the specific needs and interests of the students whom they will supervise in the working collaboration that is so desperately needed by all involved and by the community as a whole.

Preventive Work with "Well Families"

Peggy Papp
Olga Silverstein
Betty Carter

The following is a description of an experimental community project which was put into operation in January of 1971 under the direction of Peggy Papp at the Nathan W. Ackerman Family Institute.

The program was designed to be preventive by offering a service to families before their problems escalated into crisis proportions requiring professional help. This involved reaching them at a particular point in time—precrisis, and long before the crisis appeared. It was aimed at offering a service in a particular way which was non-threatening—one in which the family didn't have to define itself as "sick" in order to obtain some relief.

The project consisted of families from the community at large meeting together in groups to discuss family concerns. Each group was led by a family therapist, trained at the Institute, and met once a week, either in a church or in each other's homes for a period of six months.

This orientation towards prevention and education rather than relief of crisis and acute distress shaped our method of intervention in unexpected ways. It forced us to expand our concepts, experiment with new techniques and re-evalute our ideas on how families change.

Prevention

Recently the American Orthopsychiatric Association surveyed its members to determine what they considered the top priority in the mental health field. *Prevention* headed the list of 25 choices. Obviously to prevent is better than to treat and yet to contemplate prevention is to have the mind take a continuous series of steps backward to an earlier starting point much like the contemplation of the beginning of the universe. Where and when does prevention begin?

Certainly most work in the mental health field can be considered preventive and yet a prevailing doubt of the entire profession is that we begin too late with too little.

In 1971 Marc A. Nebejan, a Dutch psychiatrist was sent to the United States on a World Health Fellowship for a two-fold purpose. One, to learn about the Family Therapy movement in the United States; two, to study the creation and operation of prevention programs. Although he felt he learned much about Family Therapy, he discovered there was almost nothing that would qualify as an authentic prevention program. "I asked all the people I visited if they knew of prevention-action centers or units which I could visit. The answer was practically always "no." This surprised me because I had assumed that this field was fairly well developed in the United States."

Family Therapy in and of itself can be considered preventive when it is successful in disrupting destructive three-generational patterns. Yet "therapy" begins only after a problem has been designated as "serious" and in need of "treatment." There is no place in our communities for families to go when they first begin to feel something is going wrong which they don't understand and can't cope with—vague anxieties, uneasy togetherness, inexplicable tensions. Only after a child develops a serious symptom, parents are on the verge of divorce, or someone is designated as "disturbed" will families face the guilt and anxiety, not to mention the expense, of going to a mental health agency. Seeking professional help becomes a drastic step invariably accompanied by the underlying conviction that someone has failed, consequently someone is to blame, consequently someone will be found guilty and exposed. It is little wonder families put off going for years, sweeping the problems under the rug hoping they will disappear. By the time families do go for help they are usually in a state of panic or despair; a scapegoat has been chosen and accepted the role; destructive patterns have formed deep wounds; guilt is high and forgiveness low.

The Community Groups were aimed at removing the stigma of sickness so that motivation for change did not have to be based on desperation. We also wanted to challenge the prevailing belief that unless a family is in a crisis it is unmotivated to seek change.

The program was offered to various churches and schools in the neighborhood surrounding the Institute. It was presented as being for the "average family with everyday problems; the kind that beset us all in this very hectic, pressured and frightening times in which we live." The emphasis was on self-study rather than treatment or cure. The stated goal was to "understand how your family operates; to evaluate and revitalize family relationships." The setting of a group offered the opportunity to share this self exploratory experience with other families.

Clergymen, headmasters and principals were especially interested in the program because of their alarm over the increasing breakdown of families. One minister warned us "You better hurry up. There are hardly any families left!" Clergymen offered their pulpits for a discussion of the program and headmasters sent urgent letters to their parents inviting them to come and hear Mrs. Papp speak.

The families were self-selected, unscreened, taken on a first come, first serve basis. No evaluation interviews were given, no histories taken. Families were assigned to groups strictly on the basis of the ages of their children. In one group children's ages ranged from 7-10; in another from 11-14; and in the third from 15-17. When they met for the first time, therapists as well as families were strangers. The results so far have boosted our contention that there could have been no better way of selecting.

How "well" were these "well families"? Most of them had serious problems but none were in the middle of a self-defined crisis. Their motivation for volunteering was based on their awareness of the steam they were compressing at home. We defined our prevention as dealing with this steam at an early point in time and felt this had a crucial bearing on the ability of the families to mobilize their healing powers.

The quality of the participation of the group families was noticeably different from that of the Institute families. The group families as a whole were more motivated, less resistant and more creatively involved in the process of their own change. The incidence of lateness and absenteeism was low and many requested more frequent and longer sessions. We believe this was due to the difference in expectations and the manner in which the program was introduced. The group families came not to be cured or blamed by the therapists but to participate actively in their own understanding and learning. The emotional temperatures of the families were low enough to permit more contemplation and consequently to gain more perspective.

The thrust of the pilot program was of necessity limited to the most accessible community surrounding the Institute, which was largely white middle class. Our initial conviction, however, that the program had value for a broad cross-section of families including poverty and minority, was reinforced by a response to a write-up of the groups in the New York Daily News. Following this the Institute was deluged with telephone calls from families who represented a wide variety of economic, racial, social and cultural backgrounds. These families expressed a particular interest in working in a group with other families. "We would like to talk to other families and maybe get some ideas." "It would be a comfort to be able to speak to parents of other teenagers." "I feel there is a great deal of value in being with other families, particularly families who have children of similar ages. I would like to share some of my feelings."

Method of Intervention

Education

Our method of intervention was influenced by the nature of the contact we had made with these families. The fact that they had not come to us with an overt crisis which they expected us to alleviate immediately gave us leeway to present a conceptual framework in which to view the family functioning. Our major goals were to teach families a way of observing their own interaction; of defining problems in terms of relationships rather than individuals; of developing an awareness of family themes continued from one generation to the next. We also hoped that by presenting family operations as a universal phenomenon, governed by common principles, members would be able to examine their family relationships with less fear and guilt. The idea that anything as intense and explosive as family relationships could be studied in a thoughtful and systematic way helped to create a "safe" atmosphere and allowed families to explore with a certain spirit of adventure.

Following are the six basic concepts from which we worked. (These were written up at the request of the families and each member given a copy.)

How Families Operate

1) FAMILY SYSTEMS: the family operates as an emotional unit with no villains, heros, good people, bad people, healthy or unhealthy members. Family problems result from the way family members relate to one another and not from the behavior of any one person. What each person does affects every other person and a chain reaction is set off. These chain reactions become repetitious and predictable. If one can gain distance, one can study them, observe how they are set off, how they are reinforced, who picks up what cues, and the part each plays in the chain reaction.

2) LABELING: each family member eventually gets programmed into a specific role in the family and labeled accordingly. Labeling serves a need in the family set-up and each individual gains some identification from it. Each part plays a part in assuming his label and continuing it. Most labels are stultifying as they prevent growth and have little to do with the true nature of the person. It is possible for families to understand their own labeling process

and modify it, thus releasing family members to fulfill more of their individual potential.

3) COLLABORATION: collaboration is necessary among family members to keep conflicts going. One person cannot carry on an interaction all by himself. By studying how each person is involved in the family merry-go-round the cycle can be interrupted by any one person changing his behavior. Much frustration can be avoided by concentrating on changing oneself rather than blaming others. The happiest people are those who take major responsibility for their own happiness.

4) TRIANGLES: triangles tend to form in families because of the close intense relationships. When one person feels hurt, angry, disappointed or frustrated with another family member and cannot settle it with them, he tends to bring someone else into the relationship. Parents often use their children to make up for what is lacking between them. Children also involve their parents in triangles by playing one against the other. If one person in the triangle changes his position, the whole triangle will shift. It is preferable to have a separate relationship with each person which does not involve any other person and does not form a triangle.

5) FAMILY GHOSTS: family ghosts are passed from one generation to another. Parents tend to assume the same emotional position in their present family as they assumed in their family of origin. They come with prejudices, anxieties and expectations which are carried over and imposed on the members of their present families. If a parent can understand the way he was programmed into his family of origin and take a step to change it, he will pave the way to do the same thing in his present family.

6) CHANGE: the family system can be changed by any one person taking a different position and sticking to it.

Family Sculpting

Our main task was to personalize these concepts by illuminating the unique way in which they were experienced in each family. We had long been fascinated by family sculpting as an effective method of blending the cognitive with the experiential and decided to experiment with it as a therapeutic spine around which to unfold and re-shape the family systems.

Family sculpting is a therapeutic art form in which each family member arranges the other members in a tableau which physically symbolizes their emotional relationship with one another. Each creates a live family portrait placing members together in terms of posture and special relationships representing action and feelings. The essence of one's experience in the family is condensed and projected into a visual picture. This picture is literally worth a thousand words, revealing aspects of the family's inner life which has remained hidden. Vague impressions and confused feelings on the periphery of awareness are crystalized and given form.

One of the major advantages of this method is the ability to cut through intellectualization, defensiveness and projection of blame. Families are deprived of their familiar cues and are compelled to communicate with one another on a more meaningful level. As triangles, alliances, and conflicts are choreographed they are taken out of the rut of the concrete and placed in the realm of the visual, sensory and symbolic areas where there are vastly more possibilities for communication of feelings in all their nuances.

Another advantage of the sculpting is the adhesive effect it has on the families. It compels them to think of themselves as a unit with each person a necessary part of that unit affecting every other part. It is impossible to isolate any one intense relationship without seeing the reverberations of it throughout the family. While uniting the family the sculpting individuates at the same time as it requires each member to abstract his own personal experience, observe and interpret it. We shall now describe some of the ways in which we integrated the sculpting into our overall goals.

Re-Alignment of the Family

It was the job of the therapist to extract the meaning of the sculpting in terms of the family systems, analyze it, synthesize it and feed it back. Whenever possible, we used the sculpting to shift the family balance within the session. By physically re-aligning the family we produced a blueprint for a future emotional re-alignment. For example in Peggy Papp's group all the members in one family while sculpting had portrayed the father as the "ROCK OF GIBRALTAR" upon which the whole family stood. The 12 year old daughter placed him literally bending over backwards to support the family with one hand and hold up three businesses with the other. The son had him lecturing virtuously but sternly on a platform with pointed finger. The mother placed the father on a pedestal looking up to him for guidance. When it came time for this "ROCK OF GIBRALTAR" to do his sculpting, he threw himself on the floor and said "I'm swimming upstream in mud." He placed his wife hanging onto his feet and his 12 year old daughter hanging onto her feet with him pulling them both. He instructed his son to lie across his neck like a millstone as he declared, "I sometimes feel like I'm going down for the third time." The therapist then asked the father to change the sculpting the way he would like it. He tried to get to his feet. In order to do this it became obvious he first had to throw his son off his neck and shake his wife from his heels. Wife and son then had to negotiate for new positions based on the father's freeing himself. When the father stood up he held out his hand for his wife to join him by his side. Before she could do this however, she had to extricate herself from her 12 year old daughter who was hanging onto her feet and with whom she was overly involved. There followed a discussion as to whether or not her daughter would sink if she let her go or if she was old enough to do some swimming by herself now. Mother and daughter agreed she was and she let go of her mother's heels to join her brother. Mother still refused to move, waiting for her husband to pull her up. He refused to pull her up, waiting for her to join him. The basic family conflict had been physicalized. Responding to questions by the therapist which provoked thought and movement, husband and wife eventually ended up side by side holding hands with the children in front of them but some distance away. Through this three dimensional picture we had created a common language and a common family goal towards which to work.

Clarification of Symptoms

We found the sculpting invaluable in involving children in the groups. It provided them with a channel for expressing feelings which would have been difficult if not impossible for them to express verbally. It enabled them to become involved immediately, alleviated their boredom and restlessness and gave them a sense that their perceptions were important. The connection between certain symptoms and family interaction were sometimes dramatically clarified. In one family a 9 year old son had developed a bewildering symptom. He was given to walking around in circles whenever he became restless much to the dismay of the family. In sculpting his family, Jimmy placed his two sisters in one corner of the room playing jacks and ignoring him. He placed his mother and father in the other corner quarreling and himself alone in the center of the room. The therapist then asked him to demonstrate in movement what he did about this situation. "Well, first I go over here to my sisters but they won't let me play with them and tell me to go away so then I go over here to talk to mother and daddy but they tell me not to bother them so I go back to my sisters. . . ." As he described his predicament he began walking in circles going round and round between his parents and siblings. This was a quiet boy who seldom expressed any thoughts or feelings. The family was made aware for the first time of his isolated position in the family, his frustration in trying to find a place for himself and the connection between this and his walking in circles. This was eventually related to the broader family symptom of everybody "going around in circles."

Three Generational Themes

We traced family themes back through the generations in order to give historical perspective to current family patterns. After each member sculpted his nuclear family, the parents sculpted their family of origin. This gave an epic overview of the emotional life of the families through time. These series of pictures spanning the generations set the stage for viewing problems in terms of a wide network of continuing relationships rather than isolating them in the individual in the here and now.

Intense feelings were often stirred up in the parents as they reconstructed their families. Thinking in terms of pictures is a primitive process arousing primitive feelings. To bring one's family to life with living breathing people permits one to stand back and observe the earlier scenes while participating in them at the same time. Through this double vision one may see one's behavior and feelings as a functional part of the total family constellation. Members of the group took the parts of the primary family members of the parents. In doing so they became a part of the emotional interaction of that family often providing valuable insights.

If a parent was having difficulty with a particular child, we asked him to sculpt his family when he himself was the age of that child. This sensitized the parent to the feelings of the child, and helped the child to see his parent as a person with his own problems in growing up. Following is an example of an exchange between mother and daughter during a three generational sculpting in which an emotional bridge was formed between the past and present resulting in a new experience for both.

In Olga Silverstein's group a 14 year old girl, Giselle, with a severe stutter, sculptured her family as follows: father and brother are playing chess at the kitchen table, not talking but just slightly moving the pieces. She and her mother are standing a great distance apart gazing silently at one another. "I can't talk to mother because I stutter." During the same session the mother. Eva, sculpted her family of origin as follows: her father and brother are sitting silently reading the newspaper. Mother is sitting at the typewriter writing one of her interminable letters to the two sisters who are away from home. She herself is standing next to her mother talking and talking. She says "Hysterically trying to get some response." Mother never looks up from her typing. As she re-enacted this scene she said "it feels so hopeless. I can't reach anybody." The woman playing her mother said "there is a part of me that is aware of her unhappiness and would like to reach out but I am afraid." When the therapist asked what she would do were she not afraid, she reached over and drew Eva into her arms. This physical contact aroused Eva's longing for a close relationship with her mother and she spoke at length of her loneliness. When she eventually returned to her seat next to her daughter she looked at her for a long moment and then spontaneously reached over and drew her into her arms. Both cried and sat for the rest of the session close together. An insight had been translated into an action within the session. Since insights are ephemeral and tend to evaporate or remain intellectual we strove whenever possible to convert them into immediate action. In answer to the question on our periodic questionnaire "Did you learn anything new about any member of the family from sculpting," Eva responded "I learned to see my daughter as different and separate from me so I stopped demanding that she talk to me and now we talk quite easily. *I* talk to her." Giselle responded "I saw that my mother had even more problems in talking to people than I do. I saw how anxious she was and I stopped being so mad at her. I felt good when she hugged me. I didn't think I would like it."

Theme Centered Discussions

All three therapists work differently using their own individual styles and techniques but with the same concepts and goals in mind. Betty Carter, an experienced group therapist, followed up sculpting with theme centered discussions. The themes were chosen for the purpose of focusing family members on critical issues of individuation within the context of family relationships. They were used to continue the work opened up by the sculpting without necessarily verbalizing the parallels or having them interpreted.

For example a woman married to a busy chemist who spent long hours at the laboratory sculpted her original family by putting her father off in a corner with his back to the family. She spoke of his distance, silence and isolation from her. When asked where she would like to have had him she burst into tears and pulled the person playing her father into the family group saying vehemently "In the middle here—relating—a big daddy. What I'm always trying to get George (husband) to do in our family." In a discussion centered around "TAKING RESPONSIBILITY FOR MY

LIFE AND LETTING YOU TAKE RESPONSIBILITY FOR YOURS". She began to examine her angry dependency on her husband and her reluctance to find a life of her own. Referring back to the sculpting, she drew many parallels between her resentment towards father and husband. She concluded she would stop trying to put George into the center and thus let him be. Subsequently in a discussion around the theme "CHANGING MYSELF" she spoke of the concrete steps she had taken to take charge of her own life. Her husband, feeling relieved of her obsessive demands, became more communicative and began to talk about his own difficulty with closeness relating this to his own sculpting of family of origin.

Resistance

These are the encouraging experiences. Not all the families were this responsive to change. Entrenched re-activity as always was difficult to budge. Sometimes the sculpting was stereotyped and revealed little or the person was unresponsive to what was revealed. At other times so many issues were opened up with such rapidity we felt as though we had struck oil and were running around with buckets trying to catch it. Some children presented an idealized picture of the family either out of fear or a desire to protect their parents. It might take several attempts to elicit a meaningful experience. Denial and scapegoating as always were major roadblocks to progress. At times a particular type of interaction was born out of desperation. For example in Peggy Papp's group a highly intellectualizing doctor sculpted his family of origin denying all connections between the two families although these were obvious to everyone else in the group. At the same time, he was scapegoating his son unmercifully labelling him a failure, irresponsible, a con man. In his sculpting of his family of origin, he had placed his mother standing very close to him "spoon-feeding him." His father, at a great distance, was charming the world with a smile. "He was an angel on the outside and a devil on the inside. A real con man." He went on to describe the grandfather as a gambler who finally had a run-in with the police, spent some time in jail, had affairs with other women and was seldom home. He denied all feelings regarding this family arrangement.

Several sessions later, however, after a particularly intense blow up at home between father and son, the father made the following remarks to his son during the course of this session. "I do not approve of the way you are conducting your life." "As far as I am concerned you are a complete failure." "I am deeply disappointed in you and have been for years." "You are irresponsible, a real con man." "You have failed to give me the love I expected from you."

When the therapist read over the notes from this meeting (which were taken verbatim) she underlined these remarks and at the next session asked the father to re-create his original sculpting repeating all the lines he had said to his son, this time addressing them to the man who was playing his father. She asked the woman who was playing his mother to join him in the chorus as the mother was obviously collusive in labelling the father and excluding him from the family. At the end of the exercise the father said "Yes, these are all the things I thought about my father but could never say." Following this he was able to discuss some of his real feelings about his father for the first time. The theme of self disgust which ran through the family and was being passed on to his son, Peter, was now available for examination. Unfortunately this "insight" had little immediate effect on the father's relationship with his son as he was unable to integrate it in moments of crisis. However it had an immediate effect on Peter. After raptly observing the above sculpting Peter exclaimed "Then all that stuff doesn't belong just to me! Wow, I never knew you felt that way about your father." Peter had been moping about the house all year refusing to work or go to school. Two weeks later he took his first step to move out of the failure role in the family by making arrangements for a make-up program in school. He graduated from high school at the end of the year.

If a child can be helped to understand the family theme he is acting out he has the possibility of unhooking himself even though the parent cannot. Having caught just a glimpse of how he was enmeshed in the family net Peter was able to begin a long hard process of extricating himself from it. His efforts were reinforced by the group who saw totally different aspects of him describing him as "mature, sensitive, bright and unusually perceptive." They reacted intensely to the father's total renunciation of the boy compelling the father to control some of his irresponsible behavior towards Peter.

Change

The therapeutic emphasis in the groups was heavily and prejudiciously oriented toward changing behavior. The major question we asked ourselves throughout was "How do insights get translated into action." Insights which did not result in changed behavior or a shift in the family system we considered worthless. Changes in family relationships sometimes came about spontaneously as the result of changed feelings or a new awareness. Sometimes they did not. A common fallacy in every kind of therapy is the assumption that if someone "understands" something they will act on it. All too frequently this has not come to pass. While it is easier to change one's behavior on the basis of insight and a new perspective, it is sometimes necessary simply to change it without waiting for this. Based on Salvatore Minuchin's "First Comes Change, Then Comes Insight" Peggy Papp put into operation what became known as a "de-labelling" program. This was aimed directly at helping family members to "de-label" themselves by changing their predictable behavior within the family. Each family member was taken aside separately by the therapist for brief conferences, during which they discussed how they were labelled in the family and how best to go about changing their label. This was based on a diagnostic understanding of the process of labelling within the family which had developed over the months. They were not to let the others know what they intended to do but to observe reactions of the family to the change. The element of surprise was important in assessing the effects on the the family and on themselves. One of the most important gains was becoming aware of what happened to themselves as they tried to change. For example, a husband who had been labelled as the tyrant and critic in the family was asked if he could stop criticizing for one week. "Of course, easy," he stated. The following week the family reported a remarkable change in the home atmosphere. "It was delightful. There was no hostility between us all week!" exclaimed the wife. "It's the first time I've ever seen my father act human" said the son.

The father's endurance lasted three weeks and then he began to waver. The whole family lapsed back into their old ways. "You know this doesn't solve the basic problem in the family anyway" the husband grumbled. When asked what it was he replied "It's my wife's sloppy housekeeping of course." "And—how has that been the past few weeks" asked the therapist. "Well—wonderful. In fact she's been great. But that's only because I haven't criticized her." Much laughter from the group. Even the father saw the humor in his paradoxical statement. His emotional investment in his label was now open for exploration in terms of action, interaction and reaction in the total family. His attempted change has made waves in the entire family unit. The wife, relieved at first, found herself getting depressed as her role of being the maligned one was taken away. The son, robbed of the constant bickering, became provocative and picked fights with his father.

It was expected that anxiety would be stirred up as the families were stirred up. One 17 year old boy, whose mother was the mediator in the family exclaimed "Don't let my mother stop mediating or my father and I will kill each other." The mother, however, deciding the role was costing her too much stayed out of the interaction between father and son for a week. She reported "I was so relieved. When I was in between Bob and his father they used to argue for several hours at a time. When I wasn't there they argued for several minutes." Someone in the group suggested "maybe you weren't the mediator, maybe you were the troublemaker." This shifted the family into a new gear of perception.

The de-labelling program had been instituted with some apprehension on the part of the therapist who feared it might produce some mechanical and short lived results. It was therefore of great interest to learn via the final questionnaire that the group felt this was the single most helpful thing they had participated in.

Questionnaires were used periodically to get feedback and monitor change. We wanted to know from the families themselves what was helpful and what was not. Therapists often theorize about what has produced change without asking those who know the best—the ones who are experiencing it. The questions were directed towards observing one's behavior in the family and the effect it had on others; in understanding the family system and the part each played in it; in defining one's own goals and in monitoring one's own change. The families felt the questionnaires had been helpful forcing them to think about what they were doing and where they were going and suggested that they be used at more frequent intervals.

Use of Group

The group was used to create an environment in which all the senses were used in learning and understanding. Space, movement and sensory pictures became an integral part of the learning experience. Body and mind were engaged in reliving past experiences and transforming them into new experiences in the present family scene. The presence of the others bearing witness intensified the experience.

Free interaction among group members was somewhat limited in order to clarify issues in each family. Group process was focused around specific themes and activities. This sometimes required our putting aside immediate concerns of families such as the quarrel last night or the battle over the weekend in favor of longer range overall goals. While taking something away, we felt it added something more important. It reduced the amount of time wasted in superficial discussions and permitted families to participate on a deeper level. Rather than analyzing the process in the group, we analyzed the process within each family.

Despite the fact that our structure cut down on group intention, the valuable features of a group seemed to have been enhanced rather than lost. "It was so helpful having the others participate in my sculpting. I learned so much about my family that I never knew before." "I gained a great deal from seeing the sculptings of the other families and relating their experiences to mine." "It's a comfort to know others have the same problems and to be able to share them."

Socializing was done mainly outside the sessions and we neither encouraged nor discouraged this. The extent of the socialization varied from group to group and was done mainly through and around the children.

Summary and Conclusions

This has been a description of an experimental community project aimed at prevention. In searching for an educational, time limited, self help method we experimented with new techniques and approaches. We often felt uncomfortable with the new methods, as they were a departure from our accustomed approach. The primary question we addressed ourselves to was, "How are insights translated into change within the family system?" Much of our thinking changed in the process of asking and seeking the answer to this question. All of our conclusions at this point are tentative and paradoxical: 1) structuring tends to enhance rather than hamper the spontaneous release of feeling. It provides the possibility for more things happening, not less. 2) teaching concepts can lead away from intellectualization, not towards it. Intellectualizing is usually a defense against anxiety and feeling. The presentation of concepts promotes contemplation, provides perspective, reduces anxiety and leads towards the release of feelings. 3) limiting group interaction intensifies rather than diminishes the effect of the group. The focusing of group interaction around specific issues in each family deepens the group experience. 4) deliberately changing one's behavior such as in the delabeling program does not necessarily produce mechanical results but on the contrary can lead to insightful changes.

Mental Health Outpatient Centers: Relevant or Irrelevant to Mexican Americans?

Grace Burruel
Nelba Chavez

Introduction

Mental health has been defined as the optimum functioning of an individual.[1] It is not merely the absence of a mental disorder, but a sense of well-being as well. Considering the inadequate socioeconomic living conditions of most Mexican Americans in this country coupled with the stress of discrimination and prejudice, one cannot help but question whether mental health prevails among this population. Studies indicate that people living in Mexican American communities are subject, to a greater extent than others, to the kinds of stress which threaten mental health.[2] These pressures include poverty, poor housing, low educational levels, unemployment, cultural and identity conflict and social pathology.

Despite these conditions which hamper mental health, it is a known fact that Mexican Americans use mental health services less frequently than other groups.[3] Several researchers have attempted to ascertain the reasons. Karno states " . . . disproportionally few Mexican Americans arrive at the psychiatric clinic. Of those who do contact the clinic a disproportionate number drop out after brief contact."[4] Derbyshire reports " . . . admissions to state mental hospitals are proportionally less for Mexican Americans than for other groups in Los Angeles County."[5] In

1965, the admisson rate per 100,000 population was 100 for Anglos, 19 for Blacks, and 11 for Mexican Americans.[6]

Torrey has indicated that during 1968, Mexican Americans comprised only four percent of all patient-visits to the San Jose County Mental Health Center.[7] While the East Valley Center was established primarily to improve services to Mexican Americans, they accounted for only 11 percent of the patient visits.[8] Karno further found that in 1962-1963, Mexican Americans constituted only 2.2 percent of state hospital admissions, 3.4 percent of state mental hygiene clinic admissions, 0.9 percent of neuropsychiatric admissions, and 2.3 percent of outpatient admissions to the state mental health facilities.[9] The low number of Mexican Americans seeking help from the various mental health facilities in Texas led Jaco to speculate that Mexican Americans suffered less from mental illness than any other group.[10]

These findings pose an epidemiological paradox. Does under-utilization of mental health services by Mexican Americans mean they actually suffer less from mental disorders or does it mean these disorders are evidenced in other ways, such as antisocial behavior? Could Mexican Americans be more tolerant of aberrant behavior or the Mexican American family be more protective of their members with mental illness? Perhaps it simply means that Mexican Americans do not consider available mental health services helpful in meeting their needs.

It seems likely that the mental health needs of Mexican Americans are great but it is also clear that they have opted to not make extensive use of mental health facilities. The most logical explanation for this phenomenon may be the irrelevance of most of these services to their needs. The reasons for this irrelevancy are multiple and complex. But it beehoves mental health professionals to become aware of them rather than naively expecting Mexican Americans to use their facilities as they are.

Reasons For Irrelevancy

Although the primary reason for the irrelevance of mental health centers to Mexican Americans appears to be the traditional clinical, psychotherapeutic orientation, there are other important reasons which will also be cited and discussed in this paper.

1) *Continued use of traditional psychiatric services:*

Karno, who has sought answers to why so few Mexican Americans use mental health centers, believes there is a relationship between "therapeutic failures" and a set of factors which operate to make ethnic patients "less acceptable in or less accepting of psychiatric clinics."[11] He feels that part of the difficulty is related to the innate behavior of most Mexican American patients. Their "relative passivity, deference, and polite inhibited silence are poor equipment . . . "[12] for successful engagement in psychotherapy. Furthermore, he states that the relative lack of ability to verbalize and to be introspective are an added burden, particularly if the patient does not speak English and the therapist does not speak Spanish.[13] Therefore, it is believed that Mexican Americans do not have "the equipment" to use traditional psychotherapeutic services which emphasize ventilation, giving of information, utilization of transference and development of insight. Perhaps it is more correct to wonder if the traditional therapist has the equipment to be relevant to Mexican Americans.

Henry asserts that therapists feel frustrated "by one who cannot verbalize and by one who has no perceptiveness."[14] While we agree with this, it must be remembered that Anglo-Mexican relations have been anything but ideal. Furthermore, generally speaking, Mexican Americans grow up being treated as second class citizens and the American educational system suppresses and stifles the development of a positive self-image in them and inhibits their individual development. Consequently, when a Mexican American person seeks psychiatric services (if he gets that far) which thrive on ventilation and verbalization, he may not compare with his middle class Anglo counterpart, particularly if the therapist is Anglo and he adheres rigidly to the traditional therapeutic mode. One of two things may happen: the therapist may consider the Mexican American patient inept for psychotherapy or the patient may discontinue therapy. The therapist may label these patients "resistant or unmotivated" but rarely do they stop to examine what they may be doing wrong.

Although the points mentioned above contribute to a great extent to making psychiatric clinics irrelevant to many Mexican Americans, the major factor seems to be that Mexican Americans faced with mental disorders are also confronted with numerous situational stresses which must be taken care of before they can be helped with their intrapsychic problems. Many mental health professionals see this task as being beneath their professionalism. As a result, people may be turned away, since many mental health clinics screen their intakes carefully. Individuals may have to meet certain criteria before they are helped. If they are accepted, their external problems (housing, unemployment, lack of education or training and poor financial situation) which may very well be exacerbating or even creating the mental condition, are often ignored or the patient may be referred elsewhere where these needs may be met. It is very difficult for a mother, for example, to talk about her feelings when her children may not have anything to eat or she may be in dire need for money to clothe them. This applies not only to Mexican Americans but to other minority groups as well.

An additional element which makes mental health centers irrelevant to the Mexican American is the one to one approach, with emphasis on changing the individual rather than the sick environment which may be causing the disturbance. It is like applying a band-aid to a patient with terminal cancer. Concern has been expressed because mental health centers " . . . have become 'mental illness' centers—serving only those who broke down rather than promoting mental health in the community."[15]

The mental health movement represented a long overdue effort to focus on the relationship between the individual and the community in which he lives. This reawakened interest which was to remove the mental health professional from beyond the clinic walls and made it evident that an individual cannot be isolated from his social context. However, as Warren asserted "What were to be exciting, innovative programs, intertwined in a manner so as to produce greater aggregate effectiveness, highly responsive to the expressed interests and needs of disadvantaged citizens, have turned out to be largely more of the same, done by the same people in much the same way."[16]

The issue of whether the mental health professionals should concentrate their efforts on treating and changing an individual or on changing the social system which may be producing or at least contributing to the mental disorder is still unresolved. Warren's study revealed much disagreement among mental health professionals about giving priority to "broad programs for social intervention and to reserve individual treatment for particular instances where these larger approaches fail."[17] He also discovered that mental health officials tended to place the "stress on bringing about changes within the individual patient"[18] rather than the social system. An analysis of existing mental health facilities disclosed that the majority of centers considered individual psychotherapy the treatment of choice, or as one director put it "the backbone of our therapeutic program."[19] Peck based the following on critical evaluation of several mental health centers: " . . . there is little substantial evidence that any of these programs can unequivocally prove their contributions to either the maintenance of mental health or the prevention of mental illness."[20] He urged a "shift in professional orientation." Because of the difficulty encountered in changing a professional's basic orientation and the lack of innovative techniques, most of the mental health centers continue to be dominated by traditional forms of psychotherapy.[21]

2) *Difference in Categorization of Symptoms:*

Since the time of Kraepelin it has been recognized that psychopathology "varies in content and in type"[22] in diverse cultures. The present nomenclature employed by the American Psychiatric Association is based on theoretical constructs developed in relation to middle class Europe and America during the nineteenth and early twentieth centuries. Few epidimiological studies have been conducted to determine the model reactions of human beings in different cultures, particularly those served by community mental health clinics.

Mental health clinics have continued to utilize the same diagnostic tools with the implication that men and women from different socioeconomic and/or cultural orientations will respond similarly when disturbed. In fact, their symptoms may parallel cultural expectations or ways of behavior. For example, in the Mexican-American culture, men are expected to be forceful, strong and unyielding. Women, on the other hand, are expected to be soft, nutrient and self-sacrificing. It has been found that Mexican American men who have received psychiatric treatment primarily evidenced body or physical symptoms, avoiding the inference of "subjective vulnerability"[23] which would be interpreted as weakness by their cultural group. In general, Mexicans believe they have little or no control over physical processes; therefore, it is more acceptable to experience somatic disorders. However, women may express worry, disappointment and nervousness and still receive cultural sanction because these feelings are part of the feminine role.[24]

Torrey, who asserts that mental health services are "culture-bound," poses the following question: "How can a therapist do psychotherapy with a person from another culture whose categorization of the world differs?"[25] Since traditional therapists and Mexican Americans do not share the same frame of reference, meaningful communication is difficult if not impossible.[26] In a small study conducted in San Jose, California pertaining to the "cultural relativity of perceiving and classifying" Torrey found that 90 percent of the psychiatric residents associated the word "crazy" with hearing voices while only 16 per cent of Mexican Americans made this association.[27] This he says, may indicate greater tolerance among Mexican Americans for hearing voices which may be related to stronger religious beliefs. In addition, more Mexican Americans (86 percent) than psychiatric residents (20 percent) associated the word "crazy" with being frightened.[28] This is probably a result of a common folk belief that a *susto* (a frightened experience) may cause insanity.

Often, the cultural context of the patient, which may play a vital role in diagnosis and treatment, is ignored. Karno found that clinics processed Mexican American patients with no specific reference to ethnic identity or sociocultural milieu. Case studies were " . . . forced into the mold of 'chief complaint, present illness, past history, diagnosis and treatment'."[29]

Henry, addressing himself to the needs to understand the patient's culture, notes that "the psychiatrist's ability to understand the patient's answers to the questions depends on his understanding of the culture from which he comes."[30] Understanding of the patient's inner self will only come if the therapist understands the outer reality that has been incorporated into the inner self.[31] How can psychotherapists who do not understand the outer reality of Mexican Americans provide them with relevant help?

3) *Community Mental Health Services are provided by the Anglo majority.*

As Torrey observes, "Traditional mental health services are inextricably bound to the dominant, ruling caste of Anglos in the minds of Mexican Americans."[32] In day-to-day contact with the dominant Anglo society (employer, public agencies, recreational facilities) the Mexican American may be treated in a demeaning manner. He is often reminded "to keep his place." Therefore, any services established by Anglos become synonymous "with perpetuating this order."[33] In a recent study concerning reasons for under utilization of mental health services by Mexican Americans, it was learned that part of their reluctance to seek help was related to "pride and humility." Mexican Americans felt they were "looked down upon" because of their unfamiliarity with the procedures and red tape involved in getting help. Consequently, they were more willing to seek help from a more familiar source, such as a neighborhood physician, a priest or a community leader.[34]

Furthermore, the immigrant status of some Mexicans or their family members may prevent contact with the establishment because they fear repatriation for suffering from a mental disorder. Many Mexican Americans perceive the Anglo as "cold, exploitative, distant and insincere,"[35] regardless of his well-meaning intentions. This perception is rooted in cultural differences and in historical Anglo-Mexican intergroup and interpersonal relationships. Thus, at a time when a Mexican may need emotional support, an Anglo would be the last person to whom he would turn, regardless of his professional qualification.

4) *Differences in viewing mental treatment:*

Unlike some middle and upper class Americans, many of whom consider psychiatric care as a "status symbol," Mexicans continue to attach shame and stigma to receiving treatment for a mental illness or disorder. They are too proud and sensitive to expose their personal problems to "outsiders." Many Mexicans continue to uphold the traditional family function of solving its own problems. They believe in protecting and caring for the troubled family member rather than sending him to the Anglo clinic or hospital for treatment, which may be interpreted as a form of rejection.

5) *Mental disorders among Mexicans are less visible:*

Although it cannot be concluded that Mexican Americans suffer a lesser rate of mental illness, it can be said that mental disorders are "less visible." They are expressed in other forms of behavior such as crime, drug addiction, alcoholism and juvenile delinquency. While Mexican Americans are under-represented in respect to mental health facilities, this is not true for penal institutions,[36] both adult and juvenile. These institutions are overrepresented by Mexican Americans. Since Mexican Americans are reluctant to use mental health facilities when confronted with an emotional or mental disturbance, they would be even less likely to seek such services in relation to antisocial behavior.

6) *Location of resources:*

Many mental health centers are located too far from the Mexican American Community. Centers situated within the Mexican American Community are the exception rather than the rule. In San Jose, California for example, the mental health clinic is located on the opposite end of town. In Tucson, Arizona, prior to the existence of La Frontera, outpatient services consisted of two clinics located in the eastern part of the city. Individuals from the Tucson South area needing services were required to leave the barrios and travel across the city into a strange neighborhood in order to receive help.

Among many other deterrents, funds for transportation and/or child care can pose a real obstacle for some Mexican Americans. Under-utilization of mental health services by Mexican Americans has not been the case at La Frontera. The majority of clients are Mexican Americans. They have sought help, and are following through with treatment plans. They have encouraged their relatives, friends, and neighbors to do the same.

In order to understand this phenomenon, we need to analyze what is different about La Frontera which may account for the reasons why Mexican Americans have chosen to utilize its services. In this section, an attempt will be made to trace the development of the outpatient center, its features and current functioning.

Description of the Center

La Frontera, a mental health outpatient center, is part of a recently formed network (Tucson Southern Counties Mental Health Services) of mental health services, funded by the National Institute of Mental Health. The overall program includes most of the elements of a comprehensive community mental health program, such as 1) inpatient services, 2) outpatient services, 3) partial hospitalization, 4) emergency services 24 hours a day, 5) consultation and education, 6) training, and 7) research and evaluation. In addition, Tucson South has a drug problem which includes methadone maintenance and counseling. It has also an educational and therapeutic program for emotionally disturbed children.

Among the goals of the program are 1) to improve the social functioning of those individuals suffering from a mental disorder, 2) to prevent mental breakdowns by early diagnosis and treatment, and 3) to attempt to foster, improve and promote mental health.

The catchment area includes the southern and western parts of Tucson, plus five additional counties with a population of approximately 200,000 people. A survey of the area disclosed the catchment population to be older, with a concentration of non-whites, a lower educational attainment, lower income per family, higher unemployment rates, more substandard housing and more public assistance recipients than any other area in Tucson and Southern Arizona. This area revealed the highest incidence of criminal activity, including arrests for drug addiction and alcoholism, juvenile delinquency, broken homes, venereal diseases and rejections from the armed services due to mental disorders.

La Frontera is located in the center of the catchment area and is the first facility of its kind to exist in the area. Besides La Frontera, the only other social institutions in the catchment area are: Pima County Juvenile Center, County General Hospital, County Jail, Tucson Police Department, Youth Service Bureau (a model cities program) and St. Mary's Hospital which is where our inpatient unit is located. All other social agencies and medical facilities are located in either the Northern or Eastern sections of Tucson, which are predominantly populated by middle and upper class Anglos.

La Frontera is the only agency in Tucson and the Southern part of Arizona which has Spanish speaking social workers. There are two MSW's who are Mexican Americans and a bilingual psychologist. The remaining staff consists of two part time psychiatrists, two additional social workers, one of whom is the director of the clinic, and the other a B.A. level social worker, and two outreach workers.

Services at La Frontera become available with a telephone call, letter or personal visit. There are no long or complicated forms that have to be filled out in order to be helped and there are no waiting lists. A person may be seen either immediately, within a few hours, the next day, or at the latest, within a week.

The general atmosphere of the center is one of friendliness and warmth. Bright colors and cheerful decor contrast with the sterile atmosphere characteristic of some other clinics. We are very informal and many of our patients stop by when they are in the neighborhood to have a cup of coffee, or say hello even if they are not scheduled for an appointment.

Although fees are based on a sliding scale, no one is denied services because of inability or ability to pay.

1) *Direct Treatment Procedures:*

Direct treatment at La Frontera consists of individual, conjoint, family and group therapy. Other approaches used are community action, advocacy, outreach work, consultation and education for various groups in the community, to enhance their understanding of interpersonal functioning of people of all ages, and to help key people (police, doctors, schools) in the area to better understand the needs of people with mental problems.

Although it can be said that the direct treatment approaches we utilize fall within the traditional model, we modify them to meet the needs of the client. For example, the mental discomfort a person may be experiencing may be attributed to environmental stress. Subsequent to a differential diagnosis, we may find that a psychotherapeutic approach may not be appropriate. Instead, we attempt to deal with the current situation by manipulating the environment, mobilizing community resources, being advocates for the client and by providing a tangible service. Also, we often deviate from conventional approaches such as length of contacts with clients—not abiding strictly with the fifty minute hour or weekly interviews, by making home visits and/or telephone calls.

Many of our clients use us on a crisis to crisis (or emergency) basis, because it is very difficult for many to relate to consistent, hourly therapy sessions which would deal with strengthening their ability to cope with crisis. Instead of insisting that they engage in regular therapy, each time they contact us we try to help them learn other ways of handling their problems. This takes longer and it may not seem as effective as other approaches on the face of it, but it seems to work better with these patients, and most important, they can relate to it.

Our definition of mental health is very broad. We feel that anything that affects the social functioning of an individual also affects his mental health. In order for a client to receive our services, he does not necessarily have to be emotionally disturbed, neurotic or psychotic. Anyone who says he "hurts," whether it is internal, external or both, we take. Consequently, our clients range from one who may be unhappy because of the relationship with neighbors (we have had meetings in the neighborhood with all neighbors involved) to a severely psychotic person whom we try to maintain in the community, instead of sending him to the state hospital.

At La Frontera, we provide our clients with what we call "a complete overhaul." We get involved in almost every aspect of their life situation. The following cases illustrate this concept.

1) A young Mexican American man was referred to us because he had not been out of his room for three days. He lived in a small, cold room and the furnishings consisted of a bed and table. He had not eaten for several days.

Mental status examination performed on site, revealed he was within the psychotic range. His family consisted of one brother who lived with his in-laws and had no means to offer help to his brother.

It was necessary to hospitalize him, but while he was in the hospital we were able to find him a place to live, processed his application for public assistance, obtained an emergency loan from the credit union which enabled him to have some money until he received his welfare check and enrolled him in a training program.

Since he was a Vietnam veteran, we also helped him apply for a disability pension from the V.A. In the process we learned he had been turned down. We became the patient's advocate and we were successful in obtaining a pension plus his retroactive funds.

All of the above were done in conjunction with psychiatric treatment.

2) A depressed and nervous Mexican mother came to see us because she was afraid she was going to have a nervous breakdown. Her ex-husband was trying to take her children. Because of her mental condition, she had lost her job and was also in the process of losing her house due to back payments. She was very frightened because she thought the court would take her children.

In helping this woman, we not only assisted her in keeping the children (we went to court with her) but we also talked to the legal owner of the house, explained her predicament and appealed to him to give her some time. In addition we contacted her employer and requested he give Mrs. M some time to get herself together. She was also helped in obtaining a welfare grant.

Through supportive therapy, ventilation and mobilization of resources she was able to get back on her feet.

3) A young Mexican mother with two children living on a welfare grant of $130.00 a month, was referred by the county hospital because of a suicide attempt. When she failed to keep her appointment, we made a home visit. She lived in a small dilapidated trailer which had no electricity or running water. She had recently moved to Tucson; was very isolated and did not know anyone. The only family member was her mother who had come to see her from Mexico but her permit had expired. She was fearful of going to the immigration office because of the possibility of being deported.

Immediately, we mobilized our resources and found an unfurnished apartment. We were able to get some furniture through donations and charity organizations. We helped her apply for food stamps and she became involved in a training program. Since we did not feel it was advisable for her to be alone, we contacted the immigration authorities and they granted her mother a six month permit.

Her suicide attempt was out of sheer desperation because of her situation. Through short-term treatment and the mobilization of resources, we were able to help her.

4) A very concerned and sad Mexican couple came in because the school had rejected their deformed, 10 year old mentally retarded boy. Because they lived in a rural area, the school did not have the facilities to help their son. They were feeling very helpless and discouraged.

Our investigation revealed that the school did not have a program for that particular type of child; however, they had the responsibility of placing the child in another school and paying for the cost. Pressure was placed on the school and with our assistance the child entered school soon after. The next problem was transportation as the school was not obligated to provide this. Together with the parents and our staff the problem was solved.

In addition, Crippled Children's Clinic became involved and helped the child with his physical deformities. Because the father was a migrant worker we were also able to get him involved with medical services for the other family members.

5) A fifteen year old Mexican girl dropped in to see us because she had been feeling very nervous, frightened and had

recurrent nightmares. Her feelings were related to being afraid of a school-mate who had threatened to harm her and continuously followed her home after school. She tried coping with her anxiety by ditching class, thus avoiding the girl.

We contacted her mother who agreed to go to the other girl's home and meet with her parents. In the meeting with the parents, they agreed and consented for us to arrange a meeting with their daughter and our client. The meeting was held in a neutral place (other than the clinic) and their anger, animosity, conflicts and differences were aired out and we reached a reasonable compromise. The youngsters are by no means friends now but at least a fight was avoided and our client's symptoms disappeared.

To us this is mental health. Sitting in our offices, dealing only with the psychological aspect of the problem would not have been helpful to the clients. Possibly, we would have lost contact with them. We can count on our fingers those cases in which we have been able to begin to deal with the client's intrapsychic problems immediately. It has been possible with some because their socioeconomic situation was fairly stable and they were not under any real situational stress.

Contrary to what others have found, the Mexican Americans we have seen at the clinic do have the "equipment" to engage in psychotherapy. The difference may be that it takes them a little longer than the Anglos to begin to verbalize, ventilate and be introspective. One of the major factors which may account for this is the loyalty to the family and lack of trust for "outsiders." Developing a good relationship with the therapist is paramount prior to their revealing their innner self. Another contributing factor is that within the Mexican culture discussion of feelings and open communication, especially within the family is not encouraged. They are taught to be discreet, respectful and to be subordinate to their parents. Expressing how they really feel is not sanctioned by the Mexican culture. This is further complicated by the experience of Mexican Americans in the school system where they may be made to feel inferior because of their lack of ability to speak English fluently. Outside of his cultural milieu the Mexican American may appear more quiet and reserved than the Anglo.

The other important factor has to do with the level of education. There is no doubt that the less educated person is not as verbal and articulate as the educated one, regardless of ethnicity. As a matter of fact, the more educated Mexican American does not have any difficulty, but since he is better educated, chances are his socioeconomic situation is better too, and he may be more liberated from the traditional culture. Therefore, it cannot be said that Mexican Americans cannot engage in psychotherapy. It may appear that way but it requires knowledge of the culture in order to fully understand why this assumption is fallacious.

As to the opinion that mental health services are not relevant because of the emphasis placed on changing the individual rather than the societal forces which may be creating the problem, it can be said that we have not reached the level of societal overhaul yet. Because we have been so occupied in helping those individuals who are hurting *now,* we have had little time to implement some of our ideas which address themselves to the source of the problem rather than the symptoms. This becomes very frustrating at times and is a great source of conflict for us at the clinic. Often, we become disillusioned, as all we seem to be doing is treating the products of an unfair, unjust society. Actually, all we do is put patches on their wounds and send them out again. What we would really like to do is to enact social action programs to attack the school system, revamp the income maintenance programs, organize a movement for better housing, fight job discrimination, set up more training programs, and combat other major contributors to poor mental health. We have been involved and tried to do something about these issues; however, we have made no major impact. We realize this is almost impossible. But perhaps some day it can be accomplished.

2) *Understanding of the Mexican Culture:*

Although standard diagnostic nomenclature of the American Psychiatric Association is used at the center, we have an advantage in our two Mexican American social workers who share a frame of reference from the inside. This provides a better understanding of their situation in terms of what is normal or not within the culture. For example, a psychiatrist or social worker may diagnose a young man or woman as passive dependent because of their inability to break away from the mother or the home without realizing that this is normal, expected behavior in the Mexican culture. Furthermore, the treatment plan may include helping the individual emancipate from the family without realizing the pressure and guilt this could create if mishandled.

Since the other staff members at the clinic are very interested in and receptive to learning more about the Mexican culture, we often engage in formal or informal discussions enabling them to deal more emphatically with Mexican Americans.

Because there are no epidemiological studies concerning the modal reactions of Mexican Americans under stress, it may be fallacious to apply theoretical constructs developed in relation to other groups. This presents a real diagnostic problem. For example, there have been some cases of Mexican Americans whose symptoms resemble those exhibited in neurotic disorders. But some of the dynamics may deviate from theoretical models. For instance, they are not obsessively concerned with sexual or aggressive impulses but with something happening to them—the worst thing being suffocating or dying. In such cases we have found an extremely close relationship with the mother, an exaggeration of a culturally acceptable pattern. Does this mean they are not truly neurotic since the dynamics are different?

Another diagnostic problem is encountered in depression. Mexican Americans may exhibit the usual depressive syndrome (low self-esteem, lack of appetite, insomnia, suicidal ideations) but there may not be any clear precipitating factor, such as the loss of someone, which may have triggered the depression. Is it really a *depression* or could it be *oppression?* The literature (social as well as anthropological) is replete with descriptions of Mexican Americans as apathetic, pessimistic, passive, morose and fatalistic. Would it be possible to speculate that Mexican Americans have internalized the attributes of an oppressed people, and have assumed a masochistic position, or is it the work of a self-fulfilling prophecy? If so, what are the implications for treatment; should they be enjoined to social action or treated with psychotherapy and/or chemotherapy? At this point, we can only raise questions; we have no answers.

Obviously, language is a basic tool in treatment, but how effective can treatment be when words or terms can have different connotations? For example, a Mexican American patient was referred by another agency with a diganosis of paranoid schizophrenia. This was based on her statements that her ex-husband's ex-wife was "trying to get her" and had put a hex on her. Discussion with the patient in her own language clearly indicated that much of what she was saying was based on a very common folk belief related to *brujeria* (witchcraft). Is it paranoia or do we need to know more about the culture to separate that which is common to a group from that which is more clearly individual?

As stated earlier, the majority of the Mexican American males who come to the center exhibit psychosomatic disorders. This is more acceptable in the culture than having an "emotional" problem. Indicating or insisting that it is a mental problem is contradicted. Working with and dealing with whatever may be causing the physical problem requires a great deal of skill, patience and time. This again is not as effective as other therapeutic approaches with other kinds of patients, but it is one of the only effective ways of working with the Mexican American male. Caution needs to be exercised so their masculinity or sense of "machismo" is not demeaned or insulted.

If the Mexican American male is not the identified or primary patient, it is also difficult to engage them in family or conjoint therapy. Many Mexican Americans still adhere to the traditional practice of handling problems within the family. Asking for help may mean that the male, head of the family, cannot handle his own family problems. It is difficult to work with him but *not impossible*. His role in the family needs to be supported constantly, and must not make him feel as though one is taking over his family or telling him what to do. This also requires time and some informal contacts such as regular, short home visits before one can really begin to deal with the problems. The most effective resolution of the therapist's role in relation to the family is to have the therapist become part of the family or be "adopted" and thus, involvement in family therapy becomes much easier. A family approach, even if the main therapeutic modality is individual, is vital when working with Mexican Americans. For example, plans may be made with the patient and if the other family members are not included or informed they may sabotage the efforts or feel that the therapist is intruding and undermining the family structure, thus creating a bigger problem or placing the individual patient in a confusing situation, pulled in many directions.

3) *Tucson Southern Counties Mental Health Services are not strictly provided by the Anglo majority:*

The executive Director of Tucson South is Mexican American and six of the twelve board members, including the chairman, are Mexican American. Half of the staff at La Frontera, professional and clerical, are Mexican American. In addition, there is another staff member who speaks Spanish as a second language. The name of the center is Spanish and since we are located in the barrio the people do not strictly associate us with the Anglo establishment. As a matter of fact, it has often been pointed out that we are "too Chicano oriented." Our response to this has been that we are attempting to be relevant and responsive to all segments of the population. Perhaps what is unique or different about our program is that, for the first time, a concerted effort is being made to relate to the needs of this populace which, of course, make it very conspicuous.

When people call or come in, they are greeted by a Spanish speaking worker. Often, people comment on how nice it is to finally have a place where they can come in, speak their language, be understood and accepted. Furthermore, as it was mentioned earlier, there are no complicated forms or red tape involved in getting help so that their unfamiliarity or lack of sophistication in handling such matters is not a problem at La Frontera. It may be pointed out that it is not uncommon for Mexican Americans to be embarrassed or shy when in contact with most social institutions, related to fear of authority and their previous experiences with such agencies. This is an interesting issue but it is beyond the scope of this paper to fully discuss it.

4) *Understanding the difference in viewing Mental Health Treatment:*

The stigma associated with mental disorders and seeking mental health treatment is great with Mexican Americans. Before the name was changed, the center was called "Tucson Southern Counties Mental Health Outpatient Clinic." There were many negative feelings expressed by the people about coming to such a place and worries about being seen by friends or relatives.

Three steps were taken to improve the situation. First, the name was changed to La Frontera Center. Second, two social workers started spending half a day in the housing projects. This served two purposes: to make the services available to those who had some feelings about going to the clinic, and to bring the services home to those who had no means of transportation. Subsequently, our Mexican American client population increased tremendously.

The third step was attending meetings of various groups of people and trying to educate them as to what mental health is all about. We also had announcements on the Mexican radio stations and an article in the local newspaper. Most important, was the trust we obtained through being of service to the people. Our clients themselves have done most of the work in changing attitudes toward receiving mental health treatment.

Another point is that knowing and understanding how the people feel, we do not emphasize the word *mental*. Even if the person is psychotic, they attribute the illness to "los nervios" (the nerves). Actually, regardless of what the problem is, they think the trouble lies with "los nervios." We have learned that the best procedure is to not tamper with this belief.

5) *Services are also provided for people exhibiting antisocial behavior:*

Through our experience in working with Mexican Americans, we have seen that often mental health disorders among Mexicans, primarily males, are expressed in other forms of behavior such as alcoholism, drug addiction, other criminal activities and juvenile delinquency. Because drug addiction was so prevalent in the catchment area, a separate program was instituted to meet this need. A program for alcoholics is also in the planning stage.

We come in contact with those individuals suffering from some type of addiction, who are involved in criminal activities, through our clients. For example, a mother-patient may have a son, brother or husband who may be an addict or alcoholic which may be contributing to her problem; consequently, we also get involved in helping them, coordinating therapeutic responsibility with the drug program or other agency involved.

In addition, we work very closely with the Juvenile Court and many of our referrals come from that source. Another agency we provide services for is the Youth Service Bureau, a model cities program for youngsters. We provide consultation to them and we also conduct therapy groups for some of their caseload, which consists of pre-delinquent children.

6) *La Frontera is located in the barrio:*

Since the center is situated in the Mexican American community, it is easily accessible to the people. Many of our clients are our neighbors. Inasmuch as it is located on a main street, transportation via buses is possible. In addition, CEO has a transportation program which most of our clients qualify for. For those who cannot find any other means of transportation or who have babysitting problems we meet them at their home. Currently, we are in the process of setting up some kind of babysitting service for those mothers who need to bring their children with them.

Conclusion

Outpatient mental health centers *can* be relevant to Mexican Americans. It requires more time, understanding and reaching out, but it can be done. At La Frontera we have seen it happen. We are still in the process of growing and expanding, but in relation to Tucson and the previous programs in existence, La Frontera has a program which is addressing itself to the needs of the Mexican American people, as well as other minority groups. We still have a long way to go; however, we can take pride in what we have accomplished thus far.

NOTES

[1] Ruth I. Knee and Warren C. Lamson, "Mental Health and Mental Illness," p. 486.

[2] "New Ways to Meet The Mental Health Needs of Mexican Americans," p. 4.

[3] *Ibid.*, p. 1.

[4] Marvin Karno, "The Enigma of Ethnicity in A Psychiatric Clinic," p. 517.

[5] "New Ways to Meet Mental Health Needs of Mexican Americans," *op. cit*, p. 5.

[6] *Ibid.*, p. 5.

[7] Torrey, "The Irrelevancy of Traditional Mental Health Services for Urban Mexican Americans," p. 2.

[8] *Ibid.*, p. 2.

[9] Marvin Karno and Robert B. Edgerton, "Perception of Mental Illness in a Mexican American Community." pp. 233-234.

[10] E. Gartly Jaco, "Mental Health of the Spanish-American in Texas," pp. 482-483.

[11] Karno, "The Enigma of Ethnicity in a Psychiatric Clinic," pp. 518-519.

[12] *Ibid.*, p. 519.

[13] *Ibid.*, p. 519.

[14] Jules Henry, "The Inner Experience of Culture," p. 102.

[15] "Letters to Colleagues," p. 1.

[16] Roland Warren, "The Mental Health Drama: Hamlet or Hellzapoppin?", p. 11.

[17] *Ibid.*, p. 10.

[18] *Ibid.*, p. 19.

[19] *The Community Mental Health Center: An Analysis of Existing of Models,* The Joint Information Service of the American Psychiatric Association and the National Association for Mental Health (Baltimore: Garamond/Pridemark Press, c1964), p. 22.

[20] Harris Peck, Melvin Roman, and Seymour Kaplan, "Community Action Programs and the Comprehensive Mental Health Center," pp. 103-104.

[21] David Mechanic, *Mental Health and Social Policy,* p. 97.

[22] Marvin K. Opler, *Culture and Psychiatry Human Values,* p. 17.

[23] Horacio Fabregar, Arthur Reibel and Carl Wallace, "Working Class Mexican Psychiatric Patients," p. 708.
[24] *Ibid.*, p. 708.
[25] Torrey, *op cit.*, p. 7.
[26] *Ibid.*, p. 8.
[27] *Ibid.*, p. 8.
[28] *Ibid.*, p. 8.
[29] Karno, *op cit.*, p. 520.
[30] Henry, *op cit.*, p. 94.
[31] *Ibid.*, p. 90.
[32] Torrey, *op cit.*, p. 9.
[33] *Ibid.*, pp. 9-10.
[34] *Ibid.*, pp. 10-11.
[35] Karno, pp. 234-235.
[36] Armando Morales, "Mental And Public Health Issues," p. 6.

REFERENCES

Caplan, Gerald. *Principles of Preventive Psychiatry.* New York; Basic Books, Inc., 1964.
"Community Mental Health Centers Act of 1963." Title II, Public Law 880164, Reprinted from the *Federal Register.* May 6, 1964. U.S. Dept. of HEW, PHS, U.S. Gov't. Printing Office.
Cooper, Shirley. "The Swing To Community Mental Health," *Social Casework.* Vol. XLIX. No. 5, May, 1965.
Fabregar, Horacio, Reibel, Arthur, and Wallace, Carl. "Working Class Mexican Psychiatric Patients," *Archives of General Psychiatry.* Vol. *16,* January, 1967.
Henry, Jules. "The Inner Experience of Culture," *Psychiatry.* Vol. *14,* February, 1951.
Jaco, E. Gartley. "Mental Health of The Spanish American in Texas," in Marvin K. Opler (Ed.), *Culture and Mental Health.* New York: The MacMillan Company, 1959.
Karno, Marvin and Edgerton, Robert, B. "Perception of Mental Illness in a Mexican-American Community," *Archives of General Psychiatry.* Vol. *20,* February, 1969.
Karno, Marvin. "The Enigma of Ethnicity in a Psychiatric Clinic," *Archives of General Psychiatry.* Vol. *14,* March, 1966.
Knee, Ruth and Lamson, Warren, C. "Mental Health and Mental Illness," In Harry L. Lurie (Ed.), *Encyclopedia of Social Work.* New York: National Association of Social Workers, 1965.
"Letters to Colleagues," *Mental Health Advocacy Association.* Philadelphia, Penn., May 14, year not cited.
Mechanic, David. *Mental Health and Social Policy.* New Jersey:

Prentice-Hall, Inc., 1969.

Morales, Armando. "Mental and Public Health Issues," *El Grito*. Vol. *3*, No. 2, Winter, 1970.

"New Ways To Meet The Mental Health Needs of Mexican Americans," A report to the East Los Angeles Community. Presented by Mental Health Development Commission. Welfare Planning Council: Los Angeles Region, April, 1968.

Opler, Marvin, K. *Culture and Psychiatry Human Values*. Illinois: Charles C. Thomas, 1956.

Peck, Harris. "Some Relationships Between Group Process and Mental Health Phenomena in Theory and Practice," Reprint. February, 1971.

Peck, Harris, Roman, Melvin and Kaplan, Seymour, "Community Action Programs And The Comprehensive Mental Health Center," *Psychiatric Research Report 21*. American Psychiatric Association, April, 1967.

Soddy, Kenneth (Ed.) *Cross-Cultural Studies In Mental Health*. Chicago: Quadrangle Books, 1962.

The Community Mental Health Center: An Analysis of Existing Models. The Joint Information Service of the American Psychiatric Association and the National Association for Mental Health. Baltimore: Garamond/Pridemark Press, 1964.

"The Mental Health of Urban America: The Urban Programs of National Institute of Mental Health," Report prepared by: *Program Analysis and Evaluation Branch*. U.S. Dept. of HEW, U.S. Gov't. Printing Office, April, 1969.

Torrey, E. Fuller. "The Irrelevancy of Traditional Mental Health Services for Urban Mexican Americans," A paper presented at the meeting of American Orthopsychiatric Association. San Francisco, March 1970.

Warren, Roland L. "The Mental Health Drama: Hamlet or Hellzapoppin?" Paper presented at the Annual National Institute Regional Office Staff Meeting. Dallas, March, 1970.

Yontef, Gary. "A Review of The Practice of Gestalt Therapy," Reprint, California State College, Los Angeles, 1969.

The Medicine Men of the Future—
Reuniting the Learned Professions

Robert L. Bergman, M.D.

A few months ago, one of my colleagues in the Indian Health Service Mental Health Program was interviewed by a reporter interested in our work with medicine men. The reporter seemed sympathetic and intelligent, and indeed submitted a draft for comment before publication. It was an accurate account and my colleague was pleased. Unfortunately, it was printed under the headline, "Psychiatry Takes a Step Backward." The notion I want to discuss here is that perhaps we are ready for some steps in that direction.

Mr. Tom Largewhiskers, a 102 year old Navajo medicine man who serves as a consultant to our program says that when he began his training in 1886, his grandfather explained to him that unconscious mental processes were most important in determining whether one was well or ill. Most of Mr. Largewhiskers' other basic premises are more obscure and seemingly illogical to psychiatrists of the European tradition, and his values differ from those of the dominant (but weakening) majority. When the first men landed on the moon, a white man told him the news and asked if it surprised him. It didn't. "There is nothing so foolish, expensive, or dangerous, that white men won't do it," he said.

Working for the past six years with men like Mr. Largewhiskers, moving rapidly back and forth between two cultures and the systems of healing proper to each, and trying to find appropriate roles for mental health people in a receptive but wisely skeptical community has forced me to imagine how the ways of each system could enhance the other. Some things that I like about the Navajo way were abandoned by us in the past, other customs are simply different, but in either case, some familiarity with them has helped me to focus my dissatisfaction on the way we organize our work and to see alternatives. What follows are some of my speculations as to ways in which it would be good for our successors of the more or less distant future to be like Navajo medicine men.

The medicine men unite in themselves the three learned professions. We have separated them for centuries, and each, theology, law, and medicine, has been even further fragmented with sometimes nearly fatal results. To understand what it is like not to make our customary distinctions, imagine a society in which there is no difference between a church and a hospital. Many Navajo people find that distinction rather puzzling and one of the reasons for the considerable success of pentecostal missionaries among Indians is that these missionaries are quite ready to be both healers and priests. In a Navajo ceremony there is no way to tell what is healing and what is worship. Everything is both. Moral guidance is also an inextricable element of ceremonial practice, and outside of the ceremonial it was again the medicine men because of their knowledge, experience, and integrity who are called upon to play the leading role in the informal judicial process that settled disputes and dealt with wrongdoers until quite recently.

We doctors, lawyers, and ministers, like the good union men we are, try hard to avoid jurisdictional disputes. Psychiatrists pretend that they make no moral judgments. We call them 'reality testing' or some such alias. Only old-fashioned or low status (but high-salaried) ministers openly practice healing. Up-to-date ones call it pastoral care and in my experience become anxious and guilty when they discuss it with a psychiatrist, seemingly fearing that he will think they are taking the bread out of his mouth; and we try to hide the role confusion of judges and doctors, in the elaborate ritual called expert testimony—a ritual which seems to be increasingly embarrassing to all concerned.

As physicians, the medicine men are way ahead of us in the evolution of their role. Until white doctors came along, they set fractures, drained abscesses, treated wounds and did all they could for the physical aspect of illness. They quickly learned that our gadgetry was far better than theirs for this sort of thing, and turned over all such matters to the technicians and pharmacists—us. They then concentrated on what they always considered most important—roughly what we would call psychotherapy or, heaven help us, pastoral care. If we are wise, the same will happen to us in the next hundred years. It doesn't seem overly optimistic to predict that in that length of time biologists and technicians—only some of whom are physicians—will fairly easily prevent or diagnose and cure everything but unhappiness and death—those two basics should be enough to keep our successors, whoever they turn out to be, busy. The trouble is that unlike the medicine men we would rather be scientists and technicians than healer-priests. As a psychiatrist I am filled with envy by the lovely machinery I see in the hands of my colleagues in radiology or opthalmology. The biochemist-psychiatrists, I suppose, are grappling with some of the hardest scientific-technical problems of medicine, but sooner or later they will succeed in preventing or curing the major mental illnesses, leaving the rest of us with only the universal nuttiness and misery of human life to take care of. How will we do it? Not, I think as scientists or even as priests of science, but somehow as healers— like the medicine men. I think our successors will be more like Dr. Henry Reilley than Dr. Jonas Salk, or at least they had better be.

I believe that our shame at not being more rigorously scientific causes us a great deal of trouble already. We are so poor at our non-scientific tasks partly because we try to remain unconscious of them and therefore do not learn them well. It is well established that psychotherapists influence their patients in accordance with their own set of moral standards, but we rarely discuss those standards. If we do so at all, it is often as surreptitious dirty talk. We leave that sort of thing to the priests and then we scorn the priests. When we judge our patients or more commonly their parents, we leave the process unexamined because we disguise it so well as reality testing. The old claim that we only hold the mirror up is true if it is also true that we can make all the patient's judgments infallible and therefore can tell when his reality testing is off or on. One has only to read case reports (of course they are getting rare these days because they aren't scientific) to get at least a nagging doubt that all psychiatrists see the same reality and therefore can tell how well a patient is testing it. I do not mean to say that there is any easy answer to the question of how to make moral judgments about our patients, but the problem can only be made worse by ignoring it. Actually the moral principles traditionally inherent in psychotherapy are rather similar to those of the medicine men, and though surely not a complete moral system are in themselves useful and admirable: It is good for our patients to love and to work. It is good for us to be as helpfully interested in our patients as we can be regardless of their impulses and actions, and our being interested and accepting does not mean to encourage bad actions. It is good for us to meet with our patients for their benefit not ours, except insofar as it is to our benefit to work. Partly because we try to remain unconscious of our values, we seem to be drifting towards some different ones, namely that pleasure is better than love or work, and that it is good for the patient for the therapist to have fun in therapy too.

The covering-over of moral issues is not only determined by the wish to be scientific, but also by a fear of being unmanly. European religion for some time seems to have become the province of the clergy and women. This trend is only beginning among Indian people. Traditionally, either men or women can be Navajo ceremonialists, and religious activity is regarded as difficult, important, and admirable for anyone. I suspect that one reason for the difference is that Indian religion requires study and effort of everyone. The ceremonialist is the leader, but not the performer. In our religion, with only a few exceptions (and these are prospering), the ever increasing fragmentation of life into professional specialties has left only the clergy active, while everyone else is a passive member of the audience. Our culture equates passivity and femininity, and therefore we refer to the kind of damage religion has suffered by such words as 'emasculation.'

The rituals of medicine have also been damaged. The medicine men are taught ritual as much as they are taught anything, but we psychiatrists, who should know how important ritual is, teach it to our students only by-the-way or not at all. I suppose many psychiatrists would deny that they had a ritual. It would be interesting to see what would happen to such a psychiatrist who tried to practice without his ritual objects or with the wrong kind—a psychiatrist in a lawyer's office or a minister's study, for example. Ritual is what gives form to one person's presence with another. In the course of most Navajo ceremonies, there are times when the patient and ceremonialist chant together. A good medicine man quickly achieves a state of harmony with the patient so close that the lag between the medicine man's lead and the patients repetition becomes almost imperceptible. For a lonely, desperate person, the experience seems to be electrifying. Many patients I have shared with medicine men have said that it was during a prayer of this kind that they began to feel better. I think many therapists today feel so awkward about their ritual that they can scarcely stand to be present with their patients. We don't listen we—diagnose. Scientism is wheeled up to help us out in the form of diagnostic tests—computer scored, if possible, and instead of listening we classify. In the end it comes down to prescribing. I suspect that the excessive use of prescribed psychotropic drugs results in part from inadequate training in being with a suffering person. Prescribe something and they will go away.

Ritual can also be used to keep your distance. The forms of the law and the courts seem to do so admirably. Until the advent of tribal courts, disputes in a Navajo community were settled by discussions involving large families of neighbors along with medicine men or other leaders. Discussions were very long, but they were not long delayed, and the knowledge of psychology possessed by the medicine man was often the determinant of a consensually arrived at group decision. The formal procedings of our courts seem to drain the life out of even the most vital matters. Lawyers and judges are called upon to settle interpersonal disputes without training or experience of psychology or therapy. Blame and punishment are decided upon in an antipsychological and an immoral way. Consider a murder trial. If a psychiatrist will testify that the defendant is suffering from a severe mental illness which causes him to be extremely dangerous he is likely to be free—though still just as dangerous—within a year or two. There are at least two such people now on the Navajo reservation. If the defendant committed his crime under extreme stress such as will never occur again in his life, he will probably be locked up for years. This psychologically illogical result is justified by a concept of justice renounced by most religions many centuries ago—human revenge.

The basic difficulty is the fragmentation of life. One night a group of us was waiting for the start of a Navajo ceremony. The medicine man who also worked as an interpreter began talking about his employer, "My boss, Dr. J., knows about anthropology all the way," he said, "but he sure doesn't know about anything else. His car broke down today, and I had to fix it for him. He didn't have any idea what was wrong with it. If we go camping, I'd better be there to put up the tent. He can't do it. That's the difference between an Indian and a white man. An Indian may not know anything all the way. But maybe he does. Either way he sure knows a lot of different things. If he needs a house, he builds one. If his car breaks downs, he fixes it. If he wants a horse to ride, he can tell a good one and buy it and train it. An Indian can do all sorts of things for himself, but a white man needs hundreds of other people around to help him."

By our superspecialized division of labor we keep almost everyone out of contact with the realities of life. In any difficulty, minor or severe, we call an expert to take care of it for us. And even though many people are those experts, they only know one kind of crisis and that almost always at an emotional distance. We physicians are especially privileged: we are present at birth and death and we are one of the only groups left who routinely are in touch with joy and grief. It seems to me that the contact with life I had during medical school and internship was the most valuable part of my training as a psychotherapist. Now that internship has been eliminated from the training of psychiatrists, many psychotherapists will never have the experience of taking responsibility for people in the desperate crisis of their lives. I wonder how well therapists without that kind of experience and whose life before they began their practice was limited to school and home can empathize with patients who are struggling with real problems in the world of work. No medicine man was ever just that all his life. Medicine men begin their training at various ages. Some start in childhood, but many do not begin until middle age. In any case, the training is in the form of an apprenticeship lasting years, and most medicine men are experienced people in early middle age before they are in full practice. They do not perform any ceremony until their teachers declare them to be ready to do so, but that declaration alone is not enough to establish them in the new role. The community has the final power for that, because the Indian community will not simply accept certification by the teacher. A medicine man is fully accepted after several years of public scrutiny, not only of his practice, but of his life as a whole. Among us, diplomas and board certificates are sometimes enough to outweigh a common-sense judgment of incompetence.

Diplomas and certificates are not quite as necessary among us as they once were. Many mental health programs, including that of the Indian Health Service, now hire and train paraprofessionals. Indian mental health workers are the main strength of the Indian Health Service program, and we have found that a well trained Indian paraprofessional can do many things that a well trained non-Indian professional cannot. Our paraprofessionals have a familiarity with real life and their own communities that many young professionals lack, but I do not think that paraprofessional positions solve all the problems I have been trying to outline. Medicine men are professionals. What they have that paraprofessionals lack is status and intellectual discipline. It is almost inevitable that paraprofessionals will always be professionals junior grade, and though they may have great practical skill, only rarely do they become masters of any body of theoretical knowledge and, lacking that, they are crippled as planners, teachers and leaders in their fields. Medicine men are in real touch with the life of their community; they are also its intellectual leaders.

The role of Navajo medicine men was never invented by any one in particular. It fits into the rest of the culture so well because it grew with it. The science fiction that follows is about how things might be a long time from now if we really were to become more like our Indian colleagues, and if we do so it will have to be through the evolution of a new tradition rather than by regulation by any academic or governmental authority. No one can plan it. Nevertheless, in order to be as clear as possible I am going to attempt to describe my utopia fairly concretely.

The medicine men of our future will constitute a large professional class, with its own customs, values, and levels of status and authority. For lack of sufficient imagination to make up an original name, I call its members therapists. The essential attribute they will have in common is skill in being with others helpfully: their rituals and mythology will (since this is *my* imagination) be somewhat like those of psychoanalysis and Navajo medicine, the two healing traditions I know best. The two traditions have many similarities including what seems to me two essentials: a concept of unconscious mental processes, and a coherent ordered method of establishing intense, helpful relationships. Both traditions provide a framework of concepts and premises within which thoughts, feelings and life experiences can be ordered and examined. Almost all medicine men and many psychoanalysts are able to tolerate the existence of other mythologies, and so will the therapists of the future. They will be less embarrassed than we usually are to notice that a therapist's character is more important in determining his usefulness than is his theoretical persuasion. The beliefs of each therapist will be determined by his experiences in training and in life in general. Though the range of theoretical systems will be wide, they will have in common the ability to relate personality and behavior to past experiences, to discipline observation and relate the data observed, to prescribe helping ritual (e.g., lying on a couch or sitting on a sandpainting) and to define the individual's relationship with mankind and nature. The value judgments inherent in the definition of the relationship of man-to-man and of man-to-nature will be more explicit than we make them at present and will no longer be colored by scientific shame.

Among the Navajo people, anyone can begin training to be a medicine man who can find a master therapist willing to accept him as an apprentice. Similarly, the therapists will begin their training by finding an apprenticeship, and the decision of who is to be trained by whom will be solely decided by the two people involved. Ordinarily, the process will start in adolescence but sometimes it will be later, and ordinarily the apprenticeship will last for the full duration of training; but changes will sometimes take place, if necessary, for practical or personal reasons.

The master will decide what tasks an apprentice is ready to perform. At first, they will probably be such things as typing letters, running errands or sweeping out, if there is still such a thing. All interactions will be used to direct the intellectual and emotional growth of the apprentice. The interaction of student and teacher will combine elements of work supervision, therapy, and scholarship. Apprentices will attend school from time to time, but the main structure of their education will be determined by their needs as they become apparent in the apprenticeship. Classes, laboratories, and other fixtures of universities will be regarded as adjuncts to education, but not its essence. Success in study will be validated by the master, not by the classroom teacher, so that the need to study competitively is eliminated. Navajo medicine can only be taught in the cold part of the year and therefore apprentice medicine men always have other occupations. Similarly, unless the apprentice therapist of the future is already adult and experienced before he begins training, the apprenticeship will last only about six months of each year. During the rest of the year, the apprentice will support himself. Since apprentice therapists will be expected to be particularly capable people, and in order to help them in their development, it will be customary for various organizations to hire them readily. The choice of jobs will be made by teacher and student on the basis of personal needs. Each apprentice will customarily work in many capacities during the years of his training, and they will include as much contact as possible with dirt and crisis. Two or three kinds of work would almost always be included. For at least one period, an apprentice would be expected to perform some extremely lonely task, in a natural setting. One of the advantages the medicine men have is their long experience of nature undiluted. It seems to me that some of the overestimation of the importance of human beings from which we now suffer results from our living so much of the time in cities or on airliners

between them that we begin to believe that there really isn't anything but man and his works. The apprentices would do some kind
of work in the wilderness, assuming there still is any then.

They will work in various capacities among people of another
culture. In the earlier stages of training, the work will be simple,
but as they become more highly qualified, highly technical and
finally therapeutic work in another culture and another language
will be expected.

Medicine by this time will be very different from what it is now.
Much of what is done now in physical medicine will no longer be
needed because of preventive measures, and much physical diagnosis and treatment will be accomplished semiautomatically. Innovations in physical medicine will be made by biological scientists;
treatment will be by technicians and this work will be an important
step in the training of therapists. In fact, most such work will be
done by apprentice therapists and apprentice biological scientists
during their work assignments. This will be crucial experience for
them because it will put them in touch with death and other irre-
ducible realities. They will be the ones in closest touch with people
in trouble and will handle such terrible tasks as informing relatives
of a death.

Work experiences will greatly affect the nature of the apprenticeship itself. Anxieties and issues raised will be worked through
in the relationship with the master, and scholarly interests stirred
by past experience or future assignments will be pursued in the
classroom or independently. Through all models of instruction, the
apprentices will become familiar with as much of the intellectual
heritage of mankind as possible, including science equally with the
arts, without the usual scorn of one for the other. Their final and
greatest concern will be with what is now organized as psychology,
philosophy, theology, and law, but in the course of their work
assignments they will also develop a secondary career. It will
remain possible throughout the apprenticeship that the student or
the teacher may decide that he is not suited to being a therapist,
and the ability to earn a good living another way will ease the
anxiety about that decision to keep people from being therapists

because it is all they know, even if they come to hate it, and give the therapists a firm footing in the outside world.

As his training progresses, the apprentice will take on increasingly difficult interpersonal tasks. His first experiences will have been formal processes such as structured interviewing for surveys or other research. In his work, especially as a medical technician, he will have had intense contact with patients concerning physical needs, and within the apprenticeship he will have helped patients with concrete problems. He will be involved with his master in group and individual work and will gradually require less and less supervision. At a point determined with reference to the apprentice's development and without reference to time or other formal requirements, the master will suggest that the apprenticeship is over. The final decision will be left to patients, however. The new therapist will look for a job. If he can find a community that will accept him and continue to do so for two years, he will have achieved the full status of therapist.

His first job will be in a neighborhood clinic. The community will pay him a good salary, but less than will be available in those days to someone willing to devote himself singlemindedly to increasing his personal income. In return, he will stay in the clinic or around the community and do what needs to be done. My model for these clinics is more or less the Rosewater Foundation where the phone was always answered, "How may we help you?" Like Elliot Rosewater, the therapist will be available to talk to anyone who is scared or lonely, or otherwise feels he needs to talk. Some of these conversations may involve many people, some may be of very long duration, and some may occur on a regularly scheduled basis over long periods of time. All will be formed by the therapists mythos and ethos of healing and justice.

People will have come to depend on therapists for help in solving controversies that are now removed from the community. Much of what now goes to court will stay in the neighborhood. Disputes between large organizations may still be judged formally, as well as transient professional criminals, but personal injuries and local crime will be treated locally if at all possible with the two goals of reparation to the injured and prevention of future occurences. For example, an adolescent who commits an act of vandalism will be expected to repair the damage even if that is very difficult, but will not be extruded from the community into a trade school or any other jail. In fact jails as we know them will be gone because only severely dangerous people will be incarcerated and they in a manner different from present ones. If, on the basis of his behavior and the opinion of several therapists, anyone is adjudged to be a menace to those around him, he will be kept in a controlled environment, against his will if need be. However, this condition will be regarded as a misfortune to the chronic diseases of the present, and as at least should be the case with the chronically ill now, every effort will be made to make such a person's life as meaningful as possible under the circumstances. He will have the fullest possible access to his work and his family, and as much privacy and freedom as is safe.

Institutions of this kind, and others which I have only vaguely imagined, will be conducted by therapists and their apprentices. Therapists will develop their own interests and special skills and will spend part of their time in specialties, such as working in the more formal courts, or acting the part of what we now call advocate or ombudsman. Some will be elected to public office, but all will spend time in the neighborhood clinic, and strong tradition will cause any therapist, of no matter what status, to continue to treat patients and to maintain contact with the healing relaionship which is the essence of his identity. (The future version of the movie will be "The President's Analysand.")

Among other things, therapists will be asked to take a leading part in worship. Probably, they will be identified with one religion or another, but in those days, every religion will be primarily the responsibility of its adherents no matter what their vocation, and religion will be an inseparable part of everything a therapist does. The picture of a therapist I have in mind was partly formed by the requirements Zooey Glass outlined for a psychoanalyst to help his sister Franny:

> He'd have to believe that it was through the grace of God that he'd been inspired to study psychoanalysis in the first place. He'd

have to believe that it was through the grace of God that he wasn't run over by a goddam truck before he even got his license to practice. He'd have to believe that it's through the grace of God that he has the native intelligence to be able to help his goddam patients at *all*.

Recently, Mr. Robert Fulton, a Navajo medicine man, and I traveled together to a famous Eastern University where he gave a seminar in the school of public health. One of the main attractions of the trip for Mr. Fulton was a chance to go to the Atlantic Ocean. He is sixty-four, but has rarely been away from home. On our way east, he explained to me that every part of nature is important to the existence of everything, and a chance to pray at the ocean was something he had always wanted. The ocean, he said, is a giver of life. When the time came, it was a cold, windy day. Mr. Fulton stood on the beach with the waves washing over his moccasins, sprinkling pollen into the water, chanting a prayer for the sea and its creatures. That evening, a group of us had dinner together at the home of a friend. As we sat down to eat Mr. Fulton said, "It is my custom to give thanks after a meal, but I know that you do so before it. So I will be happy to follow your way." Our host explained that he did not customarily pray either before or after eating and didn't know any prayers. Mr. Fulton was slightly disapproving and considerably surprised. "How can there be a man without a prayer?" he said. "Every tree, every blade of grass has its prayer. That's what it means to be alive." It gave us all something to think about.

Symposium:
The Right to Treatment

George W. Dean

What I'd like to do is to trace for you the very recent, and very sketchy history of the right to treatment itself in the law. First, let me begin by saying that this right to treatment only exists constitutionally. By that I mean the Constitution of the United States where services are provided by the state. There may be a right to treatment on a contractual basis or other bases in the civil law, but in constitutional law it is the state. The right derives from the 14th Amendment, as you will see as we proceed.

Less than ten years ago, a doctor-lawyer theorized in the *American Bar Association Journal* the existence of a constitutional right to treatment for mental patients. By the mid- and late sixties, Dr. Morton Birnbaum's theories were getting their first timid application in the Washington, D.C. federal courts. These groundbreaking cases were the first enunciation of a right to treatment, although their scope was limited to individual cases and the judiciary found itself attempting to assess *adequacy** of treatment. Judge David Bazelon of that D.C. Circuit Court of Appeals is still convinved that the right exists but is measured by the patient's medical record and enforced by *habeas corpus*. In other words, treat and keep good records, or release the patient.

When any new idea or theory in any profession reaches the light of print, the predictable occurs—a paper blizzard. Law reviews rushed to be first with a special edition symposium. A lawyer contributed an article entitled "Enforcing the Right to Treatment"

---

*Neither courts nor lawyers will make choices between competing therapies, and these cases never intend to do so. The emphasis in my sentence is on competing therapies, any of which may be considered appropriate.

and a Harvard professor responded with "The Right to Treatment—An Enchanting Legal Fiction." Most psychiatrists followed the lead of the American Psychiatric Association after it had been wagged by the tail called the Group for the Advancement of Psychiatry. Their letters to the editor, their papers read, and their presidential addresses were all rather arrogantly unanimous that courts and lawyers had neither the right nor the expertise to mess around in their profession.

While this body of literature was building, the American Civil Liberties Union (again predictably) established a special project office on the rights of mental patients. Bruce Innis, the Project's attorney here in New York, began to build experience upon the D.C. cases. Five of his first six clients were immediately discharged from Bellevue when he informed the staff of his representation of these patients. At least one lawyer was finding out that psychiatrists were not unintelligent. They soon found the alternative to release—simply assign a psychiatrist to drop in on the patients more frequently and enter the visit on his record. This "treatment" or release completely frustrated all attempts to effectively ensure the right to treatment to broad masses of patients in mental hospitals. The right to *some* treatment did now exist and was generally accepted in the law, but the right was meaningless for some 500,000 patients in our state and federal psychiatric wards.

While our search for a remedy was floundering about in the pitfalls of individual *habeas corpus* writs, treatment plans and record keeping, two psychiatrists from the deep South inadvertedly rushed to the rescue. Dr. Robert O'Connor, Superintendent of Florida State Hospital, and Dr. Stonewall B. Stickney, Alabama's Commissioner of Mental Health, were soon to reap a whirlwind of lawyers. Dr. O'Connor had won every round of an uneven contest with one of his patients named Kenneth Donaldson. He had kept Donaldson in a locked ward for ten of the past eleven years. Being from New York, Donaldson did not fit well in the southern plantation syndrome that characterizes our large mental institutions in the South. He was uppity and disliked chopping cotton. Little did it matter that his MMPI could at worst be integrated as showing a paranoid personality and his entire personal and hospital history totally negated any predilection to violence to himself or others. It did show a tenacity and stubbornness to 1) get out, and 2) make Dr. O'Connor and Florida pay him for what he considered his false imprisonment. Donaldson had filed fourteen unsuccessful court actions on his own behalf when he read a newspaper article about Dr. Birnbaum. A letter to Birnbaum and then to Ennis led belatedly to his release but damages had never in the history of the loss been awarded in such a case.

In August of 1970, the scene changed to that bastion of civil liberties and human rights—Wallace Laud. Like all of us who had ever visited the back wards of a large state mental hospital, or had read Goffman's *Asylum*, Blatts' *Exodus From Pandemonium*, seen the Titticutt Follies, scanned the regular newspaper exposures, listened to the politicians' regular promises or even remembered the origin of the word "bedlam," Dr. Stonewall Stickney knew that things were terribly amiss at Bryce Hospital in Tuscaloosa, Alabama and now that he was Alabama's Mental Health Commissioner he could do something about it. Unfortunately for him but fortunately for the law and consequently for 5,200 patients at Bryce, he went about his goal in a fashion that I will charitably describe as highly unorthodox. He did not seek funds from the legislature, or use, or even apply for federal funds such as title IV—A and title XVI to reduce his population. He sought no certification for Medicare-Medicaid, nor did he attempt nursing home placement for 1,600 geriatric patients at Bryce. Using a manufactured budget crisis as a ruse, he fired almost half of Bryce's professional staff.

Stickney's plans to leave Bryce with one Ph.D. psychologist, four licensed M.D.'s and no M.S.W. social workers were not to be. Staff, guardians, patients and other professionals sought my legal assistance some 32 months ago, and I have since been totally engrossed in the legal problems of the mentally ill and retarded. With some brain-storming help from my favorite constitutional law professor, I quickly reached the same conclusion that Dr. Birnbaum hypothesized in 1964. The reasoning is quite simple: Liberty is a constitutional right not to be infringed upon except by due process of law. Yet in certain classes of people (insane, retarded, juvenile), the state can take liberty *without* due process by an altruistic promise to treat, train, educate, protect or rehabilitate. Hence, the right to treatment, training, etc., from which naturally arose the corollary that treatment could not exist in a vacuum without professionals. We voided the pitfalls of *habeas corpus* by bringing our suit as a class action. The Bryce staff could not treat everyone nor manufacture treatment records for all.

I do not intend to belabor you with the war stories of Ricky Wyatt vs. Stickney. They tell much better in a bar. The legal results are worth relating:

1) the first clear and unequivocal holding on the existence of the right to treatment and habilitation for the mentally ill and the retarded;

2) a finding that a humane psychological environment, adequately staffed to execute a treatment plan, is necessary to effectuate the right and (later after giving the state a year to devise a plan to deliver on its duty to treat);

3) a detailed and comprehensive set of standards that the state is enjoined to perform if it is to operate a mental health and retardation program.

The practical results have been quietly dramatic: 1) Alabama's Mental Health budget has doubled and will soon triple. 2) The population of Bryce Hospital has dropped from 5,200 to 3,200 and continues to decline. 3) Statewide, the professional staff has doubled and the sub- and para-professional staff have been dramatically increased. 4) Even George Wallace has gotten religion. He gave approximately one half of the revenue sharing monies to the long-beleaguered fields of mental health, retardation and corrections. I have not been able to find another state that begins to compare favorably with this. 5) The following have formally endorsed the legal results by joining the case as friends of the court—American Psychological Association, the Orthopsychiatric

Association, the National Association for Retarded Children, the American Association on Mental Deficiency, National Council on the Rights of the Mentally Impaired, the Society for Autistic Children, the United States Justice Department, the American Civil Liberties Union and last—not least, but appreciated—the American Psychiatric Association. As a direct result of this case, the U.S. Department of Justice has set up in its Civil Rights Section a special division called the Office of Institutions and Public Facilities with a staff of 18 or 20 lawyers. You may wish to call upon them on behalf of your patients or clients at some time.

By now the law was ready for Kenneth Donaldson. It was ready for him because there is an old civil rights statute that says no state official shall deprive a citizen of the United States of his constitutional rights under cover of state law. We really didn't have the firm constitutional right to treatment until the Wyatt decision. Last December a six-man Florida jury awarded Donaldson $38,500 against Dr. O'Connor and another. If any doubt about the existence of the right exists, I refer you to Drs. Stickney and O'Connor.

A wide variety of cases exploring new areas of the right have been filed in New York, Massachussets, Florida,* South Carolina, Nebraska, Tennessee and others are pending. Two days ago one of our *amici,* The National Council on the Rights of the Mentally Impaired in Washington, D.C. filed suit asking for an injunction to require the U.S. Department of Labor to enforce the clear and certain language of the Fair Labor Standards Act requiring compensation of patient labor in mental institutions.

This act has been on the books for six years and it says it just as clear as a bell: "mental patients" must be paid the minimum wage. But the Labor Department has never enforced it, and when

---

*I can announce to you that the state of Florida has accepted the standards of Wyatt vs. Stickney in a consent decree that will be out shortly in the area of the mentally retarded. In fact, it is Wyatt standards plus. We got a little sweetener in that they will not hire any more Drs.; there will be no more use of electrical devices, just all sorts of items that we were not able to achieve in the Bryce case.

they don't enforce the states don't pay. Their excuse was that no one had ever complained! Well, now someone has.

I believe that it is a safe prediction that one day, sooner than you expect, a recently-out-of-work young Office of Economic Opportunity lawyer will walk into your partially or fully state supported outpatient clinic and announce that he represents one of your ex-patients and. . . .

Paul Davis

I have worked with and have known my associates on this panel for many years—Mr. George Dean as the civil libertarian who has done so much as an advocate for the mentally ill and the retarded—and Dr. James Morris as a physician and administrator who has labored under adverse conditions for years in Alabama's largest institution for the mentally ill—Bryce Hospital in Tuscaloosa.

These two men have at times found themselves in adversary positions as federal court regulations and massive reforms have come to the mental institutions of Alabama.

I have been in a different position throughout the proceedings—a newspaperman observing the turmoil, reporting it to my readers and at times possibly getting involved in the conflict on the side of those who sought the reforms.

Most of the facts and figures about the change and the court order will come out in more detail during our discussion; therefore, I would like to discuss with you the role our newspaper played in these events.

First, let me assure you that our interest didn't begin with the lawsuit most of you know—Wyatt vs. Stickney. Alabama's two largest institutions for the mentally ill and retarded are located in Tuscaloosa, Ala., which is also the home of the University of Alabama.

On an almost semi-annual basis for 20 years, we have carried stories, or a series of stories, dealing with the conditions within these institutions. They were the snakepit stories about the stench, the human misery, the low state appropriations—all the tear jerking journalism that produced little results.

Those stories were pleading in tone. They often prompted a legislator to make a speech and cry a little bit on the floor of the Senate. But that was the end of the issue for a year.

There was an all-black institution in the southern part of the state for the mentally ill. Aside from being neglected by the state, it also was neglected by the press. Realistically, back even 10 years ago we knew that if nothing was going to be done for the all-white institutions, it was for damn sure nothing would be done for the blacks.

If upgrading of both facilities and treatment programs for the all-white hospitals was started, our state—which at that time was *gung-ho* for the separate but more-than-equal concept—would care for the blacks, too.

That logic wasn't too sound either. We weren't getting anything done, anywhere. Then there was the mass firing of employes at Bryce in Tuscaloosa—a so-called economy move—and in an effort to win their jobs back, lawsuits were filed and they simply contended that patients who were receiving poor treatment before would have it even worse now. That thought started to soak in.

Lawyers started talking and kicking ideas around. The state couldn't take these thousands of people, more than 5,000 at Bryce at that time, and lock them away without treatment. These people had rights—in fact—they had a right to a lot of things, including proper and adequate treatment.

That notion changed my mind, too. We determined that we would get involved as a newspaper with both feet, just jump right in. We would raise hell.

For more than a year, that was my job. I joined hands with George Dean—sometimes spending the night with him beside a stolen Xerox machine—making copies, taking depositions and getting perhaps too involved.

But at the same moment every document was filed in court, a copy was also in our newsroom and we went to press almost every day with a different twist to the same story. For one period around the first of last year, we kept the story on our front page for almost 90 consecutive days.

We got the federal judge hearing the case on our subscription list, along with the United States Attorney handling the prosecution for the federal government.

Copies of our stories and all our film were ordered into court. Our paper is small—a circulation of around 30,000. But we also serve a relatively small area—around 100,000 people, thus we hit probably more than 90 per cent of the homes.

We produced supplements and special sections. We're offset printers and therefore were able to run color pictures. We screamed and hollered. After a straight news story (?) we turned to an analytical piece, picture stories and then to an editorial.

When we were barred from the campus of Partlow State School and Hospital—formerly our only facility for the retarded where races and sexes were segregated on campus—we ran front page editorials demanding the resignation of top officials within the Department of Mental Health.

We stirred up enough smoke that the state's largest newspapers paid us a visit, picked up our stories, did their own and finally become involved. We had television crews from over the state, a crew from CBS, and national magazines. This was before Willowbrook. It was the first massive, successful push in this country leading to the landmark ruling that persons involuntarily committed do, in fact, have a constitutional right to adequate treatment.

The major change for our paper—a change we didn't perceive until the campaign was halfway over—was that we were no longer pleading. We, too, were demanding.

We printed it all. We went through every death, pulled them out and ran detailed stories on those who were killed, maimed and neglected. The mother of one child, who was allowed to die a horrible death due, it appeared, to a basic lack of adequate medical care, wrote a letter to us after we printed details of that death.

It was a mother's letter, but it also did more than plead. It demanded. It demanded that the state of Alabama recognize that a mother can care and love a child she cannot house—a child she visited regularly—a child that she loved.

That letter was written in pencil on a dime-store pad. We took it, with her permission, photographed it, and ran it from the top of page one to the bottom. It was strong. It destroyed all the myths about the tender loving care the state had too long told us existed.

We told about the state's physician who could suture a retarded child without any pain killer because the retarded can't feel pain. We told how he brought in five aides to hold the people while he sewed them up, those who do not feel pain.

We caught a lot of hell for telling our story. But today, the populations of these institutions are shrinking rapidly, budgets and staffs are doubling and adequate treatment and normalization are coming.

We're not through with our story. We know that when the spotlight is turned off, the reforms will cease and slowly stop.

But, we're also dedicated to help and we're doing that with the same front page coverage of the "good side," the halfway houses, the community workshops.

My friend Mr. Dean says that's not necessary. He says the state is expected to do good, that we're always to look for the bad. I subscribe to that theory; but often in looking for the bad, which is not difficult to find, we stumble upon some good and we print that, too.

Tearing down playhouses for the good of the people is a great life. It needs to be done in every state across this country.

If you have a rather alert newspaper, you might start there and shake a few of those people as this lawsuit and Mr. Dean did us. But if you get those news folks wide awake and ready to move, you'd better stand back and give them room and not be surprised if they reach a point where you'd like to say thanks and ask them to go home. They may get to where they like the involvement and just shake everything from the snakepit in your state to the governor's mansion.

We did it in Alabama.

James E. Morris, M.D.
Thomas Fanning, M. Div.

For almost two decades we have seen a growing emphasis on

treating the mentally disordered in the community. Throughout the nation, there has been a dramatic shift of attention from institutional-based custodial care to community-based active intervention and treatment. The decline of inpatient population of public mental hospitals in the United States from 559,000 in 1955 to 308,000 in 1971 is a further reflection of this trend. Statistics show that, concurrently, however, these same public mental hospitals were being used more extensively than ever before, handling more admissions and discharging more patients.

Despite predictions to the contrary, the public mental hospital is not fading out of the picture. Though many communities enjoy the availability of quite comprehensive mental health services, they find themselves unable to manage satisfactorily some types of psychiatric disorders. The public mental hospital is unique in being the only facility able to manage, in even a potentially adequate manner, the "difficult" patient or the problems of severe, recurrent and chronic mental disorders. Patients with pronounced self-destructive impulses, those whose destructiveness and aggression endanger the welfare of others, or the individual in a community treatment program who shows increasing emotional or mental decompensation all might well benefit from inpatient programs the public institution offers. Despite major emphasis on community oriented intervention and prevention, statistics show that during the past decade total admissions to the state's mental hospitals have just about doubled. It appears that the public mental hospital will continue in the foreseeable future as an important resource within the treatment complex of the mental health care system.

Undoubtedly, the trend toward reorganization of many state institutions into geographically oriented unit systems represents a keen awareness of the need for a close working relationship between hospital and community mental health programs. Therapeutic utilization of each other's services as indicated does provide a broad and comprehensive array of treatment possibilities to any individual patient.

While there has been much recent attention directed toward the shortcomings of the public mental hospital in meeting patients' needs, only in a few states has sufficient financial support been made available to upgrade treatment programs significantly. Society, though, has seemed less disinterested in the institution's patients and, like other citizens, feel they have certain rights. Significant in this regard is the attention focused on the right to treatment. The courts have ruled since 1966 that a person committed to a mental institution has a right to treatment. Additionally, the courts have held that the lack of staff or facilities or inadequate funding cannot be used to justify a state's failure to provide adequate treatment. A very real issue is not so much the right to treatment but the right to *adequate* treatment.

What is adequate treatment? By what standards, objective and subjective, might we measure the adequacy of treatment? Obviously, these are difficult and complex questions to answer.

The lawyer-physician, Morton Birnbaum, has suggested that treatment standards be cast in terms of minimum staff-patient ratios and doctor-patient consultations. Other jurists, including Judge David L. Bazelon, have called attention to the need for individualized treatment plans. In the 1972 ruling in Alabama, Judge Frank M. Johnson set forth specific standards required of a mental institution. These fall into three categories: (1) a humane psychological and physical environment, (2) a qualified staff in numbers sufficient to administer treatment, and (3) individualized treatment plans.

As the mental illness model is being gradually replaced by the behavioral disorder model, other types of standards might be considered. Alfred M. Wellner has proposed that the right to treatment should include for each patient: (1) a statement of goals, objectives, and, in measurable observable terms, the behavioral criteria for return to the community, (2) a statement in operational terms of the strategies, procedures, and techniques to be used by all staff to reach these goals, and (3) a meaningful, appropriate, and effective method of monitoring the progress of every individual in an institution and a feedback mechanism to permit staff to alter its approaches if progress is not satisfactory.

Thus far, all of these standards are concerned with availability of means to provide treatment and procedures to assure that adequate treatment occurs. What if a patient has the benefit of treatment in a modern, comfortable and humane physical plant by well-trained, adequately numbered staff, utilizing the latest treatment techniques, and shows no improvement? In other words, what if the "adequate treatment" doesn't work? This brings up another legal issue: Should the unimproving patient involuntarily committed be detained in the institution or returned to society? Closely related is the proposition recently set forth that an individual has a right to deviancy as long as he poses no danger to himself or others. The courts may very likely have to answer these questions.

The limited state and federal funds available for mental health are being divided primarily between community and state hospital programs. Accountability for effective treatment results from programs supported by public funds is becoming more closely scrutinized than ever before. For example, we are now frequently hearing phrases such as: cost analysis and cost benefit, evaluation studies and quality control, analysis of job function, output, throughput, and productivity, utilization and peer review. These topics are not confined just to the operation of the public mental hospital but also are related to community mental health centers.

It appears that the present emphasis is not only on the right to *adequate* treatment, but also the right to *effective* treatment. How does one measure the effectiveness of treatment?

Obviously, the determinants for treatment effectiveness are based on the ability to measure the results of the treatment modalities used. Whether treatment effectiveness or results can be truly quantified with present measuring devices is doubted by many. Today's multidisciplinary approach to treatment and the systems school of thought (family, social, educational, vocational, economic, psychological, health, and other basic human services) are examples of the complex set of factors which almost defy numerical measurement.

In the entire field of health care services, accountability is becoming the by-word. Pressures from consumers and society, generally, are pushing mental health facilities toward utilization of the more scientifically and numerically measurable treatment modalities which show visible results. By their very nature, some widely accepted treatment approaches, such as psychotherapy, do not lend themselves to quantifiable measurement. If these valuable techniques are to be retained in the treatment armamentarium, the need for a carefully planned program evaluation becomes apparent. The accountability premise emphasizes the importance in mental health of a documented, careful appraisal of the extent to which a particular program or treatment modality is meeting its stated goals. Individualized treatment plans with continuous assessment of what progress is being made toward reaching the treatment goals might be employed with individual patients.

How does the right to treatment issue affect the outpatient and community mental health centers? The patients, or clients, are not involuntarily committed and, consequently, have no constitutional right to treatment. Obviously, these centers grant the right to treatment as an ethical and moral obligation to the population they serve.

If we accept the premise that the public mental hospital is not the natural habitant of man, then the movement nationwide to lower the inpatient census to the barest minimum becomes more meaningful. Community clinics and centers are being called upon much more frequently to provide aftercare and transitional services for the large number of patients being returned to the community. These largely supportive services are vital to the rehabilitative process for these individuals.

The challenge of educating the community to develop tolerance for the former state hospital patient, his residual symptoms and aberrant behavior, is great indeed. Some communities have already created their own "back wards" where this tolerance has not existed. The community mental health facilities are in the unique position of most effectively assisting their populace in developing an attitude of acceptance.

The growing trend of consumer involvement in the structuring of provision for mental health services is quite keenly felt at the community level. The emphasis on results-oriented programs and accountability, as has been mentioned previously, is making its presence known in community mental health facilities.

The courts have followed up their original decision of the right to treatment with standards to assure that the treatment is adequate. It would now appear that attention is being directed toward the effectiveness of treatment and accountability. Though the courts have not yet become involved in this particular aspect of treatment, this is a possibility.

All of us in the mental health field need to begin now, if we haven't already, to implement program evaluations. We should measure the measurable and carefully appraise and document the more immeasurable. The end result just might be not only effective treatment but higher quality treatment.

PART III

Youth Beyond the Clinic Walls

Communication, Social Control, and Youth

Albert Scheflen, M.D.

Introduction

In classical Western philosophy we have conceived behavior as an expression of inner thoughts and feelings. We have given human behavior an inner, organismic causation.

When we consider human communication we are likely to use the time-honored way of thinking about it. Since we regard non-speech behavior or "non-verbal" communication as an expression of emotions as Darwin suggested a century ago, so in everyday culture and in psychological science communication is viewed as an interaction of thoughts and feelings through the media of speech, gesture, and facial expression.

In the last fifteen years however, a very different view of communication has evolved through the work of Birdwhistell (1952, 1966, 1970); Bateson (1956, 1972); Goffman (1963, 1970, 1972); Scheflen (1966, 1968, 1972, 1973) and many others. In this view we look first at systems of behavior which are general for man and traceable to primate and mammalian societies in general. We notice that these behaviors are continuously performed in any social groupings so we can abstract their lawfulness and regularity. Only when we have described such an ordering of behavior among the participants do we go back to a focus upon the individuals who are doing the behaving. We note then that certain people perform these customary activities in traditional or else in non-traditional ways and we can therefore speak of normal or deviant behavior or of useful or idiosyncratic styles, but we do not regard the individuals as *the* cause of the ongoing stream of events. And we will allow that unique behaviors do occur by innovation and that some people do the unexpected; but we do not believe that human communication ordinarily functions to foster the deviant or the idiosyncratic expression of individualism. We hope to show instead, that communication ordinarily serves to maintain social order and serves to control the behavior of separate persons and factions.

We shall enlarge upon this point of view, describing briefly five types of human behavior and their prehuman origins. We shall describe how these behaviors are usually integrated in small groups of people. We shall relate this approach to the elements in social control. We hope to demonstrate that many psychological explanations of behavior have been *post hoc,* and have been manipulated by the ruling class. It will then be possible to relate the research to the theme of youth and the youth movement.

Types of communication behavior.

All people learn to communicate. A behavior is communicative because other people recognize what is transpiring when the behavior is enacted, and therefore can either join the activity or entertain thoughts or make comments upon the propriety or significance of the behavior. From our research over the past twenty years I have concluded that five distinguishable types of communication occur regularly, and are necessary for adequate description of human interactions.

1) Territorial behavior. All mammals and birds mark off an area of physical space which they occupy and maintain as a group territory. Within this territory smaller groups take possession of a sub-territory, and within these zones individuals may claim and use a parcel. These territories can be fixed areas or regions or channels in which the animal grazes, wanders, or migrates; in all cases the boundaries are marked so that they can be seen or smelled. The territories are defended against any invasion by strangers of the same species.

Men mark off territories heirarchically, and employ a variety of communicative behaviors for markers. Man may mark national boundaries within which there are state, provincial, local, institutional, familial, and personal territories. Markers employed include walls, fences, lines, and maps; the maps and lines are backed by written and traditional legal sanctions. Whenever a group assembles, its rooms and furniture arrangements define a restricted zone; or else the participants arrange themselves in a square or circle facing inward, and thereby establish a temporary territory marked by their bodies. They will defend these territories against intruders: If a person enters such an aggregation or passes through it, conventional postures are demanded. We call these "rites of territorial passage."

Here are two examples of such rites: 1) When a person is about to enter an assembled circle of acquaintances in a public place, he approaches, then steps two or three feet outside the perimeter of backs. Here he flashes a greeting with his face, and awaits a recognition signal before taking a place within the ring. 2) When a person must cut through or go very near an assembled circle (as in a corridor), he lowers his head slightly, curls his shoulders, brings his arms close to his sides, and keeps his gaze forward. He may, additionally, verbalize some excuse. This posture of passage through a territory obtains as well for moving through a building, or a neighborhood held by some other group of people.

So city-wise Italian-Americans walk this way through a Black neighborhood, and, conversely, Blacks walk this way through an Italian-American neighborhood. They do not saunter through, chest out and head erect, swaggering from side to side and peering this way and that. To do so would invite an attack. The attack would be called, of course, something other than territorial defense, and would be attributed to the perversity (savagery?) of the attackers.

2) Reciprocal and bonding behavior. These territorial arrangements not only exclude outsiders, but also keep the insiders together. The occupants are enjoined from leaving the territory. We all remember how we were taught as children to stay in our own yard, then to stay within our own block, and concomitantly, to stay within our own religious, political, class, and ethnic subdivisions.

Among primates, a local territory usually contains from fifteen to seventy-five members who interact in face-to-face relationships. Gibbons, unlike other primates, aggregate in smaller groups, in territories containing two parents and two or three offspring. But other species congregate in larger kin groupings. In man, extended family networks of 15 to 75 people existed until the fifteenth century. Then, in urban and industrializing Western nations, the nuclear dwelling unit evolved.

Within these "family" groupings, customary behaviors are observed. These provide mutual service and maintain social bonds. Examples of such bonding behaviors include mutual feeding and grooming, courting, greeting and leave-taking rituals. The behaviors are reciprocal: chimpanzees kiss, shake hands, and pat each other on the buttock (Goodall, 1970). In the light of such evidence, the traditional explanation that the handshake among men evolved from gesturing, "I have no concealed weapons," seems unlikely.

When humans greet, they not only shake hands and speak, but make several other highly characteristic gestures as well. Around the world, two acquaintances show recognition by flashing a two stage elevation of the eyebrows (Eible-Eibesfeld). And when a guest enters a host's territory, the host looks at his guest while his guest looks down in territorial passage rite posture as he crosses the threshold. It has also been shown by these investigators that the presentation of the palm universally occurs in courtship and in greeting.

There are some obvious and interesting characteristics common to these examples. Among primates, the behavior is enacted in face-to-face configurations. These exchanges do not require language, even though man usually includes ritualistic exchanges of speech during courting, greeting, and departures. Each of these behaviors are also interactive, one animal performing one step, whereupon the other performs the next step, etc. These activities are designated "reciprocals," and serve to hold the group together, and maintain it as well.

In addition to the foregoing examples, a special set of reciprocals maintains the internal status organization of the face-to-face group. This refers to behaviors similar to those used to maintain the leaders of the group against intruders from the same species. These behaviors are termed "threat behavior." The threatening animal faces an intruder, draws his body to full height (or widens it), then bares his teeth, bites the air, grimaces, and makes a noise. Only humans maintain borders and status by killing.

Somewhere in mammalian history, these behaviors for demonstrating dominance and territorial defense and courtship evolved so that body contact was unnecessary. The gesture sufficed. These were the beginning of *kinesics* (coded, non-verbal body communication). Like other primates, humans display the chest, widen the body, thrust the jaw, and raise the voice to assert dominance or status within groups. Again, this does not require physical contact. The notion that group stability is maintained "by tooth and claw" among pre-humans is inaccurate, according to present information.

3) Actonic behavior. The third type of communication behavior is actonic behavior (Harris, 1964). These behaviors involve the manipulation of objects. Because chimpanzees use tools, this behavior too must be considered to have a long evolutionary history.

Perhaps 100,000 years ago men began to manipulate the soil, grow crops, accumulate harvests and physical object resources. From these early beginnings we can trace the evolution from the use of farming, through the development of manufacturing, and to the entire enterprise of control (and defense) of wealth and productivity.

In small groups, simple actonic acts can be singled out, such as maintaining the group setting by adjusting the seating and regulating the temperature, using combs to service others, moving chairs to establish a meeting place, or erecting boards to display symbols.

Also people may be observed to manipulate their clothing and hair in grooming behavior to attract or hold attention. Some will pat, poke, and grasp others, seeming, thereby, to maintain affiliations, enforce status or control restraints. Some will use pipes or cigarettes as props. Though it has been traditional to associate these props with oral need expression, observations indicate that the manipulations, the gestures, the lightings serve other purposes: to punctuate the stream of speech, to announce an intention to speak, to signal a break in proceedings, and a variety of other communications. The reliance upon prop behavior in regulating conversation and making and breaking relationships would appear to be a compelling, fresh explanation for the smoker's difficulty in giving up his habit.

In contemporary human societies, a great number of face-to-face groups are bonded together under the umbrella of business organizations. These entail ownership of resources and the distribution of goods and supplies. The ruling class maintains orderliness within the society not by soldiers and laws alone, but by businesses which control production and distribution of food and other products. Parenthetically it is worth noting that those outside the business, devoted to personal services, such as we, plus the academicians, have an assigned function even within the existing business order. They are expected to improve technologies for actonic behavior, employ language and science to rationalize the existing order, train children and novitiates to believe in it, and to remove or straighten out deviants who raise doubts and questions. They are not supposed to develop conceptual revolutions or remove conceptual inhibitions unless such activity heightens the ability of group members to "adjust" and to "work."

4) Language. A fourth type of communication behavior is language. Speech has been a well-developed medium for some 50,000 to 100,000 years. This complicated symbol system probably evolved from the vocal exchanges of earlier primate forms. Most animals have regular territory and mating-related calls. Moreover the chimpanzees do show combinations of calls which may be considered a rudimentary word system. The speech system (or linguistic system) includes not only conventionalized vocalizations, but also derivative activities such as written language, painting, and music. Within linguistic activity are many "symbolic gestures," e.g., the sign of the cross and the Boy Scout salute. These gestures can be translated directly into speech symbols. Another set of gestures are called "iconic;" in these, the hands outline a thought (e.g., "I caught a big fish"—hands held some 18″ apart). The languages of the world vary widely in the proportions of vocalization, symbolic gesture, and iconic gestures. Southern Italians, for example, are rich in symbolic gesture language, and Australian aborigines conduct many hour-long ceremonies quite without words. The American language, heavily indebted to English and Hebrew, is weak in symbolic gesture forms, but rich in iconic gestures.

5) *Clothing.* Personal adornment affords still another kind of communication. All neolithic peoples used clothing to designate caste and rank and group membership. Today, hair styling, clothing, uniforms, badges, emblems, houses, and the furnishings of houses serve the same purpose. Notwithstanding the obvious protective aspects of houses, the communicative function of these conventionalized embellishments is to identify our membership in the larger society and to preserve that order.

The Human Transaction

Having teased apart five types of behavior for the purpose of descriptive adequacy, let us now consider particular instances. We find that all types of communicative behavior occur in combination. Speech is used to coordinate and regulate workers in a manufacturing plant. And speech is used to advertise the product, as well as to demarcate geographical boundaries for distribution through various agreements. Similarly, in a business or professional meeting, participants pair off to meet. Attenuated courting rituals (flirtation or rapprochement inducement) are used to establish alliances at the meeting. And dominance displays are used to gain the floor, force a point, or maintain decorum. Badges, postures, accent, and facial set indicate categorical memberships and roles of the assembled participants.

In all these instances there are organizing forces which coordinate the collective communication behaviors of the participants at the meeting. These are the traditional and customary formats for such meetings.

The format is a plot, a scenario, a program, for what *ought* to occur; it establishes who, what, when, and where. A college commencement ceremony is an example of traditional pageantry with a programmed sequence. Another is the athletic contest within a stadium.

Architecture

In typical group assemblies, human behavior is conventionally programmed through its physical architecture. Many group activities occur in preestablished meeting areas. The customary territorial grouping behavior then can be seen to be reflected in the architecture. When people meet in open fields or in streets, they structure the space by the placement of their bodies. The football stadium is a monolithic example of the human organization of space for interaction. Looking from above, we note several zones, each with boundaries. There is a fence or wall, a circle of seats, a fence, the field. The seats are the *external zone,* the field the *internal zone.* Each zone has subdivisions. In the internal zone, one sub-region includes a court in the center, an open space across which transactions occur. Surrounding this court is another sub-region where officials and substitutes sit and stand. The external zone has the seats for spectators and facilities for those who serve the spectators. The external zone is surrounded by a territorial boundary and monitored by guards who regulate access to the territory.

Other architectural arrangements in Western cultures appear to follow this basic paradigm. The living room, for example, has furniture positioned so that participants face each other across an open central space. In large rooms, servants may occupy a peripheral zone within the room. Or, at a business meeting, participants arrange themselves in a circle or square, facing one another. A conference table may establish the spacing. In a circle at the periphery, aides sit or stand, perhaps consultants and well-wishers of the participants. Similarly, service people such as bartenders or waiters occupy stations just outside the main arena of a night club.

In activities within the home, of course, we do not ordinarily observe an outer zone of spectators as we observe at the stadium, but at times one is temporarily established. For instance, the children may be permitted to sit outside on the steps while an adult party commences inside, but are not allowed to participate. Similarly, psychotherapy is sometimes conducted behind a one-way mirror, behind which are spectators without intervention rights.

The work surface of the table has several variations: the ticket counter is one, a store counter another. Physicians sometimes use their desk. In each instance the desk or counter serves as a boundary zone marking function. Within the zones, status is frequently designated by chair arrangement and design in the American settings. For example, father has a large chair placed at the head of the table or at a special place within the living room. And the one-to-one therapist has a special chair at a particular place in his office.

Each of these positions within the zones of interaction has certain rights and restraints. We learn these as we grow up under such rubrics as "manners," custom, etc. Thus the participants in an outer zone do not have the rights to play in the game or to enter discussion at a conference until they are invited to do so by the chair. And people in the region surrounding a central zone may have the responsibility of commenting upon, but not of leading the discussion. Or they may have the duty of waiting on the participants, but not of participating in the discussion. Unless we are specially honored guests, we enter the host's living room, survey the arrangement, and avoid that particular chair which belongs to the head of the household. The patient who enters an office and sits in the large chair in front of the desk or behind the couch is a deviant. He is considered to have some special motivation.

Looking at the behavior of people together in this light, we notice that the rituals are used to pass from one zone to another, as in the "rite of territorial passage." Often one is invited to take a more central position by a person of status. Sometimes one approaches the central zone, takes a posture of territorial passage, and awaits recognition. Then at some break point in the conversation, he may proceed to a seat in the central zone. The psychotherapist is usually accorded rights to determine where a patient sits in his office. He says to the new patient, "Why don't you sit there." Or, some therapists, fancying themselves to be non-directive, may indicate, by a wave of the hand or pointing the eyes to a particular chair without realizing it, or may even do this while saying, "Please sit anywhere you wish."

The point of outlining these spatial matters is this: One's behavior at a transaction depends in some measure on the zone and location he is occupying. It is a deviancy for him to ignore these matters. And it is a piece of blind existential romanticism for the theorist then to claim that what he does at a given human event can be explained alone in terms of motivation or the expression of personal thought and feeling. We shall discuss this later in greater detail.

The programming of an interaction

The sequences of human transactions occur with great regularity. Events happen in time schedules. For example, the Club meets every Tuesday at 6:00, people eat at noon, make love at a particular time—all in a regular sequence. Most transactions are scheduled in time, and the content is scheduled within that framework. By the same token, the same regularities govern the psychiatric interview.

Some aspects of the agenda are determined by logical necessity. For instance, in order to wash clothes, it is necessary to gather the clothes, get the soap, carry the clothes and soap to the machine, and so on, all in a relatively firm and predictable order (Harris, 1964). In language transactions, the patterning is often based more on tradition. In a business meeting (as codified in Roberts' Rules), there is a call to meeting, old business, reports of committees, new business, and adjournment. In a church service, there is the call to worship, singing of the hymns, passing the plate. There are innings in baseball; quarters in football.

Despite the fact that such regularities pervade human activities, we are inclined to deny hotly that love-making or psychotherapy are equally programmed. I recall that in my old church, the hymnal contained 390 hymns. Any of those songs, but no other, could be sung during the time slot for singing. From my observations of psychotherapy, I've concluded that all the themes usually enacted number less than 390. Moreover, the sequence of a particular session of one-to-one therapy is highly predictable and regular. It often goes as follows: introductions, 1-2 minutes; phase one, 20-25 minutes; repeat phase one, 20-25 minutes; termination, 1-2 minutes.

Looking at the "slots" provided by this sequence, the interview consists first in the therapist sitting and listening to the patient talk. At the end of this phase, the therapist and patient move into a rapport phase in which they come closer; the therapist talks more, and is generally more active. Finally he offers the special contents of his particular school of therapy, such as offering advice, giving an interpretation, or hand-holding. If a particular interview contains two or more repeats of the basic "phase one," then the doctrinal point is more strongly stressed on each repetition. Accompanying these phases are characteristic postures. During phase one, the therapist takes a "low involvement" stance (back in his chair, not facing the patient directly, and legs or arms crossed). Now at the phase change, he moves to higher involvement (legs and arms uncross, he moves somewhat closer, and faces the patient more directly). Then he moves back to his original position and the phase is repeated.

The "posture of rapport" as it appears on camera, and the "posture of confrontation," are similar. In our culture, a man and woman may stand together talking at a cocktail party; but once they face each other directly, others, especially a spouse or the hostess, interrupts. The full *vis a vis* is characteristic of courtship; the 20 degree off-line is characteristic of flirtation. Both *vis a vis* positions are observable within psychotherapy interviews, but the courtship posture of direct *vis a vis* is proscribed by the rules of cocktail parties. When it occurs, other group members will intervene.

The programming of human events dictates *when* a particular thing is to be said or thought, as well as *what* is the acceptable range and type of statements. Free association, for example, is not the rule of everyday interaction, and in most contexts "expressing ourselves" will cost us something. In short, our location in time and space in the stream of events, constitutes an important source of constraint.

Metacommunication

In some customary transactions, familiar participants come together in order to carry out some particular activity. They have in mind a common schedule—an agenda. They take usual positions and launch into the task at hand. When the matter is not so cut and dried, the setting, the distribution, and the appearance of the others present, and the general context may tell us what program is expected. When we do not know the particular program on the docket, we are still likely to know about "things of this general type." And in such cases, the situation is usually defined for us explicitly (Goffman, 1957). Someone tells us what to do beforehand, or the transaction begins with a written program or a chairman's (or host's) statement of the ground rules.

When people communicate about what is taking place, we say that they are "metacommunicating," i.e., they are communicating *about* communication. The instance of explicity defining the agenda is but one type of metacommunication. At any time in the proceedings, people may pause to ask about what is next, or to pass judgement on what is happening. Or they may pause to discuss a change in the program or hold a "post-mortem" after an interaction and discuss what has happened.

In turn, the process of talking about a transaction is but one kind of metacommunicating. Much, perhaps most metacommunicational behavior is not in the linguistic mode. Rather it is *kinesic*. In fact the term and concept, metacommunication, originally derived from the observation of non-language behavior.

Bateson postulated that animals have a signal to distinguish between programs of behavior that are similar in structure (Bateson, 1955). For instance, two male animals meet and square off; in one instance they fight. In another they play. In both, they rush, approach, bare teeth, etc. Somehow, in some way it is possible for "This is play," to be signalled. Bateson called this a "metacommunication."

In looking for specific signals of play, Bateson suggested that among humans, the smile may have that effect. Two working class men may meet in a bar; one calls the other a foul name, the other gives him a poke and smiles. The smile distinguishes what has happened from an insult, and this wisdom is reflected in the folk saying, "When you say that, pardner, smile."

The *meta*communication can be kinesic, or lexical. I can say, "Oh, I didn't mean that." But more often I will give a kinesic signal. The frown is a well known indicator to express disapproval of deviance. Ordinarily, it puts an end to the unacceptable behavior. I recall my father's frown when I would attempt to eat peas with a spoon. Another kinesic meta marker is the nose-wipe. This is performed when a lie is being told, a woman is showing too much thigh through letting her skirts ride up, a man is acting too swish. Another common kinesic marker which serves as a sort of apology is the eye rub. It is equivalent to saying "I could not help it." For instance, if a man looks up a woman's dress, and the woman catches him looking, he will eye rub.

Now let us return to the description of the interview hour. We have noted that it follows a program; it goes in a stepwise fashion. At each step, or juncture point, the transition is marked by a flurry of kinesic behaviors (of a meta significance), which may be called "cues": they imply, "Now we are going to do such and such," or "We cannot do such and such." In observing psychotherapists, very clear examples of this appear. For example, many self-styled "non-directive" therapists use a hand flip or an eye-point to indicate who in the family is to speak. If one ignores such cues, it is possible to maintain the illusion that the speaking order is "spontaneous."

When we know the traditional programming of a transaction, we can watch a particular example, and note that a flurry of meta-communicational behavior occurs at each transition point or step in the proceedings. In this way any ambiguities of procedure can be anticipated and resolved in advance with a kinesic cue. Thus next speakers are indicated by shifts in head and eye address or with hand cues in much the way the performance of an orchestra is conducted. When the participants search each other's faces in uncertainty someone may offer a suggestion or directive or glance at some symbol which represents the customary proceedings. But metacommunicational behavior also appears whenever some deviance occurs in the expected procedure of that group. The monitors mentioned above: frowns, wiping of the index finger, the reproving stare, appear when someone tries to initiate another kind of transaction, such as flirtation at a formal meeting, or when someone says the wrong "thing." Then if these kinesic warnings do not suffice to extinguish a deviation, the other participants may verbalize their disapproval or even take sterner measures. *In short any transaction is continuously monitored and regulated, so that usually the customary procedure called for in that setting by that program is maintained.*

Transcontextual Behavior and Deviancy

In some kinds of human transactions the expression of individual ideas or thoughts, or even a revelation of emotional states is officially called for by the program. In meetings, for example, certain participants may take turns describing the attitudes of themselves or their constituents on an issue. And in psychotherapy the patient is specifically enjoined to tell how he thinks and feels about certain items. Furthermore there is usually an opportunity for status figures to speak metacommunicatively when they strongly disapprove a turn of events.

So there are specific slots in human experience which call for statements of value, attitude, reaction and other aspects of thought or feeling. But such expressions are slotted and constrained in human communication. Not only are lexical statements of this kind regulated but kinesic expressions, too, are to be carefully controlled. One is not supposed to set his face in exhibitionistic configurations of disgust or contempt, for instance, when his boss is speaking and he will pay for such behavior later when he applies it to the utterances of a spouse. Furthermore we hardly expect people to make accurate statements of thoughts and feelings even when there is an allowance for such metacommunicational activity in the programming of a transaction. In courtship, for example, one traditionally verbalizes an expected set of laudatory and romantic statements rather than what he may at that moment feel. At a dinner party a wide range of ideas may be allowable, but an even larger range is more or less prohibited. And at formal negotiations we must regard most of what the participants say as tactical, not as soul baring. In short, we must not confuse the various metacommunicational actions of the participants as simple expressions of their thoughts and feelings. And we cannot regard these intraorganismic events as the *cause* of what is happening.

But consider a class of expressions in speech or kinesics which are not metacommunicative to the events in progress. Suppose that a person reacts audibly or visibly, not to what is going on, but to something which as far as we can see has nothing to do with what is in progress. Suppose, for example, he shows attacking or aggressive behavior at a conversation, as though he were engaged in a battle or an argument. Or suppose a participant begins to cry, or pick his teeth, or give a scientific lecture in the middle of a courtship. In such cases we can claim that the participant is expressing something personal. He is reacting to a program in his own head. Psychiatrically we would consider such behavior to be deviant, and we would classify one who regularly acts this way to be neurotic or psychotic or whatever.

Bateson (Bateson, 1972) describes such behavior from a communicational viewpoint. He terms it "transcontextual," in contrast to behavior which is appropriate to the setting and programming, i.e., to the existing context. The term, "transcontextual," implies, of course, that the behavior which appears does belong to some other customary context.

Here is an example: A young psychiatrist in residence, A., was driving two older men to a house. Both were therapists much admired by A. All were talking in the car, and as one of the older men stepped out, he remarked to A., relative to something A. had said, "That's very interesting," but with a curious inflexion. A. was dumbfounded.

Now let's say there's a program for the way three males behave driving around in a car. Let's suppose, also, that A. was acting boyishly despite the fact that he was the driver, and in that sense on a peer level. The older man carried over a technique from classical psychotherapy to confront him, rather than carrying out the program of "men talk" that A. had anticipated. Psychiatrists get very accustomed to making interpretations. In another sense, what he did could be interpreted as "bad manners." His behavior would have been proper for another context, but he was behaving cross-contextually. Because A. and he had a relationship in another context, it is quite likely that A. gave kinesis which cued the older man. Of course each had within him the capacity of "appropriate" behavior, but in the particular example the two men together evolved inappropriate behaviors.

All transcontextual behavior ought not to be labeled deviant, lest we foster complete conformity in the existing order of human communication. A person may behave transcontextually because he does not know the particular program which is in progress. From his point of view, he thinks he recognizes a particular context and does what is appropriate to the programming he knows. This occurs, for example, when people from the outside get involved in the in-group agendas of an institution. The working class patient knows nothing of the institutionalized agenda of insight therapy. He is used to going to a doctor, telling him his complaints, and being offered means of doing something about them. The psychotherapist's silence strikes him as strange, and he cannot grasp the idea that the treatment actually *is* the description of his symptoms. Also, what appears to be a transcontextual performance occurs when a foreigner attends the usual procedure of another culture. The British and British-Americans, for example, use large interpersonal distances for conversation, and move together at less than two feet for confrontation and courtship. When these people relate to a close-distance people, such as Eastern European Jews or Latins, they misinterpret the close approach. They may react as if in confrontation or courtship, but more likely they step back and think their partner is either very aggressive and forward (if Jewish) or very seductive (if Latin).

I would like to give two examples of performance illustrating transcontextual and contextual behavior, wherein the therapist labels a performance deviant.

A therapist is talking to a patient about the patient's childhood. Unwittingly or unconsciously the therapist exhibits courtship behavior with his body and voice tone. The patient responds with courtship behavior, responding to the kinesic communication, rather than to the language communication. The therapist then may say, "You are behaving seductively, because you think I am your father and you felt sexual toward him." Here the therapist has fooled himself and placed a double-bind upon the patient.

There is a more common example: The therapist uses what is termed maximum distancing and closed behavior toward his patient. He sits as far away as the chair placements allow. He holds his legs crossed and his arms folded, while turning some 90 degrees away from the face-to-face position. And he blows smoke into the space between them while using formal vocal tones. The posture is usual in the first sessions of psychotherapy and in other formal transactions among strangers. And the patient, of course, behaves in a similar manner. But suddenly the therapist accuses the patient of being remote or withdrawn or afraid of closeness, and this behavior he explains as an expression of the patient's personality. He does not implicate the relationship or the situation and observe that the patient is behaving contextually. He rather denies the actual context, says that his patient is behaving transcontextually or deviantly, and blames the patient's personality. He is now into the politics of blaming. He is, wittingly or otherwise, using the concept of deviancy to control or manipulate the patient.

Communication in politics and social control

This sort of blaming is characteristic in human communication. A situation which is built into the economic, political, social, and ecological system in general is blamed upon that particular individual or faction which first shows a transcontextual or undesirable response. As has been described elsewhere in detail (Scheflen, 1972), this mechanism constitutes the main method of social control in a Western society. And the communicational modality of blaming is language.

Here, briefly, is how this mechanism seems to work. In Western thought, the aristotelian logic prevails. It combines two axioms which all of us are taught from day one. First, we learn that there is *a* cause or explanation for all events (including all human actions). Secondly, we learn that people somehow cause these human events. These beliefs make it difficult to examine contexts and systems. Instead, we continue to search for causation in our own actions or motives, or else in those of the other fellow. From those axioms, it follows that life is a cowboy movie, peopled by good-guys and bad-guys, and the main lexical-cognitive activity becomes the fixing of blame.

Thus a wife maintains that she is aggressive because she must compensate for her husband's "deep" passivity, dependency, homosexuality, or whatever. He rejoins by blaming her, saying he acts passively because his wife is an aggressive, domineering, phallic bitch. To be sure, both parties may exhibit the traits of which they are accused, but the reciprocal interplay of these behaviors in a larger system is ignored. The politics of blame are employed to explain the condition of the marriage. If one establishes his case, he believes, he can control the partner. If the therapist gets lost in the blame game, and ignores the dynamics of the interaction, he becomes part of the problem rather than the solution.

This blaming or scapegoating procedure operates at all levels of the social system. If the dirtiness of the ghetto is explained by claiming that the residents throw garbage in the streets, they are culpable and nothing is required of the government in the way of improved sanitation. If the ghetto unemployment is a consequence of one factor—that Blacks don't want to work—then nothing need be done about civil rights or the American economy. And if violence is an innate trait of "primitive" people like the minority group members, then we must simply hire more police. We do not have to do anything about slum environments, discrimination, unequal education or anything else about the context of the inner city.

The blame game is also played internationally. A cause of the War is found and it is of course a group of people—the enemy. The Vietnam War is enormously profitable to the corporate structure and to the labor leadership as well. It keeps a huge young labor force off the job market and insures relatively high union wages in those many industries engaged in bombs, aircraft, oil, etc. But this matter is carefully not discussed. Instead the right wing blames the Commies and the liberals get suckered into defending the Viet Cong and blaming the American politicians.

Scapegoating cannot be avoided, however, by belonging to an "in" establishment. For institutions too blame their problems and failures on their members. When this can be accomplished undesirable members can be eliminated without censure, or they can be kept working hard behind the eight ball. And such misplacement of understanding allows an institution to keep its practices and policies without reform.

The case for individualism

But surely, you will say, the idea that individuals cause social and ecological events has its good side. One can, for example, get credit for things that go right and then be promoted up the ladder of success to the good life of the upper middle class.

In fact this is exactly the promise of the idea of "the individual." One can use certain variants in dress and speech style, move away from the local control of bonding and territorial behavior in the family or origin and be free to climb a career ladder. He thus has enough independence to move from city to city or country to country in the service of the military, the government of the corporate structure. This mobility makes him very useful at these broad levels of the social structure. In return for this he can say "I am an individual." He thus replaces the territorial and reciprocal constraints of the original small group by those of other groups and the conceptual controls of parental discipline and church by the value, goals and blame systems of institutions and governments. The individuality thus obtained is illusory. We have been taught as Americans to not look at how we are controlled. We are individuals.

Communication and expression theories in social control

Psychotherapy has gone a long way to defeat Freud's dream of personal liberation and rationalize the politics of blaming. The concept of insight is often used as a strategy instead of as a tactic in understanding our life experience. Thus blaming ourselves becomes a way of life and we can endlessly contemplate our navels in an attempt to correct our behavior. But we can therefore lose sight of the contexts which determine much of human action. At a time of ecological crisis an endless preoccupation with insight constitutes an ego trip which can make us unadaptive as a people. This contracting of our field of awareness may have gained us the label "shrinks."

Psychiatry also has elaborated systems of diagnosis and a rationale of behavioral explanation which fosters and supports the process of political control by blaming and crediting. Those who do not conform to the status quo can be judged deviant, removed for hospitalization and brainwashed to proper insight. Many psychiatrists are now writing papers which ascribe the activist behaviors to insecure childhoods in the 1950s, to unresolved oedipal conflicts, to drugs—to all sorts of intraorganismic processes. These authors thus act as though there are no conditions which justify protests, that there are no proper contexts for these political issues to be aired. To claim or infer this is to behave politically. This kind of behavior has won us the term "psycho-police from the New Left."

Psychiatrists have also made an interesting about face in their own theorizing. Originally Freud and others developed motivational and other psychodynamic theories to account for the phenomena of their practices, namely the recurring use of deviant type or transcontextual behavior. Their patients, we might say nowadays, were consistently ego-tripping instead of behaving in accordance with prevailing contexts. But gradually this theory of deviance came to be the explanation for all human group behavior. This theory has become widely accepted in middle class America maybe because it so well suits the conceptual practices of a majority group.

Expression theories of communication wrap up this kind of politics in a neat pseudo-scientific package. They assume an Aristotelean or presystems paradigm of A First Cause and find this within the organisms who participate in social processes. Thus some trait of the person or faction, acquired by heredity like a disease or an instinct, or acquired in early life experience, like dependency or hostility, causes the behavior of that person. Then by reducing communicational processes (and thereby social process) to an interaction of individual expressions, the proposition of individual blame is officially sanctioned.

Conclusion

By my description of communication I have tried to alter the customary way of looking at things. A society is maintained by very ancient and continuous processes in which people take part by using traditional coded behaviors. They have thoughts and feelings about these ongoing communicational activities. These may modify a person's contributions but they do not cause the totality of communicational phenomena.

I believe that conscious thought and feeling are *meta* to the traditional motor activities of man, that they constitute a system of behaviors which judge and evaluate what is going on. Thus thoughts and feelings are usually *post hoc*. They are reactions to, but not causes of, human activity. They reflect our belief in their causative role, and afford an illusion of controlling events. In reality, we can, at best, only influence. We as people do, to be sure, sometimes take an evaluation and make a plan which we proceed then to carry out; but this kind of behavior is so extraordinary, that it must be classed as either controlling, tactical, or deviant.

Youth culture and the new politics

Finally, I would like to relate the contents of this paper to its relevance in the outpatient treatment of young people. Those in their early years who are to the left of mainstream America, deeply mistrust psychiatry, for they see it as another institution for maintaining the *status quo* in ideation and behavior. Some also distrust psychology and medicine for their tendency to explain social phenomena, like protests and drug usage, by individual illness. They distrust human sciences in general for the endless attempts of researchers and theorists to use genetics and other organismic approaches to explain away the problems of the larger society.

But they also distrust language in general, for they know that axioms of real truth constitute but one other form of political propaganda in the service of behavioral control. Many do not read. Some try not to speak much at all, preferring a few phrases (with multiple unspecified meanings) and a variety of gestures. Many detest the entire system of dominance hierarchies among nations, among institutions, and among individuals, and try instead to form egalitarian groups. They negatively value the very kinesic and territorial tactics that my generation tried to master—the use of charisma, the dominance display, the need to be right.

I believe these young people profoundly understand a principle I am trying to explain here in formal terms. I think the behavioral systems revolution in the sciences of man (which began in the mid-1950's), and the cultural revolution now in progress, are two manifestations of the same epistemological change.

Pediatric Paradox: Adolescents as Change Agents in the Family

Arlene Katz
and Andrew Guthrie, M.D.

Introduction

At a recent conference workshop, mental health professionals were assigned the task of discussing youth and the directions they might take. The act of holding such a conference implies that professionals can come to some agreement, or engage in what is euphemistically called goal-oriented behavior.

Within this small community were representatives of various sub-cultures: the young, the minority group, the silent majority, etc. It became apparent that this skewed microcosm of society fast became polarized, with each group viewing the others with the same fixed labels—radical versus old guard. The latter was akin to forty therapists in search of a patient, the former was rubbing its collective head as it batted it against a brick wall. Each brick was made by a specific training model, talking its own language, sure that it had *the* answer. The question before us is how to get beyond those walls.

In this paper, we report on a collaboration between a family physician and a consulting psychologist that has, so far, surmounted many interdisciplinary barriers and has provided an effective model for community mental health intervention.

The natural course of any experimental work in community mental health can be linked to diving in at the deep end and swimming to the shallow end, but when first able to touch bottom, telling someone about it. Having reached that stage ourselves, we shall present our findings in the light of our model of intervention. However, the *content* of our model largely evolved during the study, as it continues to evolve as new information enters the system. While we can describe its structure and the basic orientation of the participants, it is in the nature of our model to allow change in its content.

Model

The family physician is one of a naturally existing network of caretakers in a community. As such, he comes to know his community, to appreciate its culture, and observe how different families have adapted to changing circumstances. In surveying the literature, three studies were described that utilized a psychiatrist as consultant to a physician. The model was that of an "expert" teaching his own expertise to the medical practitioner (family physician, internist, etc.), (Zabarenko *et al.*, 1971).

The alternative proposed in this work uses a systems approach, focusing on the ways that the person, family, and community interlock, and pays special attention to the interface of the different community caretakers (Auerswald, 1968). Each profession has become increasingly specialized, indeed a sub-culture of its own, and has developed its own language and frame of reference. Often, a *closed system* pattern develops where the profession becomes an enclave in the larger community. The stage is set for fragmentation of health service, resulting in the difficulty of effective inter-agency communication, and reinforcing the isolation and anomie of the people who come for help, e.g., adolescents and the elderly.

We feel that systems theory is a particularly suitable basis for our consultation model, for it instructs us to examine each professional in the light of his position at the interface of the systems that call upon him for help. As a key member of a community network of social supports, the pediatrician is in a unique position for several reasons: 1) He knows the person and his family *before* a crisis occurs, 2) He can see the family in the context of the culture and the expectations of the community, and 3) He has a knowledge of local "resources," and can help to postulate the precise strengths and weaknesses that existed in and between those sub-systems that most influenced the growth of the person that he sees. Indeed, in a recently published study in Canada, it was found that the pediatrician was the one most often turned to in an adolescent's crisis (Munan, 1973. Also Mead, 1972).

Background

In the private offices of pediatricians and family practitioners, the care of episodic problems, preventive medicine, and continuing care of chronic medical illness has helped to define the various job roles; the office nurse, nurse practitioner, child health associate, and the pediatrician have developed a delineation of duties and programs which encompass the spectrum of physical problems presented by patients. A recent study (Machotka *et al.,* 1973), comparing the basic scientific and clinical knowledge of Child Health Associates with medical students and pediatric residents indicates the clinical effectiveness of this job role in the delivery of medical care. The primary goal has been to increase the availability as well as the effectiveness of services. Each pediatric nurse associate represents a 50-75% extension of the pediatrician (Sanzaro, 1970).

Many other problems which are present at the offices of physicians are as yet beyond the capacity of this team to deal with in an efficient and appropriate manner. Scholastic failure and/or underachievement, aphasia, learning disabilities, behavioral problems, and adjustment reactions, among adolescents and their families, must frequently be referred to other community agencies, such as mental health clinics, or the urban hospitals and clinics for evaluation, recommendations for management, and therapeutic programs. A recent and revealing study from Yale University (Duff *et al.,* 1972) indicates the change in the spectrum of clinical problems that are being seen in an ambulatory service. Of 25 children studied, 12% presented with physical problems, 36% with psycho-social problems, and a combination of these were seen in 52% of the cases. By its very nature, the evaluation of a psycho-social problem family is time consuming because of the amount of data necessary for arrival at a diagnosis and developing a plan of management. Frequently, this requires the involvement of several disciplines and the coordinated actions of a team approach. It is not feasible at the present time to evaluate and manage disorders in the physician's office. The particular alignment of job roles, the commitment of time, and the existence of prevailing attitudes, often negative, towards the psychological, social, and behavioral complaints include this. This has been especially true of the recent spectrum of adolescents' symptoms which are discussed, often for the first time, in the confines of the office of the family physician.

The authors, a consulting psychologist and a pediatrician with an interest in adolescent medicine, first met while volunteers in an urban "outreach" program, involving a mobile medical unit, specifically designed to establish contact with an estranged group of street youths. The informality of the program, the elimination of the artificially developed boundaries of one's training within a specialty as well as the ease and effectiveness of communication between the staff and the target population contributed to the visible indices of improved patient acceptance and compliance.

At approximately the same time, several adolescents and their families established contact with the pediatrician in his suburban office with complaints of family turmoil, anti-social behavior, sexual acting out behavior, and running away, as well as symptoms of drug use and depression. Each had then been referred to an urban clinic setting for a "family evaluation." The diagnostic unit involved also offered "crisis intervention" during the approximate three week period of evaluation.

In each of these (five) instances, the referral to already existing programs (e.g. mental health clinic, group sessions conducted by "self-help" organizations, psychiatric care, and drug-abuse oriented programs) had met with failure or resistance because of patient dissatisfaction and a lack of commitment. Three of the youths, however, did express their willingness to seek alternative methods to have their needs met. Two finally accepted the invitation to participate in group meetings with the consulting psychologist.

Pilot Study

Both of the cases described in this paper were females, 15 years of age, whose families had been known to the pediatrician over a long period. They naturally turned to him both for routine medical care and in times of crisis. To quote one of the girls:

> I remember when I first got into trouble. . . . My parents called Dr. G. He's really busy, but he came. That's funny: I thought they would go to a priest or something . . . But I'm glad they went to him.

These two girls had similar families of origin: both grew up in the context of a large extended family (somewhat characteristic of the family structure of this suburban area). Both had attended parochial schools, and were later transferred to public high schools. They were both the oldest sisters in their families, as had been their mothers. In neither of these families had a close relationship been established between the adolescent and either parent.

The goal of the group was to consult with these adolescents to help them differentiate self from family of origin. They were both encouraged to explore their roles in their families. Initially, they explored the role each played in the group. This involved increasing their awareness of verbal and non-verbal communication. A democratic atmosphere was encouraged where feelings could be shared. Meetings were held after regular office hours in the familiar surroundings of the pediatrician's office. The concept of communication as a dialogue, was shared, as well as the importance of reciprocal feedback in which each participant adds a bit of information that enables 1) Clarification of a message, 2) Information on a self in the context of other selves, leading to 3) Differentiation of selves within a subsystem, thus promoting a goal-oriented behavior. Thus we developed the idea of an *open system* on an experiential and conceptual level (Satir, 1967, Bradt, 1971). The experiential exercises demonstrated the possible levels of verbal and non-verbal communication. These included individual and family sculpturing, and the re-creation of families in space. But, a special emphasis was placed on the *resolution of a conflict,* and not just on re-creating an interaction. Postures portraying the Satir roles (Satir, 1967) were used as a transition point, helping the group members to begin to observe their parents as a communications system, to see their parents as people, and to explore the triangle between the adolescent and her parents. As a first step in "de-fusing" the family emotional system, it is important to differentiate people into roles. We therefore explored parents and families as a set of interlocking roles, with emphasis on the expectations that each has of the other. This promoted an examination of the non-verbal cues that typically evoke an emotional response. For instance, one group member spoke of knowing when her mother was in a bad mood by "her cold stare." Her usual reaction was to shut off to her mother and so avoid contact. By becoming aware of her automatic fear response, she was able to explore other alternatives and control her emotional reaction in this interaction. From passively reacting on an automatic level, observation (awareness) led to a way of modifying the pattern.

These examples fit the paradign proposed by Bowen (1971) for family psychotherapy with one family member, and for the differentiation of self from family of origin. The differentiated person strives to put himself in what has been called the "I" position. He assumes responsibility for his own happiness, comfort, and well-being. To those more familiar with Satir's communication roles, it is closest to the levelling posture (as distinct from blaming, placating, rationalizing, etc., characteristic of a person fused in an emotional system). For adolescents, the process of levelling is perhaps facilitated by contact with peers who are at varying levels of differentiation.

As expounded by Bowen, "If one member of a triangle can change, an entire extended family can change." It has been suggested that adolescents are not able to differentiate in a family because of economic dependency. Nevertheless, the initial steps have been demonstrated by our group members in their increased awareness to their family role and the working of the emotional system of their family, as well as by their increasing ability to control their emotional reactiveness. In the case of one group member, this has resulted in a major alteration of the parent-child triangle:

> Carol reported that, for the first time since they were married, her parents were going away for a holiday together. As might be predicted, her parents became more anxious and bickered increasingly in the week before their anticipated departure. Carol became aware of this, and noted that it was typical of their behavior before any trip.
>
> Rather than being triangled into their fight by her emotional reactions, Carol levelled with her mother and said "I don't know if you ever notice it, but you always fight before you go away anywhere." Her mother agreed, but didn't know what to do about it. She finally stated "Maybe it would help to think about things before I say them; then perhaps we won't automatically get into a fight."

Earlier, Carol had noticed that her mother began to act increasingly abrupt with people. She saw that her mother (as the oldest female in the family) was the focus of an extended-family conflict concerning the legal competence of an elderly great aunt. From her viewpoint outside the emotional system, Carol observed the interactions of her great aunts and uncles, and her mother's reaction to them. After discussing this with the group, the great aunt and the family were referred, via Carol's mother, for appropriate consultation with resources for the elderly. A family crisis was prevented.

This was only one of several occasions where one situation generalized to the whole family, and also to situations in other subsystems in the community. In Carol's case, this could be regarded as the role of change-agent in the extended family and community. Both girls began to pursue goal-oriented activities.

> Carol reported that she has begun running a Sunday School group of 5th and 6th grade children. She stated, "I've taken some of the things I learned straight from our group. We talk a lot about their feelings and the roles they are taking—as distracter, blamer . . . I began by telling them—"It's your group . . .

and I want you to be scared of me."* And it was amazing!
They started telling me their feelings about what I said. They're
so open! I got them before they had to be closed. I believe anybody can be opened up—look at me! I surprise myself sometimes."

Summary and Conclusions

In this paper, we have described a model for community intervention utilizing a pediatrician and a consulting psychologist, and
report on a small pilot study. We argue that this provides an alternative approach to community mental health problems. In particular:

1) Adolescents seem more ready to come to family practitioners
with their problems, and at an earlier date, than to professional
therapists or mental health centers.

2) The pediatrician himself is an *integral* member of the social
network. He has known the person for a considerable time, knows
his family, and often possesses much knowledge of the culture and
expectations of the community.

3) The familiarity of the group setting, in the pediatrician's
office, with an informal structure, reinforce the principle of our
model—that the individual cannot be considered as somehow
divorced from the systems in which he has to live.

4) Once group members are able to examine their position in
the set of sub-systems that we call family, extended family, school,
etc., it is often possible to recognize early signs of other crises,
thereby providing a measure of preventive service, as well as a
means to facilitate communication in the network.

We claim that this collaboration model has many advantages
vis-a-vis conventional community mental health care in certain
circumstances. It shows considerable potential for those populations that traditionally show reticence in turning to community
mental health outlets.

Role of the Consulting Psychologist

1) Presentation and explication of the workings of family

---

*It is interesting to note Carol's timely "reversal." She makes a point more
effectively by saying the opposite.

systems: The psychologist provides feedback about the progress of group members. Each is described in terms of the role he or she plays in the family system. The focus is on an exploration of family communication and significant family triangles, and also methods of intervening in the family system.

2) Liason with family: As necessary, conjoint family meetings are held, with the possibility of the psychologist and pediatrician as a co-therapy team. Thus family process issues are highlighted on a conceptual and experiential level. The psychologist is available to family members as needed.

3) Group meetings: These are held as described above, being flexible in terms of time, place, etc.

4) Community network: The psychologist can act as a liason between group members and other necessary community agencies. The psychologist becomes a participant-observer in the existing network.

Role of the Pediatrician

1) Case finding and triage: In addition to recognizing those patients who present with symptoms of adjustment reaction to adolescence, it is necessary to select for referral the youths who share similar concerns, reactions, and who are positive in their interactions with peers.

2) Parent advocacy: The parents have on occasion requested advice, support, and reassurance concerning their roles during the course of group meetings. The physician has met with various parents at the time of office visits for episodic medical illness of siblings, as well as for "routine" physical examinations. Telephone consultations had occurred during the early weeks of the project, and questions asked most frequently dealt with parental anxieties over progress or apparent lack of obvious change in behavioral patterns of the adolescent.

3) Reinforcement: Initially, the parents expressed feelings of doubt about the value of the group sessions, which was understandable in view of the youths' refusal to participate actively in previous therapeutic modalities. Within 5 months, both sets of

parents, on separate occasions, had asked whether the program would continue, since they felt more positive about the sessions, and were now expressing their anxieties over possible consequences to their daughter and the family, should the group meetings cease.

4) Liason with other community supports: Several opportunities have arisen within each family to communicate with other support personnel within the community, such as guidance councelors, school sub-masters, clergy, and a psychiatrist. This function has been of further value in offering counseling to other family members, and providing relevant data concerning each family.

5) Communications network: The role of a pediatrician has had the additional value of providing information to the consulting psychologist, which has resulted in the future planning of group functioning.

Directions in Community Medicine

The experience with this model, which goes beyond the walls of a practicing pediatrician's office, leads to the following comments:

1) A mental health consultant is proposed as an additional member in group pediatric practice.

2) The need for innovative alternative models for managing the social, behavioral, and psychological problems of children, youths, and their families which present to the offices of family physicians, appears essential.

3) Training programs for pediatricians and family care specialists should incorporate an experiential practicum on coping with families with problems, and children and youths with adjustment difficulties.

4) Finally, active intervention and involvement by the pediatrician in the difficulties of family life expressed by parents or discerned from the symptoms of children should be expected to yield more productive results than might be expected with the symptoms of estrangement and alienation of adolescents who have already interrupted the fabric of their family life.

REFERENCES

Auerswald, E.H. "Interdisciplinary versus Ecology Approach," *Family Process,* 1968, *7,* 202-215.

Bowen, M. "Principles and Techniques of Multiple Family Therapy," in J.O. Bradt, and C.J. Moynihan (Eds.), *Systems Therapy,* Washington, D.C. Published by the editors, 1971.

Bradt, J.O. and Moynihan, C.J. "Opening the Safe—A Study of Child-Focused Families, in J. O. Bradt, and C. J. Moynihan (Eds.) *Systems Therapy,* Washington, D. C. Published by the editors, 1971.

Duff, R.S., Rowe, D.S., and Anderson, F.P. "Patient Care and Student Learning in a Pediatric Clinic," in *Pediatrics,* 1972, *50,* 839-846.

Machotka, P., Ott, J.E., Moon, J.B., and Silver, H.K. Competence of Child Health Associates, *AJDC,* 1973, *125,* 199-203.

Mead, B. "Counseling Adolescents," an invited address to The American Academy of Family Physicians, Sept. 1972.

Munan, L. "Health Needs of the Youth Subculture," *AFP,* 1973, *7*(1), 104-7.

Sanazaro, P. A report of the Council on Pediatric Practice of the American Academy of Pediatrics on the Delivery of Health Care to Children, in *Lengthening Shadows,* 1970, 229.

Zabarenko, R.N., Merenstein, J., Zabarenko, L. "Teaching Psychological Medicine in the Family Practice Office," in *JAMA,* 1971, *218*(3), 392-396.

Symposium:
Youth in the Community

John R. Unwin, M.D.

Youth in Society and the Clinic

I see no hope for the future of our people if they are dependent on the frivolous youth of today, for certainly all youth are reckless beyond words. When I was a boy we were taught to be discreet and respectful of elders, but the present youth are exceedingly wise and impatient of restraint.

The foregoing is a quotation—written by Hesiod in the 8th century B.C., and I offer it to you, partly tongue-in-cheek, to remind you that current concern about our young people has been, to a certain extent, reverberating back and forward through recorded history. It would seem that adults have always tended to foresee the impending disintegration of civilization at the hands of each successive youth generation—including those of which you and I were members. This obsessive despair on the part of adults is answered, appropriately and vengefully, by the slogans of contemporary youth, who still tend to insist that anyone over the age of thirty is impossibly irrelevant, prematurely senile—and probably impotent. Justice is not, however, totally blind—the U.C.L.A. student who plagiarised the slogan "Never trust anyone over the age of thirty" from George Bernard Shaw, himself celebrated—or bewailed—his own thirtieth birthday some three years ago!

My task is formidably broad—to attempt to give some focus to contemporary youth as it presents itself in clinics, whether they be the more conventional hospital-based or private outpatient clinics, or the more innovative type of "store-front" or "walk-in" youth clinics pioneered by such young physicians as David Smith in Haight-Ashbury.

Because the area to be covered is so vast, I have the choice either of presenting rather emaciated over-generalizations or of choosing circumscribed topics which allow some perspective. With your permission I will touch on some topics which may permit us to reassess some of our traditional concepts about youth.

There are numerous factors which differentiate contemporary youth from previous generations. The most obvious is the sheer numbers of young people in our society—you are all quite aware that some 50% of our population is under the age of 25, that about 20% are teenagers, and that they are a particularly visible and audible crop. And though their relative predominance will be displaced in the near future by the geriatric population, the absolute numbers of youth will continue to rise for some time yet.

It would seem that it took the large size of the youth population and the evolution of a well-defined youth sub-culture to force us to realise that we are dealing with an age-group constituting a separate and critical period of development, with specific and unique maturational tasks in the biological, psychological and sociocultural spheres. Prior to the 1960s we had tended to leave this segment of our population vaguely adrift between the devil of childhood and the deep blue sea of adulthood—abandoned by child psychiatry if they were big enough or sufficiently obstreperous, accepted regretfully and somewhat timidly by adult psychiatry if they could dodge past such labels as "acting-out adolescent" or "juvenile delinquent." More recently this fertile though rocky terrain has been claimed by those of us who specialize in the area of adolescent or youth psychiatry.

Such specialized attention to this age group was encouraged by the Expert Committee of the World Health Organization which reported on the Health Problems of Adolescence in 1966 and, in recommending that increased attention be paid to this age group, stated . . . "adolescents differ physiologically and psychologically from children and adults, and these differences should be better understood, more widely taught and more consistently remembered. Only when this has been done will it be possible to take adequate account of such factors as the rapid growth of adolescents, their high degree of activity, the inter-relationship of their growth and their endocrine systems, and their requirements for a healthy personality development." Fritz Redl also pleaded for a global approach to any consideration of adolescent development in his address to the International Congress on Adolescence in Edinburgh in 1966, while Duche, Schonfeld and Tomkiewicz recommended that "the understanding of adolescent personality development and the significance of specific behavior would be enhanced if the mental health specialists were to correlate their findings not only with the chronological age but also with the level of (biological) development."

In the field of somatic development, John Tanner of England has warned us that the use of chronological age as a criteria of maturity is invalid, because of:

1. the wide variation in the age of onset of puberty and of the adolescent growth spurt (the velocity of growth during adolescence being equalled only by that of the second year of life);

2. the wide variation in the actual rate of growth during youth;

3. the trend for a progressively earlier onset of puberty and for youths to be taller and heavier than those of earlier generations.

Some examples may help underline the relevance of these trends. Muus records that "the average height of American sailors in the War of 1812 is estimated at 5 feet 2 inches—which explains why the decks of the USS Constitution did not need to be more than 5 feet 6 inches high." Similarly, the knights' armor in medieval European castles would fit a ten to twelve year old American boy today. If the present rate of gain continues to the year 4000, adult man will be 11 to 12 feet tall! And if the current trend for puberty to commence 4 to 6 months earlier per decade continues, by the year 2240 girls will begin menstruating at the age of 4 years. Should boys keep pace, population control will take on a new dimension! In fact, there is evidence that these trends are already leveling off; and there are exceptions to every rule—no girl of the Bundi tribe in the Highlands of New Guinea has menstruated before the age of 17, and no girl in the Peruvian Andes has become pregnant before 18.

The essential significance to us of the foregoing is that, with the progressively earlier biological maturation, the psychological reactions by the youth, his peers and parents to the newly-released sexual and muscular capacities are in evidence at progressively earlier ages. And the time-worn phrase "When I was your age . . ." becomes even more meaningless. At the same time we should note that, given two 15 year old boys, one may have all but reached his adult body stature while the other may have already started puberty. Yet they will share the same locker-room at school, comparisons and teasing are inevitable, and problems related to sexual identity and self-concept may arise. Number 2 can always try harder, but if the basic equipment isn't there . . . !

I suggested at the beginning that there is a need to reevaluate some of our standard concepts of youth—after all, were Holden Caulfield alive today he would be in his forties, and to take "Catcher in the Rye" as typifying today's youth would be about as appropriate as a group of Freudian analysts gathered around a piano singing "I want a girl just like the girl that married dear old dad"!

It is particularly in the area of personality development that our theoretical models bear reexamination. What is the "normal" phenomenology of this age group, and to what extent do the so-called "behavior disorders" constitute an extension of "normal" developmental processes toward psychopathology?

It would seem to be reasonable to state that, in North America, psychiatry's approach to youth has been molded primarily by psychoanalytic concepts—pioneered particularly by Anna Freud and epitomized by the title of her address—"Adolescence as a developmental disturbance"—at the above-mentioned Edinburgh congress in 1966. These now-classic concepts of the normality and necessity of turmoil and rebelliousness during youth have been reiterated in the recent report on normal adolescence by the Group for the Advancement of Psychiatry and by Peter Blos in the U.S.A., while from Argentina Knobel has written of the "normal abnormality of this period," explaining behaviour disorders as a "real exaggeration of the syndrome of normal adolescence."

It is imperative that we reevaluate the idea that normal adolescence implies inner turmoil and that a quiet, non-rebellious passage through youth suggests unhealthy development. We should note that these conventional concepts are essentially extrapolations from clinical cases to the general youth population at large. Within the context of contemporary youth dissent, Erik Erikson writes of " . . . that majority of young people who would otherwise choose only banal and transient ways of either voicing dissent or of displaying conflict—and about whom, therefore, psychoanalysis knows so very little. From this point of view, our patients often appear to be inverted dissenters, too sick for the sanctional malaise of their time, too isolated for joint dissent, and yet too sensitive for simple adjustment."

More important, we should note carefully the crucial research findings published in the past decade by those who have studied non-clinical, non-disturbed youth. I am referring here to the work of Dan Offer in Chicago, Douvain and Adelson in Ann Arbor, as well as Grinker, Golden and his associates, and Kysar and his co-workers. In summary, these authors have found that healthy youth development does not by any means always involve turmoil, that appreciable psycho-social dysequilibrium is not essential for proper maturation during this age period, and that there can be several pathways of development, including those which are smooth and undisturbing for the young person and his family. In the same vein, studies of student activities during the '60s do not bear out expectations of underlying psychiatric disturbances; such phenomena should not be automatically envisaged in orthodox psychoanalytic terms—the writings of Erikson, Keniston, Halleck, and Margaret Mead offer a broader multifactorial framework involving psychosocial, anthropological, transcultural and existential parameters. As Keniston has written, "the dissent and non-conformity of young people in America and abroad is difficult to explain with conventional psychological concepts" and "the restiveness of the best-educated generation in American history . . . is not easily captured with psychiatric diagnosis."

The area of social development of contemporary youth is far too complex, not to say bewildering, for me to do anything more than touch on a few themes *en passant*. The social scientist J.M. Thompson of the Western Interstate Commission for Higher Education provides some perspective on the socio-historical matrix within which today's youth finds itself enmeshed; Thompson has written as follows: "Today's . . . younger generation as a whole is the effect of recognizable and familiar causes . . . (which) would include the following: (1) The Nuremberg Trials have had the effect by now of implanting in the conscience of individual men the axiom that one's allegiance is to humanity before it is to systems and that systems do not provide justification for an individual act against humanity. (2) The exploration of the landscape of deprivation, poverty, despair, and inequality has been so thorough and so well communicated that, to sensitive youth, wealth is no longer possible as a transcendental goal. (3) A new objectivism in public school curricula has given youth a skeptical mind which he has turned on political, religious, social and economic systems. (4) A world-wide communications network has made actual sensory data an instrument in forming concepts of the world and has thus rendered old abstractions, used for the same purpose, obsolete." Part of the communications network to which Thompson refers involves, of course, television, which has played an unprecedented—though poorly studied or understood—role in the total education of our youth. It has brought into the home a new source of authoritative opinions and facts which are often sharply in contrast with the ways in which parents and teachers, even national leaders, value and interpret society and history. As Marshal McLuhan has noted in his unique punning style: "The family circle has widened. The worldpool of information fathered by electric media . . . far surpasses any possible influence mom and dad can now bring to bear. Character no longer is shaped by only two earnest, fumbling experts. Now all the world's a stage."

Particularly significant to present-day youth is the difficulty they experience in forming an identity, when so many alternatives and options are offered without clear guidelines as to how to choose and achieve goals, especially in a society in perennial rapid transition. In this, of course, they share the confusion of adults, faced as we all are with a speed of change which, as Kahn and Wiener of the Hudson Institute note, "has reduced the reliability of practical experience as a guide to public policy and has diminshed the usefulness of conventional judgment in dealing with social problems . . . Policy makers in many fields, given so much new information to assimilate, so many new variables to assess, and so little experience directly relevant to new problems, can no longer be as confident of the applicability of traditional wisdom—and can no longer rely as much on the intuitively derived judgments that once seemed so adequate to resolve issues and to achieve fairly well-understood social goals." Add to these observations the recent social commentaries of Jean-Jacques Servan-Schreiber, Alvin Toffler and Dennis Meadows and it is not too difficult to comprehend why a good number of our young, particularly if their earlier life experiences have not afforded them the rather phenomenal personality elasticity which our technological society seems increasingly to demand, retreat into various group or individual manifestations of alienation, be it the drug subculture or various forms of educational and social withdrawal. Those young people who experience the present as uncontrolled and the future as virtually unpredictable, can hardly be expected to agree with the late Maurice Chevalier that: "growing old isn't so bad when you consider the alternative"; they are more likely to embrace the philosophy: "if you're sailing on the Titanic you may as well go first class!" The very large numbers of distressed youth who sought help during the sixties for a multitude of problems, especially related to mental health and welfare, found our clinics poorly prepared and frankly reluctant to accept and assist them. Whether the presenting problem was drug misuse, venereal disease, unwanted pregnancies, or a host of mental health problems, youth found that their appearance, attitudes or arrogance were more likely to evoke from existing clinics moralizing rather than good management, theology rather than therapy. Most major medical organizations and associations in Canada have in recent years

admitted their failure to respond appropriately to (let alone anticipate) the health and welfare problems presented by youth, and
have initiated special efforts to remedy the situation; that we still
have not contrived the necessary approaches and facilities to an
adequate extent, despite improvements in many areas, caused the
Canadian Commission of Inquiry into the Non-Medical Use of
Drugs to comment in Volume I of its Final Report early in 1972:
"Few physicians can bring themselves either to give or to accept
advice on the handling of troubled young people today"; " . . . the
entire subject of psychotropic drugs has left the medical profession
divided, indecisive, and poorly prepared to deal with, or even
understand it. It is, in fact, the first large scale public health
problem in which medicine has not assumed a major leadership
role and which few individual physicians have faced squarely."
I would note, from my own reasonably broad knowledge of the
Canadian drug scene, that these comments about medicine in
general can not be seen as excluding psychiatrists and allied mental
health professionals. As you might well imagine, there were some
indignant and injured responses from official professional associations and from individuals—though the validity of such protests
may have been somewhat undermined when a non-official but
widely distributed publication called *The Medical Post* asked, in
an editorial written in response to the Commission's comments:
"Is society ready to have its family doctors devote more of their
time and energies to straightening out troubled youth at the
expense of 'legitimate' office visits or hospital care?"

As you know, largely in response to inappropriate attitudes on
the part of health professionals, but also as part of the conventionally unconventional disdain for established institutions, plus
fear of parental or police intervention, young people themselves
initiated the opening, in practically all cities and large towns in
North America, of "store-front" type youth clinics, staffed at the
front-line level by youth who were attuned to, and usually part of,
the alienated subculture; psychiatric and allied professional assistance was provided, usually on a voluntary basis, via a screening
and mollifying network of medical and other health students,
interns and residents. As the above-mentioned Canadian Commis-

sion (which includes Dr. Heinz Lehmann, a psychiatrist very prominent in the field of psychopharmacology), noted: "The very emergence of innovative services the major function of which is to act as mediators, moderators and translators between patient and therapist, is a dramatic indicator of how relatively inept and unresponsive the medical profession has been." Let me suggest, having kept in reasonably close touch with the U.S. drug scene, including membership in the American Psychiatric Association Task Force on Drug Abuse and the American Social Health Association Committee on Drug Dependence and Abuse, that the comments I have quoted from our Canadian Commission should not be thought of as applying only to those members of our professions who live above our common border.

The evolution of these innovative youth clinics, a major proportion of whose work has been in the mental health area, is outlined, ironically but probably appropriately, in the March 1972 issue of *Ramparts*. Many of you will be familiar with the difficulties which these dispensers of legitimate health care have faced—particularly in the early days of their existence; these clinics were subject to police and citizen harassment, delaying tactics from various governmental bodies, bureaucratic requirements which not infrequently smacked of frank discrimination, etc. Their financing has always been tenuous and inadequate, except in a few more enlightened areas of the continent. Interestingly, though in Canada the admitted extent of drug use in high-schools has tripled in the last two years or so, the initial major challenge for these youth clinics—medical complications of drug misuse—has dropped off markedly in the past year; the prime health problems now treated in most of our Canadian innovative youth clinics are venereal disease and frank psychiatric problems, not drugs. In fact, several centers designed specifically for the emergency management of youth drug crises have recently closed for want of clients. At the same time, young people with complications of drug misuse are now more willing to present themselves directly to the emergency or psychiatric departments of our general hospitals, the word having spread through their remarkable underground channels that certain hospitals at least have changed their attitudes and practices in relation to youth. In Montreal we have been advised by the Deputy Minister responsible for health and welfare matters in Quebec that doctors may treat minors for such pressing problems as drug reactions or V.D. without obtaining prior parental consent. This step, if it withstands testing in the courts, may engage many physicians who were previously reluctant to get involved with the health problems of minors because of possible legal consequences if the parents objected.

It is not my intention to discuss in any detail the techniques appropriate to work with youth; the basic approaches which are most effective and which youth finds acceptable have not changed during the recent turbulent years, no matter what the milieu in which one works with youth, and there is quite good literature available on the subject of the outpatient therapy of youth—notably the books "The Adolescent in Psychotherapy" by Don Holmes of the University of Michigan, and "The Fragile Alliance: An Orientation to the Outpatient Psychotherapy of the Adolescent" by John Meeks of the University of Texas. One will find, for example, that in working with dyssocial youth, whatever psychiatric label you give him or her, and no matter what the setting, the same phases or stages of therapy are encountered: 1. Engagement in therapy; 2. Testing of the therapeutic setting and of the therapist; 3. Inhibition of behavior, frequently accompanied by marked depression; 4. Consolidation of the therapeutic alliance; and 5. Development of neurotic defenses or attainment of health.

In closing, let me mention some of the miscalculations which I feel those of us who have been working with dissident or alienated youth over the past decade have made:

1. We have underestimated the extent to which dissident youth have been, as has always been classically true, testing limits and searching for reliable and appropriate controls—outer or inner.

2. We have underestimated the almost frantic search by youth for credible, accessible adult models who can serve as identity components, should the young person decide to dip his foot into the future to test the temperature.

3. We have not sufficiently appreciated just how much the group phenomena of contemporary youth have been a parody or carica-

ture of many of the central dilemmas faced by our total society, and how often the solutions attempted by youth might serve as starting points for consideration of the alternative—approaches we will have increasingly to devise for social problems—just let me note in passing some of the similarities between youth clinics, with their community orientation and use of indigenous or detached workers, and the models we are now being offered for the development of general community mental health clinics.

4. Finally, we have sometimes over-identified with youth—perhaps because we have been beguiled by the combination of charm, flair, artistry, vulgarity and exaggeration with which youth coats its caricatures of the modern dilemmas of society—as Aristotle said of youth, "all their mistakes arise from the fact that they exaggerate everything they do and that they do it with passion."

Paul D. Steinhauer, M.D.

Abruptio Familiae: the Premature Separation of the Family

I suspect that many of you who work extensively with teenagers are as impressed as I am by the number of middle and even early adolescents who are abruptly splitting off from their families and deciding to make it on their own. Historically speaking, what is unique about this is not the age at which they are leaving home: only a few short generations ago, it was understood that our parents and grandparents would leave their families at approximately the same age because of financial pressures. They had to seek work, to support themselves, to contribute to the support of their families. This is not the case for most of today's middle-class teenagers who choose to take off. Their families are able and willing to support them. Indeed, they frequently exert considerable pressure on their teenager to remain at home and stay in school. But still they leave, and in a manner that is often traumatic to them and disruptive to their families.

The stated reasons teenagers present for leaving home despite parental opposition may vary considerably. To some the decision to leave home is seen as merely the final step in an emotional estrangement that has in effect existed for years. To others it seems the only escape from parents who are seen as hostile, lacking in understanding, insatiable in their demands for control and unable to tolerate any spark of developing independence. Still others present their unilateral decision to split as a positive and necessary step towards maturity and independence that their well-intentioned but over-anxious parents cannot seem to understand or appreciate. In all of these, there may be more than a germ of truth.

Now I'm not suggesting that all teenagers should live out their lives in the bosom of their families. The teenager's achievement of independence and his family's acceptance of his autonomy are among the major developmental tasks of adolescence. The adolescent's move towards greater freedom of thought and action will generate tensions which may strain considerably even the best of family relationships. But some teenagers seek to abort these tensions by physically splitting off from their families, leaving the conflicts between their parents and themselves unresolved. It is as if they sought to achieve independence through physical separation, as if by moving out they could escape from the introjects of their parents. But mere physical separation will not ensure and may even hinder the resolution of these conflicts, a resolution essential to the attainment of true independence and maturity. The proof that their attempt to achieve independence through physical separation is premature is to be found in their need to continue the struggle with their parents or to totally reject them and all they stand for. In contrast, the adolescent who is emotionally ready for separation can tolerate a comfortable and at times even close relationship with his family without needlessly having to defend his autonomy through avoidance or endless battling.

The normal process of individuation, of achieving emotional independence, does not begin in adolescence. The infant, as we all know, is helpless and totally dependent on his mother. As the child grows older, his ability to do things for himself increases. He learns to feed himself, to ask for what he wants, to play, to walk. He becomes more able to exist apart from his mother. Nursery school, school and his increased involvement with his peers normally lead to a decreased reliance on the parents. The more a child has been allowed to assume responsibility and to function independently prior to adolescence, the greater his chances of establishing full and comfortable emotional independence during his adolescent years. Generally speaking, we in America begin stressing and training for independence early, but we grant *real* independence relatively late. Putting it another way, we go through the motions of encouraging independence, but then balk or panic if the teenager looks as if he thinks we mean it.

Both teenagers and their parents have mixed feelings and may vacillate as the adolescent gradually moves towards greater independence. In many cases these will be successfully resolved, not without some anxiety and struggle on the part of both parent and teenager, but without major disruption of family relationships or of the teenager's continued progress towards maturity. Many teenagers want to have their cake and eat it too. They want to be independent, but aren't ready to give up the protection, the comforts and the security of home and family. They can't admit to themselves that they still need their parents: to do so they would see as an admission of intolerable weakness at a time when strength and independence are valued above all else. They attempt to handle this contradiction by externalizing what is basically an internal struggle. Thus instead of recognizing that their conflict is between two opposing and incompatible inner drives—the drive to cut loose and the need to remain protected and secure—they externalize the conflict and see themslves as struggling to escape the clutches of a dominating parent. They provoke repeated battles, the aim of which is to keep the parents at a distance and reassure themselves that they really are independent after all. They may use continued reliance on ther parents as a defense against recognizing their own difficulties (i.e., it's only their bugging that keeps me from doing well at school, etc.).

But parents too, often have difficulty as their teenager struggles to establish himself as a separate individual. For another of the tasks of adolescence is the teenager's development of his own personal value system. Whereas once his parents were the absolute authority on what was right and wrong, now some or even all of the values they propose—and even practice—are examined and rejected. Now this displacement of the parents from their earlier position of absolute authority on what is right/acceptable is an indispensible part of establishing oneself as a whole and separate person. But some parents cannot tolerate this, and their reactions may merely intensify their teenager's need to devalue them and to repudiate their standards as he struggles to establish and assert his autonomy. They may find his increased self-assertion, his different moral standards (sex, drugs), his at times seemingly self-defeating or self-destructive behavior both frightening and upsetting. Rather than respond to these as a part of the normal process of maturation, they may interpret any deviation from their traditional values as a rejection of them.

There's no denying that communication—and therefore the channel for identification and resolution of conflicts—between teenagers and their parents can, under the best circumstances, be seriously strained. The ability to listen and to be objective under pressure requires a degree of emotional detachment that rarely exists between teenagers and their parents. Their struggles with each other may be open, or may be carried on covertly beyond even the awareness of the participants themselves. But while the struggle can be hidden, it cannot be avoided. They struggle to live in peace with feelings stirred up but never resolved throughout a lifetime of intimate contact with one another. They struggle to come to grips with their love, their hate, their need to hurt, the pain of being hurt, their fear, their sex, their need to establish control over themselves and each other, their drive to cut loose and their desire to remain dependent and secure. These struggles frequently create intense anxiety in both teenagers and parents, and what starts primarily as a struggle to master their own feelings often is transformed into a battle across the line between the generations. It is precisely this struggle that some teenagers—with disastrous results—seek to abort by their announcement that the time has come to split.

But while the normal process of individuation may be expected to stir up some degree of tension in both adolescents and their families, a number of features typical of today's society seem likely to aggravate these basic tensions and to increase the tendency to turn to premature separation as a potential—though misguided—solution.

We are living in an era of rapid change. As has been pointed out by authors ranging from Paul Tillich to Alvin Toffler, the greater the rate of change within a society, the greater the degree of uncertainty, confusion and existential anxiety produced within that culture. The parent of today, like Sholem Aleichem's fiddler on the roof, strives desperately to strike a precarious balance between the security inherent in an acceptance of traditional values and the almost unavoidable uncertainty as to how relevant these are to the world of today. How do we meet a changing world's ever-accelerating demand for adaptation and yet retain our identity and our integrity? Is there even any point trying to keep our bearings or should we, like Kafke and Sartre, merely concede that the world is absurd, and that all one can hope is to learn to come to grips with its insurmountable absurdity.

Yet at the same time that we parents are questioning what we really believe, we are faced with the emergence of a powerful, youth-oriented counter-culture which challenges many of the attitudes and values we once considered axiomatic. In place of the puritan ethic we have Abbie Hoffman declaring that work is the only dirty four letter word in the English language. Formal education, our sexual mores, our emphasis on self-reliance and planning for the future have all very much come under the gun. Much that is being questioned has badly needed challenging for a long time, but I am concerned that the pendulum has swung so far that we are in danger of replacing one set of questionable credoes and hypocrisies with another. Take, for example, the slogan "Do your own thing." This is understandable as a reaction to decades of forced, often meaningless conformity and as an assertion of the individual's determination to remain an individual in a computerized and impersonal society. That same phrase, I suggest, is being perverted by some to glorify hedonism, egotism and narcissism for their own sake. What happens to man's relationship to man—what is the future of society itself—if we all merely do our own thing without any sense of responsibility or commitment to our fellow-man? The frantic, compulsive search for constant and effortless personal gratification in which the pursuit of pleasure, regardless of how it's obtained, becomes an end in itself is by no means confined to youth. But a generation of kids brought up on a diet of constant gratification sees frustration not as an inevitable part of life—which it is—but as an evil that always can and always should be avoided. Shades of the pleasure principle!

Many kids, on hearing this, would respond, "Who the hell are you to question my right to opt out of the rat-race? We have just as much right to our life-style as you have to yours." If I could be sure that the person speaking had a true choice, I would totally agree with him. But by true choice I mean that I would want to be sure that he was both intellectually and emotionally capable of producing, but that he chose not to in conventional terms. Many kids who vigorously insist that in opting out they are voluntarily choosing a particular life-style are really copping out. They think they're making a choice, but actually they're neurotically unable to stick with any situation or relationship involving sustained effort and containing the possibility of failure or pain. So they pull out, covering their tracks with a "who-needs-it" attitude.

Finally, there's the widespread abuse of the concept of the generation gap. The term generation gap implies that conflict between the generations is not only inevitable—which it is—but that it is by definition insoluble, which it definitely is not. This provides a readily available, socially acceptable cop-out for both rebellious and immature teenagers and wishy-washy or uninvolved parents. In view of all these socially sanctioned rationalizations for avoiding the painful resolution of family tensions, and in view of the increased and more attractive alternatives available to the teenager of today who decides to split (communes, student welfare, etc.) is it any wonder that premature separation is being turned to increasingly as an alternative to hanging in and working through the tensions involved in the struggle towards individuation?

This brings us to the question of how we, as clinicians, deal with families where an adolescent either has or is threatening to leave home at a time or in a manner that seems premature or inappropriate. We may be approached by the parents of an adolescent who already has one foot out the door, or by a teenager who has been living away from home for some time and has recently decided to seek help for reasons of his own. In either case we may be under considerable pressure from the parents (to persuade the teenager to return or remain at home) or from the adolescent (to agree with him or convince his parents that by moving out he did the best possible thing). While time limitations make it impossible to discuss in any depth the complexities and individual variations that occur in dealing with these similar yet still unique situations, certain basic principles apply. These arise largely out of clinical experience, but are derived from an understanding and application of the principles discussed above. At first glance, they seem so obvious that one might wonder why they need repeating. In actual fact, however, they are all too frequently ignored, at times with results that verge on the disastrous.

1. Our greatest chance of helping both teenager and family at such a point of crisis lies in our potential for objectivity and non-alignment. At a point where successful communication between parent and child has broken down so that the identification and resolution of family conflicts has ground to a halt in the face of widespread mistrust, denial, projection, acting-out and distortion, we as therapists may be able to straddle the generation gap, making ourselves available to both teenagers and parents as concerned but impartial listeners able to understand and reflect back what we hear, committed to clarifying issues rather than imposing solutions. Our understanding of some of the underlying intrapsychic, familial and social factors deep to the stated sources of tension may do much to help us identify first for ourselves and then for the family the real origins of their tension and distress, which once located, may be accessible to successful resolution.

2. Except in those rare cases where there is a clear and definite reason why the decision should be made by the therapist (e.g. a suicidal or severely psychotic adolescent) the decision of who lives where should remain that of the family, despite the frequent attempts of family members to push the responsibility onto the therapist. In some cases the therapist may legitimately be in a position to help evaluate or advise regarding various alternatives. If so, he can of course do so, but unless there is a definite therapeutic

reason for choosing a particular alternative, the decision should remain that of the family.

3. As therapists, it is our job to bring out and clarify issues, to identify areas of conflict within the family and to explore potential alternative solutions. In the course of doing so, a proposed physical separation may be avoided. But keeping the bodies together must never become our prime focus. More important is the task of doing what we can to free the teenager and his family to get on with the process of maturation, to resolve their internal conflicts and, if they are willing, to work on resolving their conflicts with each other. These can be worked on whether or not the adolescent leaves home. Independence and maturity are not necessarily gained nor need the bonds of concern and affection be permanently severed by even a premature and ill-advised separation. To assume that since a physical separation has occurred there is nothing more we can do is an error of the greatest magnitude. In some cases, we may be able to be considerably more helpful to both teenager and parents after an ill-advised and premature separation than we could before.

We must resist all pressures to manipulate, to coerce or to support pathological defenses. We do as much of a disservice by an inappropriate referral to a treatment center in response to parental pressures as we do in agreeing with a 15 year old girl from the inner city that life can be beautiful if she just drops out of everything and homesteads it in Alaska with her 16 year old boyfriend, her puppy and a year's supply of hash.

5. Be aware and beware of your countertransference, and particularly your need to be omnipotent. The potential for overidentification with either the adolescent or his distraught parents must always be guarded against.

Sherrill A. Conna, M.D.

Ecology and Mental Health

All matters pertaining to the survival and well-being of humanity are our appropriate concern, and to the extent that such matters involve human behavior, they are our particular concern, and responsibility. Ecology, derived from the Greek word, *oikos,* meaning home, is that division of biology which treats of the relations between organisms and their environment. Depending on the level of organization being considered, one may think of external ecology, which deals with the total organism and its environment, or internal ecology, which deals with any complexity down to individual cells and their environment. The term "spaceship earth" is not metaphorical—it is descriptive of fact.

Internal ecology has been part of the concern of biochemistry. External ecology, that referred to as being in crisis, has come to our awareness because of pressures of industrialization and population. Opinions vary from, "It's too late already," to, "There is no problem." That obviously means the situation is not well understood and reflects opinion without sufficient data, and means, at least, that we should take heed.

The crisis or impending crisis, can be seen as the ultimate assertion of reality principle. We either learn the laws of nature and how to live with them, or we seriously damage ourselves and our progeny, and ultimately we perish. There may be a great opportunity here—we recognize the imposition of reality as fostering growth. If the demand does not exceed the capacity of the ego to rise to the occasion and master the situation, the demand results in growth.

In the last few years, hundreds of environmental action groups have formed throughout the country, disseminating information, working for recycling of materials, seeking to influence government at various levels. The Environmental Protection Agency at the federal level, sets standards and has certain emergency powers. The automobile industry has deadlines for reducing exhaust pollution drastically. Industry is cleaning up. Efforts at correction of grossly inadequate sewage treatment are being made, including consideration of other than water and plumbing for disposal of human wastes. The Environmental Quotient, an annual assessment made by the National Wildlife Federation for each of the past three years, reflects little improvement but much increase in awareness, and deceleration in the rate of pollution. These facts suggest that progress is being made, so this paper happily is not the prophecy of doom that I thought it might necessarily turn out to be.

That is not to suggest optimism, however. Improving the quality of our environment, whether or not in a crisis stage, depends on the degree of cooperation by everyone. It is germane, therefore, to consider factors which contribute to the difficulties in getting cooperation, and perhaps suggest some partial solutions.

Western culture's emphasis on individuation and its sophisticated technological development foster the attitude that mastery and control of nature are virtues, or givens. Eastern tradition has emphasized man's continuity with nature and the necessity of establishing harmonious relations with nature. Nations and cultures seem to have developmental stages, as do individuals, and arrogance toward the environment smacks of grandiosity and feelings of omnipotence, at worst, and of overcompensation for feelings of inadequacy, or ignorance, at best. In individuals we call these things psychopathology, (except for ignorance). To the degree it's a cultural norm, I think we must admit the presence of many individuals with that psychopathology, giving each other a group concensus. Individual development, self realization, self fulfillment, are excellent humanistic values, if not carried to the absurd extreme of disregarding the rest of the world—whether other political groups, other races, the environment, or whatever. Individuation is important because it makes possible social relations. To keep it in perspective, the most gratifying human experiences may be described as temporary ego fusions between individuals—e. g., ideational, emotional, sexual—which calls first for one's being an *individual*. In short, the ego attitudes of intimacy and generativity, in Erikson's sixth and seventh stages, involve highly social activity in a giving way, as compared to the first stage, that of basic trust, which is highly social in a receiving way, and the next four (autonomy, initiative, industry, identity) which are more matters of one's development of himself as an individual. Too much of our western culture is hung up in stages two to four. Such opinions as we must develop an SST because other nations have it, and we must preserve our prestige; or we will win the Viet Nam war even though it is rotten and we should never have gotten in it, reflect such hangups.

Possibly the ecological situation will force us to grow up—to develop the level of object relations characterized by more cooperation and less competition, both with people and with the material world, and possibly that could lead to understanding and cooperative efforts between western and eastern cultures. It is sheer nonsense to engage in competitive games, fearing destruction by each other, while we destroy ourselves with pollution from the waste of our games! The ecological crisis should help us to realize that, truly, the enemy is within each of us.

We have other difficulties in hearing the message. The existence of the bomb causes us to use a psychic mechanism to deal with the threat of annihilation. The mechanism is often denial of the possibility, or isolation of affect associated with such a possibility, such that little effective work is done to reduce that possibility. We are affectively blunted to thoughts of annihilation.

The bomb also fosters an attitude of pessimism and feelings of futility about the future, to which ecology pertains.

Our educative efforts must engender hope and must suggest concrete tangible action for correcting the ecological situation. Hopelessness breeds total denial, not constructive action.

Sound ecological practices should be made economically sensible. There should be tax advantages to such practices. Rather than emphasize the cost of cleanup, the emphasis should be placed on what is saved by living more sensibly, with less passive consumption.

The fact of our being in ecological trouble today, and that obviously meaning we are not living right, lends great credence to the various liberation movements now ongoing. These movements are healthy to the extent that the truly oppressed are seeking liberation. What greater oppression can there be of young people than to destroy their world. As advocates of humanity, we must use our expertise in the service of humanity, both in direct work with people, where we seek to aid them in achieving freedom from tyranny from within, and in promoting humanistic decisions at policy making levels in the hope of decreasing tyranny from without.

Discussion of Youth Symposium

Unwin: We must remember that there is as much drug misuse among adults as there is among children and youth. Any Commission designed to study one certainly ought to study the other. Our society is, indeed, a drug society, but our profession has taken rather a cavalier attitude toward most of the use and abuse of the psychoactive drugs. In one study at UCLA, there were many more admissions of students to the health unit for having used an excess of Nytol and Sominex than for the use of marijuana and LSD. A reliable study in Canada indicates that the over-20 population uses marijuana to a far greater extent than the under-20 population.

Of course, the number one problem of drug misuse is alcohol. In 1968, some 46-68% of high school students admitted to at least weekly use of alcohol. Jellinek said that at least a third of the alcoholics in North America begin their drinking habits between the ages of 14 and 18. Yet alcohol is excused as socially acceptable, and its users unstigmatized in comparison to those using other things. This despite the fact that each year, some 300,000 people die from either the acute or chronic effects of alcohol.

Question: The use of various medications by adults has been minimized by many as a contributory cause of drug-use by young people. There seem to be many other possible etiological factors cited in the literature of far greater significance .The parent-drug-use-factor is considered an easy mark, but spurious.

Unwin: Certainly there are other things. But I cannot minimize the role of drug-use by adults. Take it the other way around. Young people often give us the chance to look at ourselves. The mirror may magnify our blemishes, but they're there nonetheless. Their identification with us is, of course, unconscious, but we are more significant models than we realize. Basic research has shown that the children of parents who use drugs are more likely to use drugs than are others. If a mother takes tranquilizers daily, her child is three times more likely to use marijuana, five times more likely to sniff glue, and eight times more likely to shoot heroin. The parental model and the response of youth seems incontrovertible. There is a need for more credible adult models.

Question: I wonder if Dr. Unwin can attempt a definition of the intrapsychic or psychological issues in drug abuse.

Unwin: There was a cigarette advertisement showing a very elegant woman coming down an equally elegant marble staircase, and saying to an aristocratic gentleman, "I smoke them because I like them." This is exactly what a great number of young people will say about their use of marijuana. There are, of course, numerous other reasons for using any of the drugs—more than can be outlined, and ranging from peer pressure to the need to respond to such pressure because of internal demands. Where self-esteem is at stake, the dynamics are varied. Certainly those who have to anesthetize themselves are in much more psychological trouble than others.

Question: I'm not sure that there is anything terribly wrong with the use of drugs among young people, who may need them in order to cope with the world more easily. After all, is there much difference between them and the person who is given chemotherapy by a psychiatrist, and who has just as sufficient ego strength to cope with *his* world if it could be put to work?

Unwin: Fair enough. That's all right if you want simply to use a mental health model. But it doesn't bring in any social, historical, or existential parameters. I'm convinced that a person who has one joint of strong Jamaican grass per month is not in any danger. But what does bother me is the question of whether a 13 or 14 year old can judge what harm these can do. Obviously the same things apply to adults, and perhaps it is condescending to impugn the judgement of the young. But I confess it still bothers me. It is, indeed, a problem when, at an early age, a character is being molded with the built-in attitude that even the *everyday* problems of living need to be escaped from. The parent who comes home at night and says, "For God's sake, Martha, mix me a martini, quick! I've had a terrible day," is establishing an attitude of escape in his observant child. Chemicals are seen to make life "happier."

Steinhauer: I would like to second these thoughts. Not only do parents bear the blame, however. The media, of course, are culpable as well. And not only in relation to the use of drugs. The attitude of immediate gratification is pervasive. "You can take that trip now if you use that ubiquitous credit card." "Don't wait to buy that car—Our terms are the best in the country." This orientation toward immediate acquisition of pleasures cannot help but mold an attitude among young people which leads, in turn, to experiencing presumed pleasures in the here and now. Conversely, there is not the drive to put things off in favor of sound preparation.

The tendency to break away from the exigencies of living is a universal one. The use of drugs is but one way of "copping out." Adults also find ways (perhaps more socially acceptable) of retreating. But there is, of course, the possibility of facing life, and making a successful adaptation to it.

Essential first is facing the difficulties of living and avoiding the mechanisms of denial. And second, to borrow from Paul Tillich, is to "take it into the self," to have "the courage to be," and deal with life by doing what has to be done. There are all sorts of escapes—economical, psychological, chemical, and social. Reality certainly can't always be pleasant. But we can gain knowledge, a facility at coping, and, indeed, pleasure, by confronting reality successfully. Most pathetic are those who protect themselves from anxiety by restricting their lives. By avoiding any situation that might be painful or anxious, they may, indeed, make themselves very comfortable, but they restrict growth, fulfillment, and transcendance.

Question: In all the presentations, one theme appears as a thread—that youth reflects problems which exist in our culture. For instance, there seems to be a rejection of materialism by youth. There are reasons, of course, and partly it arises from a marvelous idealism. But there is danger in its complete rejection. And we professionals have a role to play in helping them to adjust to the conflict and its meaning to them. But there are insidious forces that *are* cultural and that are bad, from any point of view, and I feel impotent to do anything about them.

Conna: Kids do look at materialism cynically, but they also look at it somewhat objectively. It's not the carrot it once was. They are not as success-oriented as they once were. Nor, in fact, should they be. After all, there are some changes taking place, among which is the fact there is likely to be considerable more leisure time in their generation than there was in ours. The culture is in a state of constant change.

Obviously our effectiveness in dealing with youth is not going to be dependent one little bit on our capability in changing the culture. In that sense, both you and I have a right to feel frustrated and impotent. Culture is too big for any of us to handle. But we might feel better by doing what we can do (and doing it well), within our own sphere of influence, with the hope that if enough people do the same, there may be some impact on the overall culture.

Steinhauer: Materialism does not necessarily have to be looked upon as a bad thing. It has had its place in cultural evolution, and may still be useful to some, as well as problematical to others. In the pioneer orientation, success consisted of turning painful experiences into pleasurable ones by successful acquisitions. On one side, turning pain into pleasure could be called "masochistic," whereas on the other side, it may be termed a valuable "work ethic." For many people, having things may be partly productive, since it could cause them to be more human than they would otherwise be. Unfortunately, many individuals are sterile, and are not able to do anything with their newfound possessions. The media appeal to that part which has to do with the consumption of goods, rather than to the use of the goods for personally productive ends.

Erich Fromm has described two therapeutic goals: 1) to help the individual adjust to the society he finds himself in, and 2) to find self-realization. Of course self-realization may include developing feelings which will enable him to change society in the direction of greater humanism. My approach, consciously or unconsciously, is to focus on one or the other, depending upon how disturbed his function is within the society.

Question: There has been a lot of blame placing concerning youth and its problems. Society, parents, educators, each, in turn, has been focused in on as the causation of young peoples' ills. This bothers me. When does the youth himself bear the responsibility for his own difficulty?

Unwin: Somewhere, kids have to get the confidence that life is worth going on with. It's then that they can assume some real role of responsibility for themselves. But the responsibility for their difficulties before and after has to be divided, depending upon the perspective from which you see the concept of responsibility. Certainly they have to take the consequences for their delinquencies. But if responsibility implies something of the causative factors in causing them to be delinquent, then there are a multitude of determinants. In the long run, it is they who carry the ultimate responsibility for their lives. Influences among the youth culture itself are important to name as etiological features. And let's not forget that the youth culture itself is changing considerably, even now. After all, even Abbie Hoffman has been advocating getting out the vote. Eldridge Cleaver has departed from the old militancy of the Black Panthers. Timothy O'Leary has become an object of ridicule and pity. Even though the influences upon today's young people may well be different ones, and Hoffman, Cleaver, and O'Leary are the idols of another generation, there is no question that this bunch of youth *is* somewhat straighter than the last.

Young people are advocating specific social and environmental reforms, rather than projecting abstractions such as cynicism, criticisms, and conjectures of hypocrisy and relevance. They're pushing for legal reforms, congressional action. The biggest worry I have is whether this new activism is in time to overturn such problems as pollution.

Conna: The issue of responsibility isn't something that hinges on what happens in the adolescence and young adulthood of an individual. Nor is there a special force applicable during this period by which we can change irresponsibility to responsibility. The capacity to live one's life responsibly derives, actually, from his process of feeling, rather than his intellectual capability. The person who has had a fairly good first year of life has the foundation for relating to other people, and finds it gratifying to do so. He sees it as much more fun than being alone. He also develops and nurtures his ability to empathize. I dare say that the reason we start taking the responsibility for, say, our own toilet training, is not only the joy of self-mastery, but also that it pleases mommy. We have some rudimentary ability to identify with her.

Thus early experience in object relations, including the ability to empathize, is primary. If that's there, there is the capability for taking responsibility. Conversely, if there is no possibility of his taking responsibility, it is probably because he has never been able to *feel* responsible. The extreme of this is psychopathy, and there's no dealing with it intellectually. Fortunately most irresponsible people are not psychopaths. What I might have to do is present a relationship to him for awhile without any demands at all, so that he might feel cared for unconditionally. After an indeterminate time, he may be able to respond to demands with some degree of responsibility. That's what therapy is, in the long run, anyway.

Steinhauer: There are two issues that come up frequently enough in psychotherapy of young people that I think might be worth speaking about, since they revolve around the question of responsibility.

First, adolescents are great crusaders. They will rail against the inequities of the school system, or the hypocrisy in the political arena, and, in self-righteous fashion, use it as the rationale for a retreat from learning or an apathy about political action. He will similarly retire from family responsibilities because of his cynicism concerning the family system. Because we have our own personal investment in education, politics, or family, we might get seduced into feeling that the way to cope therapeutically with this problem of irresponsibility in the young person is to find perfect arguments against his arguments, and we might therefore engage in a debate that is worse than useless. He's been into this too many times with teachers and parents. We really play into his defenses when we do this, and we divert him from his more central tasks.

Second, either overtly or covertly, we are asked, by him or his parents to take over some of his ego functions, on the grounds that he can't handle these things himself, and needs us. There is a tendency, among therapists, to fall into that trap too easily. We must never forget that by doing so, we prevent him from learning certain things about the very responsibility he's asking us to assume for him. For it is by the absolute necessity of his taking over for himself that he will learn it and grow by it.

Also, by taking over for him, we are giving him a nonverbal message that we judge him to be incompetent to do the task by himself, or that he is too weak to take the responsibility for his life and errors. We can easily be seduced into taking this attitude, which, in the long run, turns out to be condescending. By so doing, we may very well perpetuate a self-perception that maintains pathology.

Question: In the course of this discussion it has appeared to me that the problems of youth have a universality that transcends local cultural patterns. Geographic location, political issues, national and international struggles, economic factors, all seem secondary. The difficulties among youth in Canada are evidently similar to those on a college campus in the United States. I wonder whether there are, indeed, differences in the youths seen in the clinical settings in the States and those in Canada.

Unwin: In general, I dare say that the problems are not unique in any specific cultural setting. There may be a little less extremism among youth in Canada, though I don't know whether that's a vice or a virtue. However there is less and less nationalism among the young, what with the world-wide network of communications and travel. Internationalism is much more the key word. If one were to meet kids from the universities in Australia, Costa Rica, Montreal, or Madrid, there would be no avoiding the similarities in their mode of functioning. It is McLuhan's "global village."

America has turned out to be the whipping boy. It is America which has the problems—America which is causing world difficulties. Actually it is not at all America, but technological societies all over which are in truth duplicating exactly what is true in each. Drug misuse is found in any industrialized and post-industrialized nation. The United States is focused upon because it is the cutting edge of the technology of the future. Other countries scapegoat America as a defense against recognizing the truth about themselves, much as the Italians termed syphilis the "French disease," and the French termed it the "German disease," etc., etc.

One word about "radical youth." Many people equate radicalism with violence. This may partly be appropriate, for it is the radical who embraces violence as a possibility. At times it is hard to argue *against* violence, even though we don't really like it. After all, it was through violence that many good people gained their ends, the American Revolutionaries included, not to mention the IRA, who were able to destroy the parliament of Ulster, or even the civil rights workers in the U.S. who did a most effective job, at times through violence or its threat. Certainly the administrations of many leading colleges were overthrown by student radicalism. Keniston found radical youth the healthy ones, whereas he termed the alienated youth the depressed and withdrawn ones.

It was Justice Douglas who indicated that youth become more palatable when we term them the "Loyal Opposition," as in Britain, where that group exists side by side with the party in power, respected as a viable group, but whose function is to afford a critical attitude toward the ruling people, causing the government to validate and justify its actions. Though often the young people appear something of a caricature of themselves, it would be well to examine the issue and see whether their exaggerated view isn't concerning an issue that identifies something significant in our society which we ought to attend to. As the "loyal opposition," we can look upon them as having significant communications for us, and we'd better heed the message.

Conna: I would like to go back to Dr. Steinhauer's comments on the danger of the therapist's taking over for the patient. There are, obviously, times when he must take over, when it is certain that the patient has not the potential for doing so himself. Indeed, as was pointed out, there is a tendency, however, to take over more than is necessary, as well. The best example of this is the potential suicide. To hospitalize all who threaten to kill themselves would be to do something anti-therapeutic 999 times out of a thousand. So skills are developed to catch that one out of the thousand for whom hospitalization is indicated. But in doing so, there are another ten, with whom the question is equivocal, and mistakes may be made. So there are errors in either direction.

As for the question of differences from one country to another, I do feel that there are certainly some significant ones. But it is not so much the national boundaries that make the difference, as it is other elements in the sub-culture. I do know, for example, that there were many different kinds of problems coming into the clinic at Worcester, Mass., as contrasted with those in Durham, North Carolina. This, I think, derives from such seemingly unimportant variables as weather and climate, among others.

Question: Certainly some major shifts have been effected in the lives of young people through the introduction of "the pill," aside from the simple fact of contraception. I wonder if the panel would comment on that.

Conna: This, of course, is a big question with many ramifications. I'll only react to it by one route. Certainly in the psychological growth of any individual, developmental conflicts can be expressed through sexual behavior—call it sexual acting out. In some it can be the expression of dependent needs, in others, an expression of power, and in still others, a kind of masochism. Anything, at times, other than mutual caring. Now one problem with the new freedom is that there is no more repression. The pill has undercut that. As a result, we are slowly removing one of the "reality principle" elements which might have served people well as a vehicle with which to resolve problems. I don't know that I'm willing to go too much further with that point. However, it does seem germane to the question that this great arena of sexuality, for the expression of needs, may be unavailable to work out problems, and others may have to be put to use to a larger degree.

A Closing

Can a Dinosaur Be Taught to Evolve? Or the Absurdity of Trying To Steer an Octopus

Mathew Dumont, M.D.

As you know, there is nothing more arrogant or materialistic than a first year resident in psychiatry. As someone who is so recently a physician, the first year resident is now struggling with a whole new role model without all the paraphernalia and accoutrements he was barely comfortable with: the white coat, stethoscope, and all the rest. First year residents have a way of responding by sort of puffing themselves up and treating non-physicians with contempt, and by approaching their patients with the kind of Aesculapian arrogance that comes in pure culture. Erich Lindemann greeted us in the Herman room of the Bulfinch Building at the Massachusetts General. He was sort of wandering around the room waiting for people to settle down, and stopped for a minute at the window which was overlooking the West End, which at that time was being devastated by bulldozers. The community was being devastated, the homes were being devastated—the lives of people were being devastated—as we later found out. He shook his head sadly as he walked to the front of the table, continued to glance out the window, and said, "Gentlemen, it is a fiction that mental illness resides within the individual." Now that is the kind of thing that grabs first year residents by certain sensitive organs. It gets their attention and makes them think—some of them. Others close their minds.

During residency, I was also a career development fellow at the National Institute of Mental Health and had the opportunity of running around the country participating in a number of sessions with Dr. Stanley Yolles and Bert Brown, and others who were at that time planning the National Mental Health program and the Community Mental Health Center program. Intermittently I would come back after many of these discussions, rather excited, and I would say, "Erich, this is what you have been talking about. They're going to have geographically bounded communities. The Mental Health program in each of those communities is going to have total responsibility for all the mental health problems going on in those areas. There won't be any more buck passing. They're going to be forced to come to grips with all of the issues relating to mental health, all of them . . . "

Erich, being both pleased with my exhilaration and a little impatient with it at the same time, replied, "Look, carry on! I have a funny feeling that our colleagues will find a way of doing the same old thing despite the new rhetoric. I also distrust things that rely too heavily on the federal government. I'm a little concerned about all this talk about comprehensive plans and construction grants, and staffing grants, but carry on."

Well, now from the vantage point of watching what is probably the twilight of that "bold new approach," I've been thinking very carefully of what Erich said about it. You see, Erich really did not believe in bold, new approaches in community mental health. In fact, the whole community mental health movement, to the extent that it was ever a movement, probably should not have been so "bold," and should not have thought of itself as quite so "new" as it did. The paradigm that Erich conveyed about what Community Mental Health was all about was not unlike the kinds of things that Bob Bergman was talking about in his description of the Navajo. He had a paradigm of people taking care of people in a natural way—natural caretaking networks. A man walks along a road and sees a child tottering at the edge of a wall. His impulse, his natural impulse, is to take that child and put it to safety. He doesn't have to calculate whether the child is going to acknowledge his act or not. He doesn't require any reward systems. He doesn't require any planning. It is an instinctive, natural human act, perhaps the most human kind of act, to want to put a child to safety.

The kind of caretaking networks that Erich envisaged as what mental health is really all about was much closer to that feeling than it was, God help us, to the Erich Lindeman Mental Health Center. That building, a solemn, huge monument named after him with some kind of poetic injustice, is a bit of urban sculpture that nobody can understand or find their way in—a staircase that makes you limp as you walk up it—designed for confusion—designed to make you feel inadequate, inferior. That's not what Erich had in mind, obviously.

As a matter of fact, what Erich's conception of Mental Health's professionalism was all about was simply a kind of studied capacity, to heighten the relief to identify the parameters, to find the interfaces, natural caretaking networks. All the overblown, self important, somewhat exploitative aspects of Mental Health professionalism were really very foreign to all of this. It would have been very nice, actually, if we could have had the opportunity to play out this conception of Mental Health professionalism. It is a conception much more humble than arrogant, and really much more ancient than new. Not a bold new approach—but something much more relaxed. Something that would not have cost seven billion dollars as they envisaged the Community Mental Health Center program to cost when it reached fruition in the creation of 2,000 Mental Health Centers. It would have cost nothing—except a little humility. It would have been nice to play that out.

Unfortunately, and now I speak for myself and not Erich, some things happened that I think makes it no longer possible for us to have the luxury of playing out that model of Mental Health professionalism. You see, I think we have suddenly emerged with a very different kind of responsibility. I'll state it now and then come back to it. Bear with me if some of this seems a little disorganized and chaotic. These are first thoughts. I have come to the conclusion that there is one superordinate job for Mental Health professionals, and conceivably one superordinate job for all professionals, and that is to prevent fascism. I know that's an unhappy word to use, and frequently I lose audiences when I refer to it even obliquely, but I work quite deep in the heart of the beast. I work in the very Zen center of bureaucracy and have access to much of what power and bureaucracy is all about, which is information.

Now let me see if I can make myself sound less paranoid and alarmist to you. I think we've entered a very dangerous time in this country. Intermittently throughout our history we have taken sudden shifts to the right. This huge pluralistic system is very much like a big pan of water that we're trying to juggle between the refrigerator and the sink. The slightest tilt, because of its hugeness, because of the pluralism involved, the slightest shift in the center of gravity sets up momentous forces that are soon out of control. Approximately once every 20 or 25 years we become preoccupied with a state of mind that has to do with order, stability, propriety, economy, and enormous intolerance to deviant behavior, and a very unhappy capacity to find well-identified enemies of the social order which we have to persecute. This is not new. It has happened approximately every generation since our very earliest beginnings.

It's different this time. What is different is the size of the organizations and the systems that are mediating this state of mind. The enormous power of the technologies that are being brought to bear in its service are quantum jumps beyond what the history of the world has ever seen before. It is, by the way, a state of mind that sociologists talk about as "ressentiment." If you're interested in reading about it the best study is by a Danish sociologist named Ranulf in a book called *Moral Indignation and Middle Class Psychology*.

When I say the earliest roots of our country were steeped in this I was being quite literal. You might if you're interested in pursuing this also read Erickson's book, *Wayward Puritans,* to get a sense of what our country was like in its origins. Massachusetts was not always a free State. Erickson's book is about the first 60 years of the Massachusetts Bay Colony, during which there were three "crime waves," and three periods of ressentiment. In 1632, Massachusetts was a theocracy. The Governor, John Winthrop, was the chief minister. Ann Hutchinson, a respected woman of the time, had developed a kind of Wednesday evening salon. Here a group of intellectuals used to meet with her to discuss issues of theology, and there emerged around her meetings a very finely tuned theological argument with the established church. It was so finely tuned that we don't understand what it involves anymore despite endless tracts written about the Antinomians, as they were called. The reaction of a Massachusetts Bay colony in its first days—it wasn't more than a decade old—was to banish this group of people to the wilderness, virtually to perish. They actually went down to Providence, later to be joined by Roger Williams, and developed a whole new colony. But what is significant is that they felt it necessary to push these people out. As soon as this succeeded, the whole concern about the American movement died away and things quieted down for a few years.

Then in 1652 there was another upsurge of ressentiment focused on the Society of Friends. This was a somewhat larger group and the issue was not an ideological one—there weren't any actual theological differences between the Quakers and the established Church. If anything they were simply a purer culture of Puritan theology. The differences had to do with their life style. What was objectionable about the Quakers in 1652 interestingly was that they insisted on wearing their hair long; they insisted on wearing hats indoors; they tended to be nomadic—they didn't stay in any one community; and they had an unfortunate tendency to want to live communally—they were the hippies of their day.

The reaction of the Massachusetts Bay Colony was very interesting. Quakers were killed. They were dismembered. Their tongues were bored with hot irons; limbs were pulled off. They were burnt at the stake. They were hung. In fact, it took a letter from the King of England, Charles II, in 1661, to order the Massachusetts Bay Colony to stop torturing and killing Quakers. There is poetic justice here somewhere, that the King of England had to tell the primordial roots of American democracy that it must stop killing and persecuting deviant groups. Indeed, the respect for authority was sufficiently great that the persecution of the Quakers did stop in response to Charles II's letter. Again, things quieted down.

Then a generation later, (1696 this time), up in Salem, Massachusetts, some events occurred which perhaps you have heard about and read about. Three adolescent girls suddenly developed some hysterical behavior. They would suddenly fall on their hands and knees and start barking like dogs, a very strange bit of behavior in anyone's society. The one physician in Salem was called to administer to them, and he responded, after examining them, with characteristic Aesculapian humility by saying, "I can't tell you what this is and I have no way of fixing their behavior. It must come from the devil." Notice that if something is unusual, and if a doctor can't fix it, it is unnatural in its origin.

Unfortunately this comment was uttered within earshot of the young ladies, and fell on fertile ears. They immediately announced that indeed they were being harassed by witches. Who were the witches? They identified three women. One was a maid working in the home of one of the girls, a black woman from Barbados who carried with her some voodoo type thinking from the West Indies. She was one of the witches. Another one was a derelict old woman who used to wander around the streets of Salem with a pipe clenched in her teeth, muttering to herself. This was apparently only a schizophrenic, derelict old lady. She was another witch. And the third was a woman, of somewhat higher social standing, but a woman who, it was whispered about, had had a scandalous love affair the year before. She was the third witch. These three women were summoned before the magistrate of Salem, confronted with these three girls, who in their presence conveniently exhibited their strange bit of possessed behavior, and the three women were executed as witches.

Unfortunately things didn't stop. More people were implicated by these three adolescent girls. So that before a year had gone by, the State of Massachusetts had murdered 22 people because they were implicated as witches. It went far beyond Salem very quickly. Hundreds were in jail.

The only reason it stopped, incidentally, just about a year to the day after it began, was that the girls pointed an accusing finger at the president of Harvard College, and the chief magistrate thought that it was very unlikely that the president of Harvard was a witch.

Almost immediately there was a shudder of recognition among those in power that maybe they had all been taken in by some bit of foolishness. Of course eventually people were released from jail, and everybody felt a little shamefaced. The first 60 years of the Massachusetts Bay Colony: the Antinomians, the Quakers, the witches!

Erickson's point is that the country this came to be, needed to have a group of deviants every generation in order to find its own identity. We need deviants, because without them we don't know who we are. They are territorial markers of our own selfness. Be that as it may, the fact is that just about every generation, this country has gone slightly mad, and it has found some group of people:—Communists, Bolsheviks, the "Yellow Peril," the "foreign-pauper-insane," the "junkie,"—to be identified as public enemy number one. Each is labeled the worst threat the country has ever faced, and as Nixon recently said about the addict and drug abuse, "My attitude towards drugs is like my attitude towards foreign troops on our shores."

Before we laugh let's take another look at the shift once again toward rage and terror! What is our preoccupation with weeding out people who are enemies of society? There are current discussions, as you know, about mandatory life imprisonment. The death penalty is being legalized once again. Incidentally according to Ranulf, writing in 1938, the best indicator of ressentiment is attitudes toward the death penalty. Insistence on this punishment reflects that state of mind which says that there are people who are so outside of our realm of acceptance that they must be killed bureaucratically by the state. As you may know, attitudes in this country toward the death penalty have taken a dramatic shift in the last few months, and now once again a majority of the population is in favor of it, whereas in 1966 a majority were against it. The last time a majority was in favor of the death penalty was 1953, according to the Gallup Polls. 1953 was a bad year if you remember. McCarthy had the country by its throats, and everybody was living in a state of paranoia and terror about Communists. The Rosenbergs were killed.

Sixty-six was a very different year. We were still talking about doing something about racism and poverty. We had almost gotten over Kennedy's death. Robert was still with us. Martin Luther

King was still with us. The riots were not quite so bad as they later became, and the war hadn't loomed so large in our minds. We still felt some sense of faith—some of us—in our country. It's very different now.

If you do a kind of content analysis of Nixon's speeches or even better his wandering interviews—like the long one he had with the *Washington Star News* that was released after his election—you realize what we are going through. The two words that appear most consistently in his interviews are "strong" and "weak," and it's quite clear that they appear as moral distinctions. The President apparently believes that it is moral to be strong and immoral to be weak. Therefore he sees that the purpose of government is not to redress inequities of power or wealth because that would be rewarding weakness by assisting it. The purpose of government is in fact to maintain the moral distinction between the strong and the weak. That's why it is therefore moral to help Lockheed Aircraft when it has some difficulties, and yet to want to kick Welfare recipients off their doles. It's a moral distinction.

But as I indicated in the beginning, things are now different from what they used to be. I mean that now the capacity for ressentiment, for this intolerance to deviance, for this concern with order and stability and propriety, and along with our capacities to be repressive, have become enormously professionalized. I'm not thinking of the obvious things like no-knock entry, preventive detention, or even concern about the press. That's the sort of thing that everybody, even those with the most blunt liberal sensibility, can be upset about. I'm talking about much more subtle things, like for example the lowering of the distinction between treatment and social control. We are seeing this in terms of drug abuse control programs. Lost in the drama of Rockefeller's announcement of the need for mandatory life imprisonment, was a much more inconspicuous item involving the significant enhancement of the involuntary civil commitment codes of the New York State Narcotic Addiction Control Commission.

Involuntary civil commitment is an enormously more insidious instrument of social control than life imprisonment. In New York and in California, two states which have such codes, it is possible to act on the initiative of a neighbor or a friend, or relative, or cop. After a physician has determined that the person is drug dependent, or in California likely to become drug dependent, it is possible for that person to be sent away for up to six years without the adversarial protections of a criminal. You see you don't need due process when you talk about civil commitment. It is not a punishment: It is treatment. It is for the person's own good. I assume you know that the programs of the institutions run by the New York Narcotic Addiction Control Commission and the California Rehabilitation Center in Corona are really prisons. Although called treatment centers, they are preoccupied with security and custody.

But even that's pretty gross, and relatively unfinely tuned liberal. Civil liberation sensibilities are upset by that. It's gone far beyond. We are in the process now of seeing a Juggernaut of social science research, unleashed for the purpose of identifying problem behavior before it emerges. First it was the business of finding the "drug abuse prone" individual. That is the best example of what's going to go in the whole host of areas.

You may remember that a few years ago the President said that he had a communication from a physician friend of his, about the advisability or feasibility of having a program that would identify "delinquency prone" people by the age of six, and perhaps having some kind of early intervention at that point before they become actual delinquents. The doctor unfortunately added—and this upset a few people—if we can't somehow repair their defect, perhaps we should find some way of protecting ourselves from them, preventively. The fact that a physician trots out an idea like that is not significant. What is significant is that the President of the United States feels it is important enough to repeat—and in fact ask the secretary of HEW to pursue its feasibility. Not so much even as to whether they're going to do anything about it, but as an effort to see how much the public will tolerate this kind of thinking. I don't know how far they've gone with that particular program, but there is now a tremendous amount of research about the capacity to identify junkies pre-morbidly by actuarial data so that we'll know, based on the kind of person he is, and what kinds of groupings he belongs to, whether he is likely to be a junkie or not when he grows older.

A better example of that sort of thing unfortunately funded by the NIMH was an effort to identify "protest-prone" behavior in colleges during the time when we were worried about students and colleges. The American Council of Education was responsible for a grant where 30,000 incoming freshmen to 33 participating schools were given questionnaires. They weren't told what the questionnaires were about, and they were stupid questionnaires— (you see you don't have to be smart anymore in social science if you have the machines). They just asked a whole bunch of apparently irrelevant questions about their background, their religious orientation, their political beliefs, their drug behavior, and what have you. Two years later a sample of that cohort was interviewed in terms of what kinds of protest behavior they actually were involved in. Then the machines did a factor analysis. The computers doggedly picked out those questionnaire items that were related to protest behavior. The investigators had done a pilot project before this with a relatively small group, and from it had determined that a very high predictor of protest proneness in students was having a Jewish name, and saying "none" when asked about religion.

The purpose of this massive study was to be much more detailed and find out with much greater accuracy how you can predict the troublemaker before the trouble.

This incidentally speaks with the language of Public Health. Apparently, it is talking about early case finding and primary prevention. Actually it's neither. It's not primary prevention which is to try to do something about the social context of casehood. It's not really secondary prevention either because secondary prevention is trying to find a case early after it has emerged as a case to treat. It's really a kind of ultra-early case finding. It's something new—finding the deviant before he becomes deviant and intervening then.

I assume you know that it's getting difficult to get NIMH support to do social science, and in fact there are large numbers of social scientists, behavioral engineers, and electronic engineers who are out of work these days. They are being drawn by the sluices of grant controls to one good source of support of basic research: the Justice Department. There are many social scientists now doing their thing under grants from the Law Enforcement Assistance Administration, which is preoccupied with this business of social control in a very sophisticated way.

Much of this relies on data banks and computer systems and registries. Just yesterday I learned from a friend that every physician in New York is being asked by the State to identify any of his patients by name and social security number who are on drugs, and this shall be sent to a State-wide registry. There are efforts to launch a national registry with the idea of having a footprint identification system for every addict in the country. You may have heard about this. The powers that be stepped back after a little bit of flack, but they'll have something else soon. It is called the CODAP Program, a client oriented data acquisition process to keep track of addicts throughout the country, presumably protecting confidentiality all the while.

There are about 5,000 computers at work in the federal government sifting information all the time, many of these concerned, by the way, with deviance, with malcontents, political activities. I suspect myself and perhaps not a few of you share a micron of tape here and there. Seven million potential assassins are being monitored by the Secret Service all the time—seven million of us are considered potential assassins! The Pentagon had another system concerned with civil disobedience, remember, the so-called CONUS Program. We don't know how many people were being watched, but they included senators and governors. Interestingly the Governor of Massachusetts was one of the people who were thought potentially could be involved in civil disobedience.

The thing would be a little silly if in fact it were not so huge, and relentless, and sophisticated, and so blanched of malice, and so relying on people like ourselves.

One of the things you have to understand about bureaucracy is it has changed the nature of evil. You don't have to be evil anymore in order to be a significant part of a monstrous evil. You can, for example, be against the war and be a significant part of the war machine. I have friends who are working in the Defense Department who would go out and demonstrate against the war on Saturday and go back to work on Monday as systems analysts, having no sense of the consequences of their behavior collectively. This goes on all the time, in big systems and small. Bureaucracy controls all of our lives. We are all part of it, and we have absolutely no awareness of the consequences of our behavior. We don't even see first order consequences to say nothing of second order consequences. This is why people of good will, people like ourselves, can be involved in very destructive social control programs and call them compassionate and rational responses to social problems. The kinds of measures that are being patterned out to control the drug problem are merely the research and development phase for a whole slew of social control programs that we will never be able to undo.

In a few years from now, if we shift back to some sort of stability, and we grow out of our period of ressentiment, we will say, "My God, we made a terrible mistake back there." This we are likely to do as we have always done in every generation. We did after McCarthy, after the Red scare of 1919, and all the way back to 1627. This time we'll be stuck with an array of capacities in government that will not be undone. They are too large, too unaccountable, and too sophisticated. They will be too locked-in for us to change. The planners will rely on us, particularly us, the mental health professionals, because we have been so ignorant ourselves. We have been so unwilling to deal with the issue of the social control implications of the treatment of mental illness. We have been too unphilosophical and we have been too little like the witch doctors in the Navajo described by Bob Bergman.

I think we have entered the most dangerous time in the history of this country, and conceivably the history of the world. If indeed we still have any belief in freedom, if we're still concerned about a pluralistic, open system, if we're still concerned about the protection of privacy, and autonomy—if indeed all that stuff means anything to us anymore, then we have entered the most dangerous time in the history of the world. We have the option of turning our backs on it, dropping out, getting high in the woods like some of my friends are doing, and not caring. Or we have an option of muddling through and continuing to draw arbitrary lines around our professionalism and acting as if the consequences are somebody else's responsibility. Or we can take a position of relentless opposition to this movement. The option is merely not a choice about being part of it, but actually being agents of control that would rely on mental health professionalism to a very large extent. When you hear of the line, as we hear from the Panthers, that you are either part of the solution or part of the problem, this suddenly has very urgent meaning, or should have for all of us.

How can we do this? I can't say in a few lines. I'm working very hard to develop a strategy of non-violent radical change involving the redistribution of our power, but that will wait for another time to pursue.

However, I want to leave you with another parable that I heard recently. It's not from Erich Lindeman. It's the kind of story, however, that Erich might have told, and it's the kind of story that I want him to know about. It involves an analyst and his patient in 1938 in Berlin: a Jewish analyst and Jewish patient. A hardworking analysand who was free-associating very well. He was working on his Oedipal conflicts, appropriately and well. It was a good therepeutic alliance. Around them, of course, was a swirl of events culminating in the so-called Kristalnacht occurrence of 1938, which put the final, irrevocable stamp on German anti-Semitism. It was then apparent that every Jew was in physical danger, and the analyst decided that he was going to flee the country without telling his colleagues, without telling his friends, without telling his patients. He took his family and what belongings and resources he could carry with him, and went down to the train station in Berlin to leave the country. He was a little astonished as he was waiting in the crowd to board the train to look up and see, standing in front of him, his patient. As the story was told to me, the two men simply nodded to each other and without a word turned to board the train. This is something perhaps to think about—and I'll leave you with this.

Discussion

Question: Dr. Dumont, how can you advise others to wage a battle against the power of the State and the dinosauric nature of bureaucracies tending toward overpowering human values and individuals?

Matthew Dumont: You have to do it by taking what power there is in State government and very quickly giving it back to people at the lower level. This is not the New Federalism, you understand. I'm not talking about city government, which is what the President means when he talks about a lower level. I mean the level of people dealing with people on a face-to-face level. The best example, perhaps, is the Community Action Program, which was an aborted effort to do that sort of thing with power. But the reason why I don't want to answer your question is because I think it's the kind of thing that we should all be talking about and struggling with rather than saying, yes, that's the answer.

It seems to me that it's time for us to be a little unsettled for a while and not to quickly translate a response system as some kind of program for action. Most of the people I talk with about these things immediately respond with, "Well, what do we have to do?" Well, it seems to me there should be a period when we have to live with the anxiety for awhile and recognize—almost work through in analytic sense—what it means in terms of our behavior, before we can say, "O.K. now let's get organized." An improvident response might possibly be as destructive as what we're trying to deal with.

I would say generally it has to do with retreating from our own position of power. I think we have to learn to abrogate the esoteric imperialistic qualities of professionalism, which at least will avoid the possibility of more harm. What we do after that is something that I don't want to pour into proverbs or flowery statements just yet. It seems to me there has to be much more discussion. Rather than protecting our training grants and our clinics and centers at a time when the funds are running out, we should say maybe we have another order of business to do.

Question: The reason I asked that is because while we are waiting for answers people are getting killed. We can't just continue thinking and being anxious. It's time to do something.

Matthew Dumont: Well, I think your question is the question everybody should be asking about their own roles. I ask it every day of myself, how can I be an Assistant Commissioner of Mental Health? The fact of the matter is, when you're dealing with issues of professional conscience, you don't get the answers from somebody else. These are things that emerge in the quiet midnight reveries that have to be undertaken. My own response is that the reason I am where I am is not because I'm cultivating a brilliant career in state government, or not because I want my tenure at some point, but because it represents an opportunity in some way, however feebly, to redistribute power. As far as I'm concerned that is the only way to prevent repression. It's more than a protest. It's a prevention.

Question: Well you partly just answered my question. I grew up in Germany and I was still there in 1940. I think a mistake has been made not to speak up, and not to make any move. You know, I'm just speaking up, and we are part of the Establishment in a way. You know, you do have a lot of power somehow, some of you do. I think that it's wrong to sit back and say, "Let's wait and see. You know, let's wait. Let's not do anything." This I can tell you is not going to help. And yet we really do not know how to do anything either.

Matthew Dumont: . . . We don't, but we have to begin to find out.

Question: The climate is changing and a lot of Vietnam veterans are coming back quite different from what they were when they left. How do you feel now about putting yourself on the line with them about the issues of war and violence?

Matthew Dumont: . . . It's certainly time, as far as my personal feelings are concerned, again, that this is the decision that I have made, obviously giving consideration to my family at the same time. I do know that there is already a response. I'll share with you the fact that having said things like this within earshot of representatives of a federal agency there were efforts on their part to try to get me fired. Unfortunately, I'm a brilliant administrator and Massachusetts can't do without me at this point. (Laughter) So that was a somewhat enfeebled effort.

Question: If you get attacked and lose your position, then you've conceded your power to do anything.

Matthew Dumont: . . . That's the trap, unfortunately, and— there were some other things I wanted to talk to you about, but let's let it stop now because I think it's more important for Eric's program to go on. In any case, let's understand that we're not alone, those of us who are interested in redesigning our roles in this way. Something very precious and very exciting can emerge from it. The alternatives are not only very destructive, but they're very dull, and I would suggest to you like taking on a schizophrenic patient in treatment, becoming involved in the redistribution of power can be the most rewarding experience that you can possibly imagine. So I invite you to join me.

LC